Lecture Notes in Computer Science 13545

More information about this series at https://link.springer.com/bookseries/558

Francesca Spezzano · Adriana Amaral ·
Davide Ceolin · Lisa Fazio ·
Edoardo Serra (Eds.)

Disinformation in Open Online Media

4th Multidisciplinary International Symposium, MISDOOM 2022
Boise, ID, USA, October 11–12, 2022
Proceedings

Editors
Francesca Spezzano
Boise State University
Boise, ID, USA

Adriana Amaral
Universidade do Vale do Rio dos Sinos
São Leopoldo, Brazil

Davide Ceolin
Centrum Wiskunde and Informatica
Amsterdam, The Netherlands

Lisa Fazio
Vanderbilt University
Nashville, TN, USA

Edoardo Serra
Boise State University
Boise, ID, USA

ISSN 0302-9743   ISSN 1611-3349   (electronic)
Lecture Notes in Computer Science
ISBN 978-3-031-18252-5   ISBN 978-3-031-18253-2   (eBook)
https://doi.org/10.1007/978-3-031-18253-2

This Springer imprint is published by the registered company Springer Nature Switzerland AG
The registered company address is: Gewerbestrasse 11, 6330 Cham, Switzerland

Preface

Online media is a critical infrastructure that is economical, political, social, and organizational. Interaction and civic participation can amplify the access to political discussion. Diverse sources, huge amounts of information, and opinions and sentiments from the public are available to journalists through online media and all these contents can be part of their reporting. Online media can contribute to public opinion by affecting politicians who can refine their positions and (maybe) change or maintain their actions, while others can use these channels in order to circulate their views. Corporations and brands have their products reviewed by users that can contribute by securing a quality collective evaluation. In this context of digital transformation the Multidisciplinary International Symposium on Disinformation in Open Online Media (MISDOOM) is an important bridge to researchers from a variety of disciplines such as computer science, communication and media studies, computational social science, information science, political communication, journalism, and digital culture, as well as to digital activists and practitioners in journalism and digital media. The main essence of the symposium is its strong multidisciplinarity and its aims to provide a discussion space for different fields and disciplines that gather around the idea of disinformation.

This volume contains papers accepted at the fourth edition of the symposium, organized in 2022. This volume also includes the abstracts of the talks given by the four invited keynote speakers. Following the success of last year's fully virtual format, MISDOOM 2022 was also held completely online during October 11-12, 2022. In total there were 65 submissions: 17 full/short papers and 48 extended abstracts. Submissions were single-blind and each submission was reviewed by at least two Program Committee members. The Program Committee decided to accept 10 full/short paper submissions in the computer science track for publication in this LNCS volume. In addition, a total of 45 contributions among full paper and abstract submissions were accepted for presentation at the symposium. Figure 1 shows a summary of the topics of all contributions to the symposium.

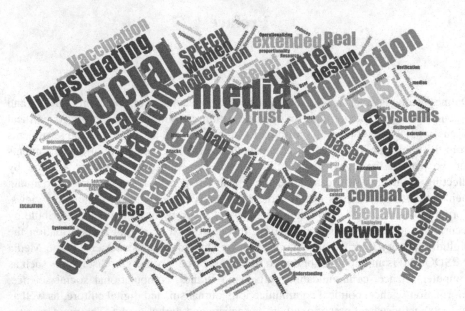

Fig. 1 Topics of MISDOOM 2022. Size is proportional to the frequency of the word in the titles of the submissions accepted to the symposium.

We want to express our gratitude towards all those who contributed to organizing and running this symposium. This includes the Program Committee, the MISDOOM Steering Committee, Boise State University, and our sponsors: the European Research Center for Information Systems (ERCIS), and the Idaho Secretary of State's Office. We hope that participants of all communities taking part in this multidisciplinary endeavor had a nice symposium and found some new insights and personal connections, especially between communities that usually do not meet so often in a symposium setting.

October 2022

Francesca Spezzano
Adriana Amaral
Davide Ceolin
Lisa Fazio
Edoardo Serra

Organization

General Chairs

Francesca Spezzano   Boise State University, USA
Adriana Amaral   Unisinos University, Brazil

Program Committee Chairs

Davide Ceolin   Centrum Wiskunde & Informatica, The Netherlands
Lisa Fazio   Vanderbilt University, USA
Edoardo Serra   Boise State University, USA

Proceedings Chair

Shiri Dori-Hacohen   University of Connecticut, USA

Communications Chairs

Anu Shrestha (Web Chair)   Boise State University, USA
Rafaela Tabasnik (Social   Unisinos University, Brazil
  Media Chair)

Program Committee

Alon Sela   Ariel University, Israel
André Calero Valdez   University of Lübeck, Germany
Angelo Spognardi   Sapienza University of Rome, Italy
Arian Askari   Leiden University, The Netherlands
Beliza Boniatti   Comsi.org, Brazil
Björn Ross   University of Edinburgh, UK
Bram van Dijk   Leiden University, The Netherlands
Britta C. Brugman   Vrije Universiteit Amsterdam, The Netherlands
Carlos D'Andrea   Federal University of Minas Gerais, Brazil
Chico Camargo   University of Exeter, UK
David Arroyo   Instituto de Tecnologías Fisicas y de la Información,
           CSIC, Spain
Dennis Assenmacher   GESIS - Leibniz-Institut für Sozialwissenschaften,
           Germany
Dennis M. Riehle   University of Koblenz-Landau, Germany
Derek C. Weber   University of Adelaide, Australia
Dina Pisarevskaya   Queen Mary University of London, UK
Ebrahim Bagheri   Ryerson University, Canada

Elena Kochkina	Queen Mary University of London, UK
Emiel Beinema	Delft University of Technology, The Netherlands
Enes Altuncu	University of Kent, UK
Eric Araújo	Federal University of Lavras, Brazil
Florian Wintterlin	University of Muenster, Germany
Gerasimos Spanakis	Maastricht University, The Netherlands
German Neubaum	University of Duisburg-Essen, Germany
Heike Trautmann	University of Münster, Germany
Hendrik Heuer	University of Bremen, Germany
Henna Paakki	Aalto University, Finland
Janina S. Pohl	University of Muenster, Germany
Jeremie Clos	University of Nottingham, UK
Jeroen G. Rook	University of Twente, The Netherlands
Joshua T. Nieubuurt	Old Dominion University, USA
Jozef Michal Mintal	Matej Bel University, Slovakia
Jukka Ruohonen	University of Turku, Finland
Kelechi Amakoh	Michigan State University, USA
Lena Frischlich	University of Muenster, Germany
Lennart Schäpermeier	Technische Universität Dresden, Germany
Leonie Heims	Technische Universitat Berlin, Germany
Liesbeth Allein	KU Leuven, Belgium
Lilian Kojan	RWTH Aachen University, Germany
Louis M. Shekhtman	Northeastern University, USA
Åukasz G. Gajewski	Warsaw University of Technology, Poland
Magdalena Wischnewski	University of Duisburg-Essen, Germany
Marco Niemann	University of Münster, Germany
Maria Clara Aquino	Unisinos University, Brazil
Marina Tulin	University of Amsterdam, The Netherlands
Marisa Vasconcelos	IBM Research, Brazil
Mehwish Nasim	University of Western Australia, Australia
Mike Preuss	University of Leiden, The Netherlands
Monika Hanley	Queen Mary University of London, UK
Nicole C. Krämer	University of Duisburg-Essen, Germany
Nicoleta Corbu	National University of Political Studies and Public Administration, Romania
Olga Gadyatskaya	Leiden University, The Netherlands
Or Levi	AdVerif.ai, The Netherlands
Orlando Mendez	Experian, Ireland
Peter van der Putten	Leiden University, The Netherlands
Raquel Recuero	Federal University of Pelotas/Federal University of Rio Grande do Sul, Brazil
Ravi Shekhar	Queen Mary University of London, UK
Robert Jankowski	University of Barcelona, Spain
Silvia Majo-Vazquez	University of Oxford, UK

Stephan van Duin   The Online Scientist, The Netherlands
Sthembile N. Mthethwa   Council for Scientific and Industrial Research,
                              South Africa
Sviatlana Hoehn   University of Luxembourg, Luxembourg
Wenjie Yin   Queen Mary University of London, UK

Keynote Talks

Hacking Online Virality

Filippo Menczer

Indiana University Luddy School of Informatics, Computing, and Engineering
fil@iu.edu

Abstract. As social media become major channels for the diffusion of news and information, it becomes critical to understand how the complex interplay between cognitive, social, and algorithmic biases triggered by our reliance on online social networks makes us vulnerable to manipulation and disinformation. This talk overviews ongoing network analytics, modeling, and machine learning efforts to study the viral spread of misinformation and to develop tools for countering the online manipulation of opinions.

Biography

Filippo Menczer is the Luddy distinguished professor of informatics and computer science and the director of the Observatory on Social Media at Indiana University. He holds a Laurea in Physics from the Sapienza University of Rome and a Ph.D. in Computer Science and Cognitive Science from the University of California, San Diego. Dr. Menczer is an ACM Fellow and a board member of the IU Network Science Institute. His research interests span Web and data science, computational social science, science of science, and modeling of complex information networks. In the last ten years, his lab has led efforts to study online misinformation spread and to develop tools to detect and counter social media manipulation.

From the Infodemic to the Information War: Disinformation Narrative Evolution, Lessons Learned, and Challenges Ahead

Maria Giovanna Sessa

EU DisinfoLab
mgs@disinfo.eu

Abstract. Recent crises have foregrounded the highly dynamic nature of online disinformation. As world-changing events such as the coronavirus pandemic and the war in Ukraine follow each other at a rapid pace, deceptive information and harmful narratives seem to adapt to these changing contexts effortlessly. The talk will debate the evolution of disinformation narratives in the past year, building on data collected in the framework of EDMO Belux (Belgium-Luxembourg European Digital Media and Disinformation Observatory) and EU DisinfoLab's monitoring of fact-checked disinformation in France, Germany, and Spain. The intersectionality of disinformation will be emphasized through empirical examples to show that disinformation is overcoming ideological boundaries for tactical convergence. The information disorder travels across different countries, languages, and platforms. The same communities are exposed to hoaxes that combines the twin crises (e.g., from anti-vax to pro-Russian stances) and other polarising issues (e.g., elections, migration policies, or civil rights). The common trait of these hybrid communities seems to be a pre-existing mistrust of government and institutions: in fact, anti-establishment sentiments resonate with people from different backgrounds. In view of these considerations, conclusions will address counter-disinformation responses with reference to the EU framework and, in particular, the implementation of the Digital Services Act. The main takeaway is the need for a systematic rather than ad hoc response, shifting away from crisis management to building resilient communities capable of facing the next disinformation challenge regardless of its topic.

Biography

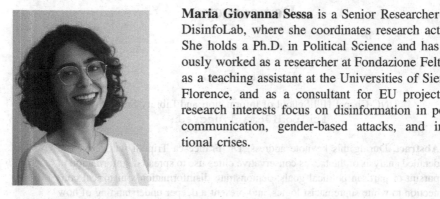

Maria Giovanna Sessa is a Senior Researcher at EU DisinfoLab, where she coordinates research activities. She holds a Ph.D. in Political Science and has previously worked as a researcher at Fondazione Feltrinelli, as a teaching assistant at the Universities of Siena and Florence, and as a consultant for EU projects. Her research interests focus on disinformation in political communication, gender-based attacks, and international crises.

The Propagandists' Playbook: How Search Engines are Manipulated to Threaten Democracy

Francesca Tripodi

UNC-Chapel Hill School of Information and Library Science
ftripodi@email.unc.edu

Abstract. During this keynote address, Dr. Francesca Tripodi will provide a detailed analysis of the tactics conservative elites use to spread disinformation in pursuit of partisan political goals, demonstrate disinformation's historical connection to white supremacist logics, and present a deeper understanding of how our society has become algorithmically polarized. Combining interviews and ethnographic observations with content analysis, media immersion, and web-scraped metadata, this talk takes audiences on a deep dive into conservative media practices. Through the mechanics of information literacy, networked media, search-engine optimization, curated keywords, and strategic signaling, Dr. Tripodi will explain how conservative pundits and politicians weave together economic, social, and religious groups into a common conversation and seed the internet with content around these filters. By encouraging audiences to "do their own research," this method of spreading propaganda mainstreams extremist logic, changes narratives adopted by mainstream media, and blurs the lines between reality and fiction. The goal of identifying these tactics is to break the feedback-loop vs. trying to reactively treat "information disorder," because disinformation is not a bug in the code, it is a feature wielded for political gain, and a great risk to American democracy.

Biography

Francesca Tripodi is a sociologist and media scholar whose research examines the relationship between social media, political partisanship, and digital inequality. She is an Assistant Professor at the School of Information and Library Science (SILS) and a Senior Research at the Center for Information Technology and Public Life (CITAP) at UNC-Chapel Hill. In 2019, she testified before the Senate Judiciary Committee on how search engines are gamed to drive ideologically based queries, a subject that is the focus of her forthcoming book with Yale University Press titled *The Propagandists' Playbook*. Her research has been covered by *The Washington Post*, *The New York Times*, *The New Yorker*, *NPR*, *The Columbia Journalism Review*, *Wired*, *Slate*, *The Guardian* and *The Neiman Journalism Lab*.

The Role of Display Advertising in the Disinformation Ecosystem

Ceren Budak

University of Michigan School of Information
cbudak@umich.edu

Abstract. The role that markets play in the disinformation ecosystem is generally overlooked and yet significant. For instance, revenue-seeking parties can set up disinformation sites and use them to monetize traffic through ads. Our ability to curb misinformation depends, at least partially, on understanding and changing these incentive mechanisms. How can we make meaningful progress in this direction? The first step is to understand the role different market forces play here. In this talk, we will take that first step and quantify the degree to which ad firms and advertisers support producers of misinformation through display advertising. By using data continuously collected on ads served on low and high credibility news sites, we will discuss (a) which ad firms and advertisers are uniquely responsible for supporting misinformation sites, (b) how these patterns are changing over time, and (c) how different ad-firm or retailer centric strategies to curb misinformation is likely to reshape the disinformation ecosystem.

Biography

Ceren Budak is an Associate Professor at the School of Information at the University of Michigan. Her research interests lie in the area of computational social science. She utilizes network science, machine learning, and crowdsourcing methods and draws from scientific knowledge across multiple social science communities to contribute computational methods to the field of political communication.

Contents

User Perception Based Trust Model of Online Sources: A Case Study of Misinformation on COVID-19

Loay Alajramy and Adel Taweel(✉)

Department of Computer Science, Birzeit University, Birzeit, Palestine
lalajramy@birzeit.edu

Abstract. Online websites have become an important source of information in all domains. Health has become one of the most Internet-dependent domains for information for the common users and experts alike. However, health information can be a critical determinant of human health and false information may cause real harm to Internet users. In this research, we aim to develop a model that evaluates the degree of trust in websites that provide health information. We conducted a quasi-experiment to assess the factors that affect user trust in health information providing websites. The experiment was conducted on pre-selected websites that provided information on Covid-19, ranging from official sources to those reported as providing misinformation. Participants had to assess the websites and determine factors that affected their level of trust. A total of 30 participated in the quasi-experiment, including both common users (46%) and health experts (56%). As a result, we identified the user-perceived importance weight of each of the studied factors that affect user trust in the studied websites. Using the identified importance weights of the factors, we developed a trust model and algorithm to evaluate the degree of trust in websites that provide health information. To evaluate the scalability of the developed model and algorithm, they were additionally applied on a set of pre-identified websites. The results were compared to the manually assessed scores conducted by health expert participants. The developed model achieved an error rate between 15%–19%, depending on the type and nature of the information-providing websites.

Keywords: Trust model · Misinformation · Online sources content · Covid-19

1 Introduction

In the first of 2021, the world Internet active users have reached 4.66B users, with nearly 60% of the world's population [1]. With this massive spread, the Internet has become one of the main sources of information because of the ease-of-access and large amount of information transmitted to it through online websites or social networks.

The health domain is one of the main domains that have a large share of the information published on the Internet. As reported, there are over 70,000 online websites specializing in providing medical information for online users making the internet an

F. Spezzano et al. (Eds.): MISDOOM 2022, LNCS 13545, pp. 1–15, 2022.
https://doi.org/10.1007/978-3-031-18253-2_1

important data source [2]. Also, many other websites, non-specializing in health, provide information in this field. About 7% of daily searches on the Google search engine, alone, are related to health [3]. Some researchers argue that sharing health information between users is very important to increase consumers' health experience [4].

With the many benefits of the availability of the health information over the Internet, however, this has a frightening and dark side, due to the ease of spreading false and misleading information. That may cause significant problems that may lead to harm or even death [5, 6]. It has been reported over 800 persons have died because of misinformation about covid-19, and other 5800 were taken to hospitals [5]. Others reported many other issues that affected communities because of fake and misinformation, such as effects on economies, marketing for untrusted products and many others [6].

Due to the rapid spread of misinformation, the World Health Organization (WHO) indicated that the spread of the information epidemic regarding Covid-19 is parallel to the spread of the virus and contributed to deaths and injuries [7].

Because of these problems, many researchers have focused on finding the factors that determine how users trust websites that provide health information. Identifying and understanding these factors, will help enhance our ability to identify websites that provide misinformation and the level of trust in these websites and thus may help decrease their spread and effects on Internet users.

Our work aims to understand how users trust websites that provide health information, and what factors affect their trust. Using these factors and their importance can help build a trust model that measures the level of trust of websites and consequently the information provided by them. The work focuses on Covid-19 as a case study, because of the global concern of the massive amount of misinformation that was published in the last few years.

2   Related Work

Fake information is news or information fabricated published with the intent to cheat people to achieve goals for the publisher [9]. This misinformation is published on social media, websites, and other information sources.

Several researchers focused on measuring the factors of trust on websites that provide health information to determine whether to publish information or not. Sillence et al. [10] used an online survey, on 1123 users (625 USA, 498 UK), to find the indicators that affect user trust in websites that provide health information. The authors focused on four types of indicators in their questionnaire: personal experiences, credibility and impartiality, and privacy and familiarity. They found credibility and impartiality as the main factors that have directly affected user trust.

Gunther et al. [11], on the other hand, conducted experiments by requesting from participants to undertake specific tasks on searching about health information, then interviewed them. Twenty-one users, who previously searched for health information on the internet, participated in this experiment. The final result of these experiments was that most of the participants focused on several factors including source or provider, website design, usability, language, and scientific appearance. However, no participant searched for information about the website or parent organization. Also, in [12], the authors found that the interface design and its beauty are influencing factors of user's trust, in addition to, the main factor they found, the familiarity of the website.

In the study [13], they found that parents rely heavily on health information from the Internet to care for their children. The authors have interviewed 15 parents of children of ages between 1.5–21 years. To trust the information, parents made comparisons between information from different sources, such as other websites, experts, or other sources. Another study found that the parents' trust is affected by the title and description of the websites, but often they did not consider the sources [14].

In [15], they found the trust in online health services is affected by separate factors, the most important of them is trust in offline services (e.g., parent organization and medical team). These factors have a direct impact on users' trust in online health services. The participants in this study, total was 93, were users who used the e-service of a hospital. In [16], the authors found that the website's origin affected users' trust in addition to other factors, such as ease-of-use, familiarity, language, references, and commercial interest and others. Although the participants in the experiment reported in [17] expressed distrust of online health information in general, but they noted that the organizational authority and clear language affected their trust positively.

In the study [18], after interviewing a small group of people, the authors found differences between participant opinions about the factors that affect their trust in online health information. But in general, the information style and website design were identified as factors that have an impact on trust. The study in [19] confirmed the existence of discrepancies in the opinions of people with little health experience and their reliance on inaccurate factors to assess the "goodness" of health information provided on websites, so they did not accurately identify the validity of the information provided, compared to people with health experience. Yalin et al. [20] summarized 37 research papers from the year 2000 to 2019 in this field, as a systematic literature review. They found many factors that affect users' trust in online health information with different levels of importance such as trustworthiness, expertise, objectivity, familiarity and others.

Trust is a difficult phenomenon to study, especially that people may not always be good at assessing the factors that really affect their perceptions of trustworthiness [22]. Also, using people's perception to determine trust factors may not always provide very reliable results, because people often lie, although not necessarily always consciously [22]. However, based on the above studies, understanding and determining how people perceive trust and how they make their trust judgement is a valid and a noteworthy approach to use for trust modelling.

3 Our Approach: User Perception-Based Trust Model for Websites

This works aims to develop a trust model that can calculate level of trust of websites based on a number of factors and their importance. However, to identify the factors of significance in determining trust and their importance, we conducted a quasi-experiment on a set of pre-identified key factors, identified as the most significant, as the most frequently reported by the literature, and a set of manually pre-selected websites, used as a gold standard, to compare against participant responses. These will help determine the importance level of each of these factors based on users' perception of how they affect their level of trust in websites and the information provided by them.

3.1 Trust Factors

This section will describe the factors that were identified for the study and the way each affects user trust. The selected factors were chosen based on those significant factors identified in the literature and those of relevance to the characteristics of the manually identified websites for the quasi-experiment.

These identified factors were divided into three types: those related to the characteristics of the website itself, the content provider, and the content itself. These factors are described below in more details.

Website Quality:

1. *Website design:* it falls under the main factor of aesthetics. The first impressions have an important effect on user trust, one of the main factors that affect the first impression for the user is the website design [21]. Many of the previous research mention the importance of website design as one of the main factors of user trust in websites that provide health information [11, 12, 18].
2. *Website performance:* the performance of the website helps to achieve user requirements and provide good experience using it, which raises user trust in the information provided by that website. Performance of the website is the main factor for the success of websites, which can be measured by the response time, loading time, page size, and others measures.
3. *Website global rank:* there are many algorithms that are used to rank websites in search engines such as PageRank, HITS, and others, however each measures the value of websites in a different way. We used the rank provided by SimilarWeb[1], because it calculates the popularity of websites by measuring the number of monthly unique visitors and the number of page views.
4. *Website domain:* is a string that defines the realm of administrative autonomy, authority, or control on the Internet. Some domains need special conditions such as high-level domain (e.g., .int, .edu, and others). As reported, a website domain increases trust and prevent distrust [23].

Website Origin:

Privacy policy: a legal document that shows how an organization or website collects and uses user's data. Many researchers reported that privacy policy affects level of user trust to provide personal information [20].

Logo: research indicates a relationship between the logo and its familiarity to users, which it has decreased the need to verify the information provided in the website [10].

Parent organization type (profit, nonprofit): according to [20], websites published by nonprofit organizations that provide information about the celiac disease have a higher rank on Google than websites by commercial organizations. That may be because other websites view it as reliable sources of information [20].

---

[1] www.similarweb.com.

Location of parent organization: Richard et al. [24] found the location (domestic or international) of e-commerce organizations affects user trust in their website. This research will study if this information applies to websites that provide health information.

Country of parent organization: many users are affected by the country of the website that provides health information. In [16] some of the participants reported that they trust information from America more than others.

Content Quality:
References: studies reported that using references, in citing the content, both online and offline references, had a significant impact on increasing user confidence in online health information [11].

Scientific and official touch: the scientific content can be observed through several characteristics, the most important is writing well, i.e., writing correctness and style, and showing the author's information, which would increase the user's trust in the information provided [11].

Multi-language: reported that websites that provide a multi-language ability helped to increase trust in websites that provide information or services for large societies [20].

From the above, the exact factors, their abbreviations and description, that will be considered to study further in our work are listed in Table 1 below.

3.2 Quasi-experiment Design

After reviewing the literature, we developed a set of questions that measure the level of importance of the identified factors and to study how they are perceived by participants in our experiment. The quasi-experiment included an online questionnaire that included 12 questions that represented the selected trust factors. Each participant is required to complete one questionnaire, for each one of the pre-selected online websites, completed separately for each. Six websites were carefully manually selected, ranging from highly trusted to low trusted websites, described in more details below.

We requested from the participants to go through specific articles on each of the six websites that provided information about Covid-19. Secondly, they, then, rate their level of trust in the website out of 10. As a third step, they answer 12 questions, on 5-point Likert scale, divided into three categories, each category on one type of the above factors that represent the characteristics of the website, the provider, and the content. These three steps are repeated for each of the six websites. We added the global rank, from SimilarWeb, to the description for every website, as a potential indicator.

3.2.1 Websites Selection Criteria

The websites were manually chosen so that they carry different degrees of trust: two websites have a high degree of trust, which are considered officially recognized as main sources for health information, in the world, and belong to official organizations (e.g., WHO, Harvard University). Two other websites with lesser degree of trust, one of them for a commercial company for the health industry, another one allows users to talk about their health experiments (e.g., pfizer). The last two websites were chosen based on the recommendations of some press reports that they are not reliable [3]. After careful

Table 1. Trust affecting factors under study.

Factor	Description
Website quality	
Website design	It represents how well or professionally the interface of the website is designed, in achieving professional look, feel, sophistication and coherence in UI/UX design
Website performance	It represents how fast is the website in its response to request and loading its information
Global rank	the rank provided by SimilarWeb
Website domain	It represents the type of domain of the providing organization (.edu,.org,.int…etc.):
Website origin	
Privacy policy	It represents whether a website/organization provides a clearly written privacy policy of e.g., user personal data, cookie usage etc.
Logo	It represents whether the website provides and includes a professionally designed logo on its pages
Organization type (profit, nonprofit)	Parent organization type profit or nonprofit
location of the organization	It represents where the organization is located and whether global, regional, or local to the user
The country of website	It represents the country of where the organization is located, how the user generally perceives the country as a trusty source of information
Content quality	
Reference	The content is well-referenced (or not): it represents how well the article is referenced to correct sources of information
Author Information	Content clearly shows author information (or not): it represents whether the information of author is clearly written on the article
Article written (scholarship)	Scholarship: it represents how well the article is written (scholarship)
Multi-language	Multi/single Language: it represents whether the article is written in more than one language (or in a single language)

manual check, we found they publish some misleading articles that contradict with WHO reports.

Ideally, selecting more than six websites would provide more accurate results, but due to the long time it took to complete the experiment by each participant, six websites were deemed sufficient to measure the user perception of each of the factor's importance.

Table 2 shows the list of the selected websites arranged depending on the degree of trust based on the opinion of the researchers.

Table 2. Websites for experiment

Website URL	Manual researcher trust assigned value
www.who.int	10
www.health.harvard.edu	10
www.pfizer.com	7
http://vestibular.org	6
http://vaccineholocaust.org	0
http://healthfreedom.news	0

3.2.2 Participants Selection

To reach a more comprehensive view of user perception of common internet users, ideally participants should include non-expert users. However, based on the results of previous studies [18, 19], users with low level of health experiences find it difficult to decide if the online health information is true or not. Therefore, to qualify the results, the experiment included more than half of the participants (56%) with those that have work experience in the medical field, to achieve more accurate results. These participants included health experts from three national hospitals from two different cities. The rest of the participants were common users, come from different specialties such as (computer sciences-CS, teaching, and others). Figure 1 shows the work experiences of the participants.

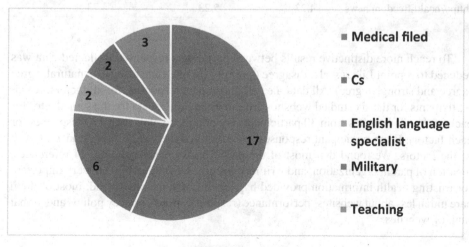

Fig. 1. Participants distribution.

3.2.3 Platform for Data Collection

We collected the data by designing the questionnaire as a Google form, to enable and facilitate conducting the experiment online, which also provides ease of use and easy access. Additionally, participants come from different locations and thus Google forms enables to conduct the experiment remotely.

4 Experimentation and Results

This section describes the collected data and discusses the proposed model. The first step in the data analysis is to calculate the average degree of trust from participant responses, on the six websites. As shown in Table 2, we found that most participants were able to distinguish highly trusted and medium trusted websites, but with less ability to distinguish untrusted websites. Table 3 shows the websites and the average degree of trust for both health and non-health expert participants. On ANOVA test, the results are statistically significant, of p-value < 0.00001.

Table 3. Trust degree for all participants

Website URL	Overall average trust (User Assigned Value) [1–10]		
	Health experts	Non-health expert	All participants
www.who.int	8.65	7.54	8.1
www.health.harvard.edu	8.3	7.46	7.88
www.pfizer.com	7	6.61	6.81
http://vestibular.org	5.76	5.69	5.73
http://vaccineholocaust.org	4.77	5.41	5.09
http://healthfreedom.news	4.23	5.23	4.73

To reach more distinctive results between participant responses, collected data was reduced to 3-point Likert scale: disagree (strongly disagree and disagree), natural, agree (agree and strongly agree). All data, i.e., all participant responses, for all factors, for all participants for the six studied websites are shown in Fig. 2 (data for the same factor for each of the six websites from 30 participants are combined, thus total 180 responses for each factor). From participant responses, we identified the level of importance of each of the factors. We found that most of the participants consider the use of references, location of parent organization, and writing correctness (scholarship) are very important for trusting health information provided by websites. On the other hand, most of them care much less about websites' performance (response/speed), privacy policy, and global rank of websites.

We found a distinct difference of change in the level of importance for the same factor that caught the attention of the participants, for different types of websites. For example, we found the website design received lower attention in trusted websites with rank 8, and takes more attention for medium trusted ones with rank 6, but in untrusted ones it takes most attention with rank 2. Table 4 shows the arrangement of the factors based on the degree of importance by participants, (i.e., their perception as of higher importance) from high importance to low for websites categorized as trusted, medium-trusted, and untrusted or low-trusted.

To improve the accuracy of results, we set a threshold to accept the factors that received more than 100 positive responses (i.e., arbitrarily set to, at least 75% of total highest Agree responses) from participants to define user trust in websites that provide health information. From this, we can deduce the most important factors to consider are (numbered from most important to least important): 1: Reference, 2: Location of the parent organization, 3: Article written (scholarship); 4: The country of website, 5: Author information's, 6:Website design, 7: Website domain.

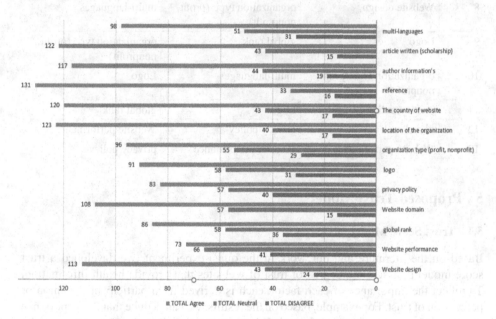

Fig. 2. Participant's answers for all indicators questions.

Table 4. Arrangement of the factors based on the degree of acceptance of participants for websites divided into three categories

Rank	Trusted website	Medium trusted websites	Low trusted websites
1	Reference	article written (scholarship)	Reference
2	location of the organization	location of the organization	Website design
3	country of website	The country of website	article written (scholarship)
4	author information's	author information's	author information's
5	article written (scholarship)	reference	The country of website
6	Website domain	Website design	location of the organization
7	multi-languages	Website domain	Website domain
8	Website design	organization type (profit, nonprofit)	multi-languages
9	Logo	global rank	organization type (profit, nonprofit)
10	organization type (profit, nonprofit)	multi-languages	Logo
11	privacy policy	Logo	global rank
12	global rank	privacy policy	Website performance
13	Website performance	Website performance	privacy policy

5 Proposed Trust Model

5.1 Trust Score Model

Based on the literature and our work in the quasi-experiment, we developed a trust score model to assess the degree of trust of websites that provide health information. To reflect the importance of each factor, each is derived from participant's opinion or perception of trust. For example, based on the results, we can deduce that the importance of using *references* is considered more important than website *domain*, as perceived by the participants. Thus, to compute the weight of the factors in our model, from user responses, we use the following equation:

$$FW = \frac{FAG}{ALLAG} \tag{1}$$

where *FW* is factor weight, *FAG* is the agree response of the factor, and *ALLAG* is the total Agree response for all the seven identified factors. The result of the calculated weights or trust scores is shown in Table 5 (shown values are approximated).

Table 5. Trust score model

Factor	Score/100
Reference	16
Location of the parent organization	15
Article written (scholarship)	14.5
The country of website	14
Author information's	14
Website design	13.5
Website domain	13

From trust scores, in Table 4, a fully trusted website will be donated with 100 points and a fully untrusted website will be donated with 0 points. To achieve additional accuracy or different weighting for each factor, to calculate the points for each in the model, additional conditions were considered for each factor. The following conditions are derived from obtained results and the literature:

1. Reference score: websites that use less than 3 references achieve 5 points, 4–6 references achieve 10 points and more than 6 achieve 16 points. Note the Reference score may change depending on the article.
2. Location of parent organization score: the website must belong to an official organization, if the location of the organization is global it achieves 15 points, for regional it achieves 10 points and local it achieves 5 points.
3. Article written (scholarship) score: the article must be written correctly with fewer writing and grammar errors. If No errors, it achieves 14.5 points, 1–3 errors, it achieves 10 points, and 4–6 errors, it achieves 5 points, more than 6 errors, it achieves 0 points. To find "writing" errors, we use Grammarly Google Chrome extensions.
4. The country of website score: website country must be in the first 20 in the number of the published scientific article to take 14 points.
5. Author information's score: the website must show the article author information to achieve 14 points.
6. Website design score: to measure the user interface value we use Wave tool[2] (web access ability evaluation tool).to achieve 13.5 points, website must have less than 20 Design Errors and Contrast Errors.
7. Website domain score: to achieve 13 points, a website must be from the top-level domain (.int, .edu, .gov, .mil), because it has allocation restrictions.

Accordingly, the proposed trust model, to calculate its trust score, is developed as an algorithm. The developed algorithm is included below.

---

[2] https://wave.webaim.org/.

Algorithm 1 proposed algorithm to compute trust score
1. Initialize TrustsScore and set it to 0
2. Initialize **RL, OL, WR, CE, DE**
3. Get reference list save it as RL
4. **if** (RL <=3)
TrustScore = TrustsScore +5
else if (RL >=4 && RL<=6)
TrustScore = TrustsScore + 10
else if (RL>6)
TrustScore = TrustsScore +16
End if.
5. Get parent organization location save it as OL
6. **if**(OL= = global)
TrustScore = TrustsScore +15
else if (OL= = regional)
TrustScore = TrustsScore +10
else if (OL= = local)
TrustScore = TrustsScore +5
End if
7. Calculate number of spelling and grammar error save it as WR
8. **if** (WR =0)
TrustScore = TrustsScore + 14.5
else if (WR >0&& WR <=3)
TrustScore = TrustsScore + 10
else if (WR >4&& WR <=6)
TrustScore = TrustsScore +5
End if.
9. Get the country of website.
10. If the country on the list of first 20 country published scientific research then
TrustScore = TrustsScore +14
End if.
11. Get author information.
12. If author information exist then
TrustScore = TrustsScore +14
End if.
13. Calculate constrain error save it as CE and Calculate design error save it as DE
14. **if** (CE<20 && DE <20)
TrustScore = TrustsScore + 13.5
End if.
15. If website URL contain one of (.int, .edu, .gov, .mil) then
TrustScore = TrustsScore +13
End if.
return TrustScore

6 Validation and Testing

To validate the developed score trust model, the algorithm is manually applied, first, on the same six websites that were used in the quasi-experiment, to compare the results of the score trust model to results obtained from the participants. The purpose is to conduct a manual evaluation of the model with comparison to the defined gold standard, with a trust degree approximate to the opinion of the researchers and participants in the quasi-experiment. To calculate trust score for a website, we use the following equation:

$$TS(ws) = \frac{\sum FW(ws)}{10} \qquad (2)$$

where TS is trust score for website ws, and FW is factor weight for website ws, for each of the seven identified factors. FW for each of the factors is calculated bnaccording to the conditions set in Algorithm 1.

The resultants scores generated by the model are then compared to the researchers' opinion in Table 2 and the opinion of the health expert (only) participants, i.e., those with health experience in Table 3 (health experts are selected to increase the accuracy of the outcome). The results are shown in Table 6. As shown, the proposed model achieves relatively good results with acceptable error rate. It is able to evaluate websites and their information effectively and distinguishes between them effectively, i.e., it discovers reliable and unreliable websites.

Table 6. Validation and testing result

Website	Manual researcher trust assigned value	Expert/trust assigned value	Trust model calculated trust value/10	Error rate from manual evaluation	Error rate from expert evaluation
www.who.int	10	8.65	8.2	1.8	0.45
www.health.harvard.edu	10	8.3	7.95	2.05	0.35
www.pfizer.com	7	7	8.15	1.15	1.15
vestibular.org	5	5.76	2.9	2.1	2.86
vaccineholocaust.org	0	4.77	1.9	1.9	2.87
healthfreedom.news	0	4.23	2.4	2.4	1.83
Average Error				±1.9	±1.585

7 Limitations and Future Work

The authors recognize that this research has some limitations, but believe that it provides a good basis for an approach to aid the users to identify websites that provide misinformation. We note some limitations that may be constitute threats to the validity of the results. Firstly our result is based on a human judgment. This implies that there may be differences in people's opinions and their focus may be on different factors to trust websites that provide health information and may not scale to websites providing different type of information. Secondly, having larger number of websites to assess and a larger sample of participants in the quasi-experiment would have improved accuracy and reduced error. However, finding large number of health experts, to spend a long time as participants, can be a real challenge.

As a future work, scaling up the research and evaluation of the trust model, on larger number of participants and larger and different types of information and websites would enable to create a scalable solution. Developing the trust model algorithm as an automatic computation in internet browser, e.g., plug-in, may prove a valuable tool to users to distill invalid information.

8   Conclusion

This paper developed an approach to identify online sources that provide misinformation, about medical information. It developed a trust model that provides trust scores of websites. The model assesses the degree of trust of websites that provide health information, using trust factors identified based on user perception of how users trust information provided by online sources or websites. To achieve, 12 factors of relevance were identified from the literature and conducted a quasi-experiment to derive user-perceived opinions of the importance of the factors that affect the level of trust in health information providing websites, using COVIDE-19 as an exemplar.

The results found 7 factors, out of the 12 studied, that are of most importance to users to determine trust in health websites. Using these results, a trust model was developed to calculate a trust score for websites. The developed model was manually validated against a set of gold standard websites and health expert opinion. As shown, the proposed model achieves good result with an acceptable error rate between 15%–19%.

References

1. Internet users in the world 2021 | Statista. https://www.statista.com/statistics/617136/digital-population-worldwide/. Accessed 29 Dec 2021
2. Sbaffi, L., Rowley, J.: Trust and credibility in web-based health information: a review and agenda for future research. J. Med. Internet Res. **19**(6), e218 (2017). https://doi.org/10.2196/jmir.7579
3. Health websites are notoriously misleading: So we rated their reliability. https://www.statnews.com/2019/07/26/health-websites-are-notoriouslymisleading-so-we-rated-their-reliability/. Accessed 02 Jan 2022
4. Brady, E., Segar, J., Sanders, C.: 'You get to know the people and whether they're talking sense or not': negotiating trust on health-related forums. Soc. Sci. Med. **162**, 151–157 (2016). https://doi.org/10.1016/J.SOCSCIMED.2016.06.029
5. Islam, M.S., et al.: COVID-19–related infodemic and its impact on public health: a global social media analysis. Am. J. Trop. Med. Hyg. **103**(4), 1621–1629 (2020). https://doi.org/10.4269/AJTMH.20-0812
6. Baldwin, R., Weder, B., Mauro, D.: Economics in the Time of COVID-19. www.cepr.org. Accessed 15 Dec 2021
7. Fighting misinformation in the time of COVID-19, one click at a time. https://www.who.int/news-room/feature-stories/detail/fighting-misinformation-in-the-time-of-covid-19-one-click-at-a-time. Accessed 15 Dec 2021
8. Daraz, L., et al.: Readability of online health information: a meta-narrative systematic review. Am. J. Med. Qual. **33**(5), 487–492 (2018). https://doi.org/10.1177/1062860617751639
9. Patwa, P., et al.: Fighting an Infodemic: COVID-19 Fake News Dataset. https://doi.org/10.1007/978-3

10. Sillence, E., Blythe, J.M., Briggs, P., Moss, M.: A revised model of trust in internet-based health information and advice: cross-sectional questionnaire study. J. Med. Internet Res. **21**(11), e11125 (2019). https://doi.org/10.2196/11125

11. Eysenbach, G., Köhler, C.: How do consumers search for and appraise health information on the world wide web? Qualitative study using focus groups, usability tests, and in-depth interviews. BMJ **324**(7337), 573–577 (2002). https://doi.org/10.1136/BMJ.324.7337.573

12. Kim, H., Park, S.-Y., Bozeman, I.: Online health information search and evaluation: observations and semi-structured interviews with college students and maternal health experts. https://doi.org/10.1111/j.1471-1842.2011.00948.x

13. Alsem, M.W., Ausems, F., Verhoef, M., Jongmans, M.J., Meily-Visser, J.M.A., Ketelaar, M.: Information seeking by parents of children with physical disabilities: an exploratory qualitative study. Res. Dev. Disabil. **60**, 125–134 (2017). https://doi.org/10.1016/j.ridd.2016.11.015

14. Benedicta, B., Caldwell, P.H.Y., Scott, K.M.: How parents use, search for and appraise online health information on their child's medical condition: a pilot study. J. Paediatr. Child Health **56**(2), 252–258 (2020). https://doi.org/10.1111/JPC.14575

15. van Velsen, L., Flierman, I., Tabak, M.: The formation of patient trust and its transference to online health services: the case of a Dutch online patient portal for rehabilitation care. BMC Med. Inf. Dec. Making **21**(1) (2021). https://doi.org/10.1186/s12911-021-01552-4

16. Peddie, K.A., Kelly-Campbell, R.J.: How people with hearing impairment in New Zealand use the Internet to obtain information about their hearing health. Comput. Hum. Behav. **73**, 141–151 (2017). https://doi.org/10.1016/j.chb.2017.03.037

17. Marshall, L.A., Williams, D.: Health information: does quality count for the consumer? J. Librariansh. Inf. Sci. **38**(3), 141–156 (2006). https://doi.org/10.1177/0961000606066575

18. Cunningham, A., Johnson, F.: Exploring trust in online health information: a study of user experiences of patients.co.uk. Heal. Inf. Libr. J. **33**(4), 323–328 (2016). https://doi.org/10.1111/HIR.12163

19. Diviani, N., van den Putte, B., Meppelink, C.S., van Weert, J.C.M.: Exploring the role of health literacy in the evaluation of online health information: insights from a mixed-methods study. Patient Educ. Couns. **99**(6), 1017–1025 (2016). https://doi.org/10.1016/J.PEC.2016.01.007

20. Sun, Y., Zhang, Y., Gwizdka, J., Trace, C.B.: Consumer evaluation of the quality of online health information: systematic literature review of relevant criteria and indicators. J. Med. Internet Res. **21**(5), e12522 (2019). https://doi.org/10.2196/12522

21. Health websites are notoriously misleading. So we rated their reliability. https://www.statnews.com/2019/07/26/health-websites-are-notoriously-misleading-so-we-rated-their-reliability/. Accessed 2 Jan 2022

22. Stephens-davidowitz, S.: Everybody Lies : What The Internet Can Tell us About Who We Really Are. Bloomsbury Publishing (2018)

23. Seckler, M., Heinz, S., Forde, S., Tuch, A.N., Opwis, K.: Trust and distrust on the web: user experiences and website characteristics. Comput. Human Behav. **45**, 39–50 (2015). https://doi.org/10.1016/J.CHB.2014.11.064

24. Fisher, R., Chu, S.Z.: Initial online trust formation: the role of company location and web assurance. Manag. Audit. J. **24**(6) 542–563 (2009). https://doi.org/10.1108/02686900910966521/FULL/PDF

Using Artificial Neural Networks to Identify COVID-19 Misinformation

Loay Alajramy⑩ and Radi Jarrar(✉)⑩

Department of Computer Science, Birzeit University, Birzeit, Palestine
{lalajramy,rjarrar}@birzeit.edu

Abstract. Since the spread of the coronavirus disease (COVID-19), a huge amount of information about the virus has been published over the internet and social networks. Along with such, there is an uncontrolled spread of harmful misinformation. This paper aims to review three state-of-the-art datasets of misinformation on COVID-19 and present experimental comparison on these datasets using various Neural Network architectures. The datasets comprise data from various sources such as articles from trusted websites and posts and tweets from social media. As for the algorithms, different Neural Network architectures (ANN, CNN, RNN, and LSTM) are used to compare the reviewed datasets to detect misinformation about COVID-19. The experiments are conducted on the datasets individually and merged together to generate models with larger input dataset. The results show, in terms of accuracy, that feedforward Artificial Neural Network (ANN) outperformed other more complicated Deep Learning methods such as Convolutional Neural Networks (CNNs) and Recurrent Neural Networks (RNNs). Moreover, merging the datasets has resulted in better performance in comparison to the individual datasets. In terms of execution time, ANN showed better performance with shorter training time.

Keywords: Misinformation · COVID-19 · Neural networks · Deep learning.

1 Introduction

Towards the end of 2019, a new infection affected a number of people was discovered in Wuhan, China. The symptoms appeared to affect mainly the respiratory system and seemed to be similar to pneumonia. It was then classified as a virus of the SARS-COV family and named as the SARS-COV-2, which is known as the COVID-19 coronavirus. This disease has spread rapidly worldwide and the World Health Organization (WHO) decided on March 11, 2020 to declare the new Corona virus a global pandemic[1]. The number of deaths around the world as of the date of writing this article has reached approximately 6.3 million death, and 517 million infected with COVID-19 [1].

Governments and international organizations have struggled to limit the spread of this epidemic by imposing closures, curfews, and imposing other means of protection (muzzle, sterilizers…etc.) [1].

---

[1] https://www.who.int/director-general/speeches/detail/who-director-general-s-opening-rem
arks-at-the-media-briefing-on-Covid-19—11-march-2020.

© The Author(s), under exclusive license to Springer Nature Switzerland AG 2022
F. Spezzano et al. (Eds.): MISDOOM 2022, LNCS 13545, pp. 16–26, 2022.
https://doi.org/10.1007/978-3-031-18253-2_2

During the quarantine period, people used social media and there was a leap in the number of active users for social media. Users used social media to post updates of the state of the pandemic and to search for updates related to the emerging coronavirus. For instance in United States, the average rate of using social media for a person raised in the year 2020 from 54 min daily (in 2019) to 65 min [2]. This caused an increased spread of misinformation that led to some serious issues like creating chaos, marketing for unreliable products, affecting countries' economies, and many other problems [3]. The WHO has described this situation as an information epidemic [1].

Lay users are generally not able to detect misinformation without prior experience. It has become imperative for websites and popular social media networks to combat the spread of misinformation. It is indeed a challenge to detect misinformation from the huge amount of information exchanged over the Internet from many trusted and untrusted sources [4, 5].

To overcome the aforementioned challenges, many researchers have developed techniques to identify misleading information, many of which rely on Artificial Intelligence (AI) and Machine Learning (ML) techniques [6]. In this paper, we use three different datasets containing tweets, posts, and articles about COVID-19. The dataset instances are labeled as fake or real and we aim to test these datasets on different Neural Network architectures.

2 Literature Review

Misinformation is defined as *"information that is contrary to the epistemic consensus of the scientific community regarding a phenomenon"* [21]. This information may be published on social media such as Facebook, Twitter, online websites or other sources of information over the web.

Natural Language Processing (NLP) is a branch of AI that aims to earn value and better understand free text [22]. Text classification, in particular, deploys ML techniques to classify text data into different categories. It has many applications such as classifying clinical reports, research papers, media articles, social media posts, and many others [23]. Furthermore, NLP and ML have been widely used to detect fake news [10, 11, 13, 19, 20]. Most of these methods depend on comparing historical annotated data (fake and real) with the new input data. The models are trained to learn certain patterns in the historical data and apply them to new data and classify them based on these patterns [6]. To annotate data as fake or real, researchers use experts or online tools like Google fact check and Snopes.com to name a few. These tools facilitate the work of researchers in validating the accuracy of their data.

In this section, we review state-of-the-art techniques used to detect misleading information about COVID-19 by grouping related works according to the ML techniques used.

k-Nearest Neighbor (k-NN)
Is a nan-parametric algorithm that classifies new input instances based on the nearest neighbors in the feature space. The final classification label is most common class among the nearest k-neighbors. Though k-NN is a simple classification algorithm, it is used in

cases where it is difficult to discover the relationships between features and target class [8].

Aiming to identify misleading information, Alenezi et al. [9] compared Long-Short-Term-Memory (LSTM), Multi-Channel-Convolutional Neural Network (MC-CNN), and k-NN algorithms. The best accuracy was achieved using k-NN (k = 3) with a value of 99% and precision/recall 99.24% and 99.72%, respectively. The main limitations of their work is using a small dataset [10] as well using Twitter only to collect their data.

Naive Bayes

Naive Bayes is a probabilistic ML algorithm that is based on Bayes theorem. It assumes that all features are independent on one another given the target class. In the case of text classification, it depends on the likelihood of a word in the fake news post as a ratio of the fake news posts that contain this word to the total number of fake news posts. This algorithm may be strong with a weak correlation [11].

Granik, M et al. [12] used Naive Bayes algorithm to detect fake news in a data set that was collected from posts published on Facebook. They achieved an accuracy of 74%. This accuracy may be weak because of high error rate may cause high risk. This risk comes from the high number of users rely on social media for information and news.

Support Vector Machines (SVMs)

Support Vector Machines are popular strong classifiers that are used in multiclass classification problems. SVMs create hyperplane(s) to separate data belonging to different classes. If the data is not linearly separable, then SVMs maps that data into higher dimensional feature spaces, through the kernel trick, to create more separating surfaces [13, 14].

Patwa et al. [7] created a dataset of 10,700 posts and news of real and fake information about COVID-19. This dataset set was manually collected and published publicly[2]. They classify the data using four traditional ML algorithm (Decision Trees, Logistic Regression, Gradient Boosting, and SVMs). They achieved the highest results with an F1-score 93.32% for SVMs. This result is acceptable given the size of the dataset compared with other published research. Dharawat et al. [15] also used SVMs and compared its performance with against Random Forests (RF) and Logistic Regression to detect misleading information. They used Bags-of-Words and TF-IDF to represent their input features, which resulted in an accuracy around 95%.

In comparing different ML algorithms for this task, Elhadad et al.[6] performed experiments using 10 algorithms on a manually collected data set and verified on fact-checking websites. The main trusted information source is the WHO, UNICEF, and the United Nations. They used different feature representation including Term-Frequency, TF-IDF using N-gram representation (i.e., unigram, bigram, and trigram), and word-embedding. The highest accuracies were recorded for different algorithms with different representations. For example, XGBoost resulted with the highest accuracy for using word-embedding. However, the highest accuracy was encountered for ANN using TF representation that resulted in 99.68%. More details on their experiments is shown in Fig. 1.

---

[2] https://github.com/diptamath/covid_fake_news.

Artificial Neural Network and Deep Learning Approaches

Artificial Neural Networks (ANNs) are strong classification technique that are comprised of a set of connected neurons in different layers. A Neural Network consists of an input layer, a hidden (or more) layer(s), and an output layer. The data is passed to nodes (i.e., neurons) from one layer to the other and each node contains an activation function that represents a mathematical transformation of data. The inputs are adjusted by weight and added the bias, which will decide whether to activate the neuron or not. This algorithm is used in the complicated and uncorrelated datasets [16].

Using NNs algorithms to detect fake news was studies extensively [7, 16, 17]. In [7], the authors achieved good accuracy with the neural network algorithm 88.20%.

Convolutional Neural Network (CNN)

CNN is a Deep Learning algorithm that is improved over the simple neural network architecture. The main use of CNN is in the field of image understanding and classification. A standard CNN consists of five layers as shown in Fig. 2. These layers are as follows [13]:

1. Input layer: receives the input data and transforms it into matrix. In case of text data, it is called word embedding vector.
2. Convolutional layer: receives the input matrix then uses several filters that execute the convolutional operation. After performing mathematical operations on the input matrix, it will output one column matrix.
3. Pooling layer: the main task of the pooling layer is to decrease the input feature vectors.
4. Fully connected (FC) layer: learns a non-linear collection of features as represented by the output of the convolutional layer. This layer is learning a possibly non-linear function in that space [16].

ACCURACY, ERROR RATE, AND AREA UNDER CURVE OF THE VALIDATION RESULTS

Metric	Feature Extraction		Classification Algorithm									
			DT	MNB	BNB	LR	kNN	Perceptron	NN	LSVM	ERF	XGBoost
Accuracy (%)		TF	99.04	98.29	95.09	99.36	96.42	98.93	99.68	99.52	99.52	99.15
	TF-IDF	Unigram	98.93	98.01	93.96	98.18	98.67	99.57	99.63	99.52	99.15	99.25
		Bigram	98.02	97.92	90.55	97.49	97.06	98.72	98.99	98.99	98.56	96.80
		Trigram	93.00	92.57	92.68	92.47	90.92	93.54	93.75	93.91	93.43	91.45
		N-gram (n=2:3)	98.56	98.08	90.97	97.81	96.64	98.99	99.57	99.57	98.72	97.44
		Characters Level	99.20	97.97	91.35	98.08	99.36	99.52	99.63	99.63	99.09	99.41
		Word Embeddings	97.33	55.45	64.80	80.61	89.16	72.12	93.86	65.99	98.72	99.52

Fig. 1. The results of the comparisons between different algorithms and different representation of features as appeared in [7].

Choudrie et al. [18] used various DL techniques to classify the input text as useful information or misinformation. High results were encountered using CNN and decision tree algorithms reached 86.7%. However, using a small dataset (147 instances) is a main limitation of their work.

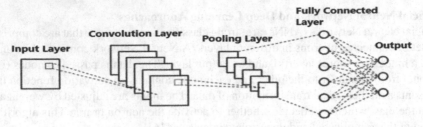

Fig. 2. The architecture of Convolutional Neural Networks [13].

LSTM algorithm has been used for detecting misinformations. Agarwal et al. [24] used the LSTM algorithm to detect misinformation and compared to other algorithms (SVM, CNN, KNN, and Naive Bayes). Their results show that the LSTM outperformed the other ML and DL methods and obtained around 97% accuracy. Similarly, it was used as a classifier for Fake News Detection with GloVe word embeddings and obtained an accuracy of 84.1% [25].

In this work, we will report our experiments on using different Neural Network architectures: feedforward Artificial Neural Network (ANN), Convolutional Neural Networks (CNN), Recurrent Neural Networks (RNN), and Long-Short-Term-Memory (LSTM). We evaluate these algorithms on different datasets and show their results.

3   Methodology

The goal of this work is to review different methods on classifying misleading information as well performing experiments using different Neural Network and Deep Learning architectures. Our goal is to build models that classify input text about COVID-19 as real or fake using Neural Network algorithms and evaluate them on large datasets. This section presents the used datasets and the proposed model used in our experiments.

3.1   Dataset

In the literature, there are many publicly available datasets on COVID-19 misinformation. In this work we use 3 datasets that we will conduct our experiments on individually and combined.

The first step is to use existing dataset or build a new one. Since there are many published data sets about COVID-19, decided to use the publicly available datasets instead of building a new one. We selected the following datasets:

1. **Fighting an Infodemic** [8]: this dataset contains articles, posts, and tweets in the English language. The size of the data set is 10,702 instances. This dataset is collected from various trusted online sources like the World Health Organization and the Centers for Disease Control and Prevention. The fake news were collected from social media networks that verified the news manually and other fact-verification online websites.

2. **Extracting Informative COVID-19** [19]: this dataset contains English tweets that are labeled as informative/uninformative. This dataset comprises 10,000 tweets.
3. **A Multimodal Repository for COVID-19 News** [20]: this dataset is created using 2,029 articles about COVID-19. The dataset contains other features as the publisher, country, Publication Date, and News URL.

3.2 Preprocessing and Merging Datasets

The first step in the preprocessing is to delete the unnecessary features (e.g., tweet id, publisher, and country of publisher ...) and keep the text-only data. Cleaning data also entails removing empty rows and deleting the non-English characters, emoji's, symbols, URLs, and stop words. Then we standardize the labels of instances between the 3 datasets (i.e., [1, 0] and [informative, uninformative]) to be able to merge the datasets.

We merge the datasets in several stages as shown in the next section. All duplicate instances in the datasets are checked and removed. The dataset is split into 80% training and 20% test sets taking into account that the test subset contains data from the three collected datasets.

3.3 Experiments and Result

We merged the datasets in different combinations. We refer to the datasets as (a) for the dataset presented in [8], (b) for the dataset presented in [19], and (c) for the dataset of [20]. As stated earlier, the datasets are merged in several stages based on the experiment as follows: (a & b), (a & c), (b & c), and (a & b & c). Table 1 shows the size of datasets and their sizes after the merge.

Table 1. The size of datasets before and after the merge.

Dataset	Total Size	Training size			Test size		
		Real	Fake	Total	Real	Fake	Total
a	10691	4476	4076	8552	1120	1019	2139
b	9931	4190	3741	7931	1056	944	2000
c	2018	1087	529	1616	268	134	402
a & b	20545	8229	8187	16416	2069	2060	4129
a & c	12555	5511	4542	10053	1363	1139	2502
b & c	11804	4782	4663	9445	1183	1176	2359
a & b & c	21997	9016	8573	17589	2249	2159	4408

On each of the resultant datasets, we generated models using feedforward Artificial Neural Network, CNN, RNN, and LSTM algorithms. The results are shown in Tables 2, 3, 4, and 5 based on the used algorithm. The tables show the accuracy metrics and the total training time for each experiment. Unit of the run-time is per second the run-time is approximate with a slight margin of error.

Note that all experiments were performed on a Dell Precision laptop with 32-GB RAM.

Table 2. The results of running Convolutional Neural Networks (CNN) algorithm.

Dataset	Accuracy	Precision		Recall		F1 score		Total training time
		Real	Fake	Real	Fake	Real	Fake	
a	91%	92%	90%	91%	91%	92%	91%	350 s
b	72%	72%	72%	67%	77%	69%	74%	340 s
c	69%	76%	54%	78%	51%	77%	53%	185 s
a & b	77%	77%	77%	76%	785	77%	77%	1550 s
a & c	84%	86%	82%	84%	84%	85%	83%	1000 s
b & c	67%	68%	67%	65%	69%	67%	68%	900 s
a & b & c	74%	75%	72%	73%	75%	74%	74%	1750 s

It can be noticed that the highest accuracy of CNN resulted with model created from the first dataset (a). The results of the other metrics are also in-line with the accuracy.

Table 3. The results of the feedforward Artificial Neural Networks.

Dataset	Accuracy	Precision		Recall		F1-score		Total train time
		Real	Fake	Real	Fake	Real	Fake	
a	90%	98%	91%	92%	88%	91%	89%	45 s
b	74%	75%	74%	68%	79%	71%	76%	50 s
c	77%	81%	66%	85%	60%	83%	63%	45 s
a & b	77%	79%	76%	75%	79%	77%	78%	55 s
a & c	85%	85%	85%	88%	82%	87%	84%	70 s
b & c	72%	74%	71%	69%	75%	72%	73%	75 s
a & b & c	76%	78%	73%	73%	78%	75%	76%	80 s

The results of using feedforward Artificial Neural Networks (ANN) gave very similar results as of using CNN with dataset (a) resulted in the highest accuracy. However, it can be noticed that the training time of feedforward neural networks is much faster than of CNN. Moreover, the accuracy and F1-score of the dataset merged of the three sets (a & b & c) on using feedforward neural networks is higher than the CNN architecture.

RNN resulted with close accuracy of using CNN but with faster training time. However, the accuracy and F1-score on dataset (a & b & c) is less than both multilayer neural networks and CNN.

Table 4. The experimental results of the Recurrent Neural Networks (RNN).

Dataset	Accuracy	Precision		Recall		F1-score		Total train time
		Real	Fake	Real	Fake	Real	Fake	
a	92%	93%	91%	92%	93%	92%	92%	225 s
b	71%	75%	69%	58%	83%	65%	75%	240 s
c	70%	80%	55%	74%	63%	77%	59%	200 s
a & b	73%	75%	72%	69%	78%	72%	75%	1030 s
a & c	75%	92%	66%	59%	94%	72%	77%	630 s
b & c	65%	75%	61%	47%	84%	57%	71%	625 s
a & b & c	72%	73%	71%	72%	72%	72%	71%	1100 s

Table 5. The experimental results of using Long-Short Term Memory (LSTM).

Dataset	Accuracy	Precision		Recall		F1-score		Total train time
		Real	Fake	Real	Fake	Real	Fake	
a	90%	91%	89%	89%	91%	90%	90%	7000 s
b	67%	72%	65%	51%	82%	60%	73%	6400 s
c	59%	76%	43%	56%	66%	64%	52%	1750 s
a & b	70%	72%	68%	64%	76%	68%	71%	15500 s
a & c	74%	90%	65%	59%	92%	71%	76%	8000 s
b & c	64%	65%	63%	60%	68%	63%	65%	8300 s
a & b & c	69%	69%	69%	72%	66%	71%	68%	18500 s

LSTM algorithm resulted in the highest running time through the training stage with no major improvement on the accuracy. Contrarily, it resulted in lower accuracy and F1-score values in comparison to the other algorithms.

4 Discussion

As shown in the tables above, there is a slight superiority for the simple feedforward Artificial Neural Network in comparison with the other algorithms. Where simple ANN algorithm Accuracy 85% for the merged dataset (a & c) compared with 84% for CNN, 75% for RNN, and 74% for LSTM. However, for the individual datasets, CNN resulted in the highest accuracy for dataset (a) and ANN has the highest accuracy for both datasets (b) and (c) individually.

We noticed through the results and data distribution in Figs. 3 that 4 that the best accuracy results were achieved with the shortest text lengths. Where dataset (a) with text length between (2–100) words achieved accuracies that varied between 90%–92% for all algorithms compared with the dataset (c) with text length between (2–2200) words that achieved accuracy scores between 59% and 77%.

On another note, when we compared the training time for all algorithms, the simple neural network was much faster in terms of training time than all others algorithms. Simple ANN algorithm took (80 s) to train the model with 50 epochs training on the largest merged dataset (a & b & c) compared with (1100 s) for RNN, (1750 s) for CNN, and (18500 s) LSTM.

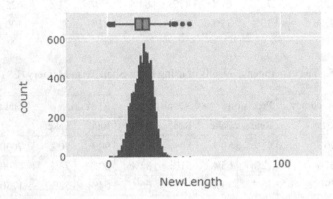

Fig. 3. Data distribution and the length of tweets in dataset (a).

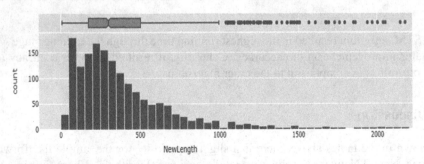

Fig. 4. Data distribution and the length of tweets in dataset (c).

5 Conclusion and Future Work

This paper aimed to detect misinformation about COVID-19 using different Neural Network architectures on different datasets. The paper presented experimental comparison between different Neural Network architectures on three datasets individually and combined. We found that a simple ANN achieved the best accuracy on datasets used in comparison to other more complex architectures. As well, merging the datasets, which resulted in a larger dataset, has increased the performance of the learning algorithms. The algorithms ranked based on their accuracy as follows from best to worst: ANN, CNN, RNN, and lastly LSTM.

Additionally, the simple ANN algorithm was the fastest in terms of training time compared to the other algorithms. We can rank the algorithms based on the training time from best to worst as follows: ANN, RNN, CNN, and LSTM.

For the future work, we plan to include other datasets and to train the models on different languages such as Arabic. Furthermore, we plan to test against other ML algorithms such as ensemble methods and other more advance Neural Network architectures such as transformers.

References

1. Coronavirus disease (COVID-19). https://www.who.int/emergencies/diseases/novel-corona virus-2019. Accessed 1 May 2022
2. Social media use during COVID-19 worldwide - statistics & facts | Statista. https://www.statista.com/topics/7863/social-media-use-during-coronavirus-Covid-19-worldwide/#dossierKeyfigures. Accessed 15 Dec 2021
3. Baldwin, R., Weder, B., Mauro, D.: Economics in the Time of COVID-19. www.cepr.org. Accessed 15 Dec 2021
4. Fighting misinformation in the time of COVID-19, one click at a time. https://www.who.int/news-room/feature-stories/detail/fighting-misinformation-in-the-time-of-Covid-19-one-click-at-a-time. Accessed 15 Dec 2021
5. Cinelli, M., et al.: The COVID-19 social media infodemic. Sci. Reports **10**(1) (2020). https://doi.org/10.1038/s41598-020-73510-5
6. Elhadad, M.K., Li, K.F., Gebali, F.: Detecting misleading information on COVID-19. IEEE Access **8**, 165201–165215 (2020). https://doi.org/10.1109/ACCESS.2020.3022867
7. Patwa, P., et al.: Fighting an Infodemic: COVID-19 Fake News Dataset. https://doi.org/10.1007/978-3
8. Flach, P.A.: Machine Learning The Art and Science of Algorithms that Make Sense of Data (2012)
9. Alenezi, M.N., Alqenaei, Z.M.: Machine learning in detecting COVID-19 misinformation on Twitter. Future Internet **13**(10), 244 (2021). https://doi.org/10.3390/fi13100244
10. Bafandeh, S., And, I., Bolandraftar, M.: Application of K-Nearest Neighbor (KNN) approach for predicting economic events: theoretical background. J. Eng. Res. Appl. **3**, 605–610. www.ijera.com. Accessed 18 Dec 2021
11. Hastie, T., Tibshirani, R., Friedman, J.: The Elements of Statistical Learning (2009). https://doi.org/10.1007/978-0-387-84858-7
12. Granik, M., Mesyura, V.: Fake news detection using naive Bayes classifier. In: 2017 IEEE 1st Ukraine Conference on Electrical and Computer Engineering UKRCON 2017 - Proceedings, pp. 900–903 (2017). https://doi.org/10.1109/UKRCON.2017.8100379
13. Ullah, A.R.S., Das, A., Das, A., Ashad Kabir, M., Shu, K.: A Survey of COVID-19 Misinformation: Datasets, Detection Techniques and Open Issues (2021)
14. Cortes, C., Vapnik, V.: Support-vector networks. Mach. Learn. **20**(3), 273–297 (1995). https://doi.org/10.1007/BF00994018

15. Dharawat, A., Lourentzou, I., Morales, A., Zhai, C.: Drink bleach or do what now? Covid-HeRA: a dataset for risk-informed health decision making in the presence of COVID19 misinformation (2020). https://arxiv.org/abs/2010.08743v1. Accessed 20 Dec 2021
16. Murphy, K.P.: Machine Learning A Probabilistic Perspective (2012)
17. Dadgar, S., Ghatee, M.: Checkovid: A COVID-19 misinformation detection system on Twitter using network and content mining perspectives (2021)
18. Choudrie, J., Banerjee, S., Kotecha, K., Walambe, R., Karende, H., Ameta, J.: Machine learning techniques and older adults processing of online information and misinformation: a covid 19 study. Comput. Hum. Behav. **119**, 106716 (2021). https://doi.org/10.1016/j.chb.2021.106716
19. Perrio, C., Madabushi, H.T.: CXP949 at WNUT-2020 Task 2: Extracting Informative COVID-19 Tweets – RoBERTa Ensembles and The Continued Relevance of Handcrafted Features, pp. 352–358 (2020). https://doi.org/10.18653/v1/2020.wnut-1.48
20. Zhou, X., Mulay, A., Ferrara, E., Zafarani, R.: ReCOVery: A multimodal repository for COVID-19 news credibility research. In: Proceedings of the International Conference on Information and Knowledge Management, pp. 3205–3212 (2020). https://doi.org/10.1145/3340531.3412880
21. Swire-Thompson, B., Lazer, D.: Public health and online misinformation: challenges and recommendations. Annu. Rev. Public Health **41**, 433–451 (2019). https://doi.org/10.1146/ANNUREV-PUBLHEALTH-040119-094127
22. Yim, W.W., Yetisgen, M., Harris, W.P., Sharon, W.K.: Natural language processing in oncology: a review. JAMA Oncol. **2**(6), 797–804 (2016). https://doi.org/10.1001/JAMAONCOL.2016.0213
23. Mujtaba, G., et al.: Clinical text classification research trends: systematic literature review and open issues. Expert Syst. Appl. **116**, 494–520 (2019). https://doi.org/10.1016/J.ESWA.2018.09.034
24. Agarwal, A., Dixit, A.: Fake news detection: an ensemble learning approach. In: Proceedings of the International Conference Intelligent Computing Control System ICICCS 2020, pp. 1178–1183 (2020). https://doi.org/10.1109/ICICCS48265.2020.9121030
25. Sharma, R., Agarwal, V., Sharma, S., Arya, M.S.: An LSTM-based fake news detection system using word embeddings-based feature extraction. In: Fong, S., Dey, N., Joshi, A. (eds.) LNNS, vol. 154, pp. 247–255 (2021). https://doi.org/10.1007/978-981-15-8354-4_26/COVER

Tracing Political Positioning of Dutch Newspapers

Christopher Congleton⬚, Peter van der Putten⁽⊠⁾⬚, and Suzan Verberne⁽⊠⁾⬚

Leiden University, Niels Bohrweg 1, 2333 Leiden, CA, The Netherlands
c.r.congleton@umail.leidenuniv.nl,
{p.w.h.van.der.putten,s.verberne}@liacs.leidenuniv.nl

Abstract. Newspapers write for a particular readership and from a certain ideological or political perspective. This paper applies various natural language processing methods to newspaper articles to analyse to which extent the ideological positioning of newspapers is reflected in their writing. Political bias is illustrated in terms of coverage bias and agenda setting by means of metrics, LDA topic modelling and word embeddings. Furthermore, article source discrimination is analysed by applying various classification models. Finally, the use of generative models (GPT-2) is explored for this purpose. These analyses showed several indications of political tendencies: disproportionate coverage of certain politicians and parties, limited overlap of political discourse, classifiable article source and divergence of generated text thematically and in terms of sentiment. Therefore, reading a newspaper requires a critical attitude which considers the intricate political tendencies of the source.

Keywords: Political bias · Topic modelling · Newspaper agenda setting

1 Introduction

Newspapers typically write for a particular audience, and from a certain ideological or political perspective. For opinion articles this is not necessarily a problem if authors and media are transparent about their positioning [6], but ideological or political bias is an issue for analysis or news reporting articles [12]. Framing the debate and setting the political agenda offers media considerable influence depending on how critical the reader is in consuming content. Media outlets have been visualised on political bias and news value scales to this end[1].

Specific newspapers shape their readers' view through how and to what extent they select, present, and discuss political issues as a subset of the collective political discourse. Unlike modern social media where each user publishes on personal account, a newspaper is formed by the collection of articles from different writers and tied together by the editor. This editorial coherence shapes the

---

[1] Visualisation of the position of media on a political bias and news value scale by Vanessa Otero https://adfontesmedia.com/static-mbc.

F. Spezzano et al. (Eds.): MISDOOM 2022, LNCS 13545, pp. 27–43, 2022.
https://doi.org/10.1007/978-3-031-18253-2_3

Table 1. Research questions

RQ1	To what extent is the ideological position of newspapers reflected in their writing?
SQ1	To what extent is coverage bias measurable in newspapers?
SQ2	To what extent do newspapers share a set of topics?
SQ3	To what extent do specific newspapers cover the shared political topics?
SQ4	To what extent can newspapers be identified given a political article?
SQ5	To what extent does text generation based on specific newspapers diverge in topic?

newspaper's ideology or political perspective [12]. By selecting what news newspapers collectively cover and how they write in terms of sentiment and theme, the scope of political discourse is determined which is the basis on which parties distinguish themselves and the public casts their vote. Inversely, politicians or parties might shape their messages into a format that make it more likely to be included.

Recent research in Germany [7], Denmark [10] and Korea [14] has quantified bias in seemingly politically neutral articles by means of modern computational techniques. Regarding selection bias work by Susanszky et al. [27] measures the extent to which demonstrations in Hungary are under reported in pro-government media outlets. Their analysis is based on a dataset containing 329 articles. Furthermore, there is research vanilla GPT-2's bias in relation to occupation-gender ratio [17] as well as political bias [20]. Following up on GPT-2 with 1.5B parameters trained on 40 GB of text and published in 2019, a larger model GPT-3 was published in 2020 with 175B parameters and trained of a filtered dataset of 570 GB [4,22].

There is a gap between these works of specific bias analysis of a subject, media outlet or source and bias on a high-level generative model like GPT-2 based on an enormous set of textual data. This paper aims to bridge this gap by tracing political positioning of newspapers based on a large collections of their articles. Furthermore, in this paper we aim to retain the bias in the generative language model and analyse it in contrast to studies reducing bias in the model.

Work by De Vries et al. [30] recycling the originally English GPT-2 model has made a Dutch version available through Huggingface. This version is partly trained on old newspaper articles for 2007. Therefore, this paper extends on this work by fine-tuning the model on more up to date Dutch articles from 2021.

Analysing and visualising political bias, scope and coherence in newspapers can uncover and unpack political and ideological orientation. Understanding these underlying mechanisms facilitates safeguarding readers by showing the true colour of sources where this is obfuscated. Therefore, this paper seeks to answer the following key research question: to what extent is the ideological position of newspapers reflected in their writing? (for sub questions see Table 1).

The research questions are answered by applying computational techniques to a collection of 96,840 Dutch newspaper articles collected for the purpose of this paper. To answer the first sub question the political bias in newspapers is quantified. The second sub question provides a high level, illustrative view of the scope of the collective political discourse present in newspapers. The third sub-question aims to uncover the specific scope of political discourse unique to newspapers compared to the shared topical perspective among newspapers. The fourth sub question looks to illustrate the coherence of articles in newspapers. Finally, for the fifth sub question we fine-tune natural language generation models on specific newspapers, to analyse the divergence in text generation.

The contribution of this paper consists of introducing the application of specific computational methods to newspaper data for quantitative political research and analysis. Specifically, analysing selection bias by means of topic modelling and word embeddings, analysing identifiability of article source by means of classification models and analysing thematic and sentiment divergence by analysing the output of Dutch source specific fine-tuned GPT-2 models. Applying generative language models is unique in this context of political bias. Some research that approaches this topic is an attempt to deep fake politicians on twitter by Ressmeyer et al. and a domain specific BERT model for the 2020 election for example [16,23]. Furthermore, the size of the Dutch dataset used for these analyses is among the larger of those used in related work.

The remainder of this paper is organized as follows. Section 2 reviews the background and related work. We then present methods, analysis and results for data collection (Sect. 3), coverage bias (Sect. 4, SQ1), discourse topic analysis (Sect. 5, SQ2-3), article source identification (Sect. 6, SQ4) and text generation (Sect. 7, SQ5), followed by a discussion (Sect. 8), limitations and future work (Sect. 9) and conclusion (Sect. 10).

2 Related Work

In this section a background context on the study of political ideology in media is constructed by discussing bias, political ideology spaces and source classification of textual data.

In the context of this paper, bias is the action of supporting or opposing a particular person or party in an unfair way through allowing opinion to influence judgment. It can manifest itself in various ways as illustrated in research by Eberl et al. [9] where political bias in media is divided into three types: visibility, tonality and agenda bias. Visibility bias is defined as the effect of a party or politician receiving a relatively undue amount of coverage. Tonality bias describes the sentiment, positive or negative, of articles towards a party or politician. Agenda bias concerns the alignment of topics or issues covered by the news and a party or politician's agenda topics. Quantifying visibility and tonality bias is a good step towards answering the first sub question of this research. A lot of work has been done to investigate visibility and tonality bias. For example, the work of Dallmann et al. [7] covering political bias in online newspaper articles uses occurrence metrics and sentiment analysis. Enevoldsen et al. [10] specifically use sentiment analysis to study tonality bias.

2.1   Dimensionality of Political Discourse

Various research studies have also been conducted on the modelling of the political ideology space. Traditionally, this space is orientated on the one-dimensional spectrum from left to right, even though this contrasts the complexity and multifaceted reality of public policy. For example, the convergence of the extremes known as the Horseshoe model, challenges this linear view by discussing a convergence of extreme right and left [28]. Similarly, the representation of politics in newspapers is not limited to a single-dimensional scale. Modern dimensionality reduction techniques have been applied to find the essential dimensions needed to distinguish party politics [1,19] using surveyed political stance data. A similar approach could be applied to newspaper data to analyse the scope of political discourse which in turn can be used to answer to what extent shared political topics are discernible [25].

Quantifying agenda bias approaches the third sub question as it covers the newspaper specific topical shape in contrast to the general political discourse. Research on agenda bias in news media using topic modelling or word embedding methods is not found, and thus leaves a void to be filled by this research paper.

2.2   Source Identification

In order to approach the extent of coherence in writing between political articles from the same newspaper, reverse analysis is applied by developing a system for the task of articles' source classification. Research work on this topic has been performed in the context of author identification of natural language [24] using a support vector machine and deep learning based approaches. Furthermore, author identification of code using word embeddings, tf-idf and convolutional neural nets shows very accurate results [2]. Another angle of discriminating articles is whether the content has a commercial or editorial purpose. The work of Kats et al. [15] shows that it is possible to differentiate between the two with an accuracy of 90%. On the basis of these research papers, it is expected to be possible to develop an appropriate system to discriminate between articles' source and analyse on what basis they are distinguished.

2.3   Text Generation

Modern natural language generation has many applications where text is generated from other forms of data or a language model [11]. In this paper, a transformer-based language model is used, specifically GPT-2 [22]. In this paper, we use it as auto-regressive model, generating natural language by predicting the next word in a sequence following up a prompt. The architecture of GPT-2 closely follows the setup as described in Radford et al. [21] which is based on the Transformer model [29]. In this paper we aim to retain and analyse the bias of a source using a generative AI model. To our knowledge no research work has been done using modern language models from this angle.

3   Data

The data used to answer the research questions is collected by scraping articles from the internet archives of various Dutch newspapers. As the second sub question covers the shared political topics of newspapers, a broad scope of sources is required. Therefore, a balanced and representative collection is the key to establishing a suitable analogue of political discourse. However, some newspaper websites have restrictions on crawling and scraping activities. Therefore, the data are limited to articles from NRC (centrist, progressive liberal), Volkskrant (centre left, progressive), Het Parool (Amsterdam regional, centrist) and Trouw (centre, protestant origins). We would have liked to have included more conservative, right-leaning or tabloid media.

3.1   Data Collection

The collection of articles for each newspaper is carried out following the same general sequence of steps[2] First, the website archive is crawled to index all the articles URLs in a specific time range (2021). Second, all these links are scraped using Python's Requests library, resulting in a collection of HTML data for each web page. Third, the HTML data is parsed to produce clean text article data. Capitalisation and punctuation are retained. Fourth, the data are saved as JSON dumps.

3.2   Results

In total 96840 articles have been collected, respectively for NRC (32043), Volkskrant (25702), Trouw (20944) and Parool (18151) as visualised in Fig. 1. To illustrate the size of these collections the number of words in each set is illustrated in Fig. 2. A subset of 15,508 articles is connected to politics through the mention of either a party leader or party name in the 2021 Tweede Kamer, the Dutch House of Representatives. This set consists of the articles from the complete set that contain either a party name or a party leader name. This political subset consists of 15.508 articles, respectively for NRC (6425), Volkskrant (3752), Trouw (2877) and Parool (2454) as visualised in 3. To illustrate the relative size, the number of words for each source is visualised in Fig. 4.

Although the total number of articles in Volkskrant is significantly smaller than the number of articles in NRC the total number of words in these articles is comparable. Thus, Volkskrant writes less but longer articles. Regarding the political subset, NRC has a relatively larger number of articles and especially compared to the Volkskrant a larger number of words in articles concerning politics.

---

[2] Sample code for data collection and analysis can be found at: https://github.com/Chris-Congleton/MSc-Thesis.

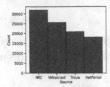

Fig. 1. Total number of articles

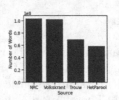

Fig. 2. Total number of words (in 100 Ms)

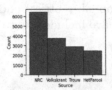

Fig. 3. Number of articles in political subset

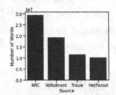

Fig. 4. Number of words in political subset (in 10 Ms)

4 Coverage Bias

Coverage bias (SQ1) is studied by evaluating various metrics based on the aggregation of party or politician mentions. The selection of party and politicians of which mention frequency is counted is based on the elected parties in the Tweede Kamer in 2021 and their respective party leaders[3].

4.1 Log Normalised Mention Frequency

The first metric is calculated on the complete data set. First of, the occurrence of each term (party or politician) in each article is counted. The resulting counts are aggregated by summation over each source. Furthermore, these values are normalised by dividing over the total sum of term mentions, all politicians and parties, in a specific source. This takes care of the discrepancy in number of articles per source. Finally, the logarithm of these values is taken to make the results interpretable as initially the normalised counts of lesser prominent parties or politicians are dwarfed by the greater. The formula is given in Eq. 1. The Log Normalised Mention Frequency is denoted with f_{ln}. S is the set of sources in the complete data set D. An article is denoted as a and the term count in an article is denoted by t_a. The T is used to denote all political terms, politician or party names.

$$f_{ln} = log(\frac{\sum_{a \in S} t_a}{\sum_{a \in S} T_a}) \tag{1}$$

---

[3] The parties, party leaders and number of seats in the 2021 Tweede Kamer can be found at: https://www.kiesraad.nl/actueel/nieuws/2021/03/26/officiele-uitslag-tweede-kamerverkiezing-17-maart-2021.

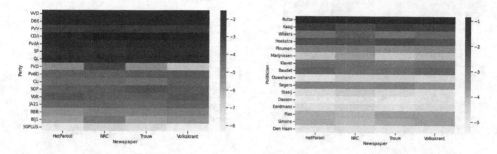

Fig. 5. Party-newspaper coverage   **Fig. 6.** Politician-newspaper coverage

4.2 Relative Normalised Mention Frequency

The second metric is computed over the complete dataset as well. First of, the occurrence of each term (party or politician) in each article is counted. The resulting counts are aggregated by summation over each source. Furthermore, these values are normalised by dividing over the total sum of term mentions in a specific source. Thereafter, in order to establish the relative term mention frequency, the average mention frequency of a term over all sources is computed and this value is used to normalise the counts per source. There are four sources thus adding the $\frac{1}{4}$ fraction to the equation.

$$f_{rn} = \frac{\sum_{a \in S} t_a}{\frac{1}{4} \sum_{a \in D} t_a} \tag{2}$$

The Relative Normalised Mention Frequency is denoted with f_{rn}. S is the set of sources in the complete data set D. An article is denoted as a and the term count in an article is denoted by t_a.

4.3 Experiments and Results

In order to illustrate the political coverage bias present in newspapers the results of the Log Normalised Mention Frequency of parties and politicians in 2021 are depicted in Figs. 5 and 6. In both figures, the parties or politicians on the y-axis are ordered according to the party seats in the Tweede Kamer. Therefore, one would expect the coverage to gradually decrease from the biggest party at the top towards the smallest party at the bottom. Two parties clearly break this idea: PVV and FVD both have contrasting low coverage compared to the other parties. Both are considered (far) right wing populist parties, which may explain this discrepancy. Interestingly, the low coverage of PVV and FVD contrasts with relatively regular coverage of the party leaders Wilders and Baudet, with Baudet scoring better in relative terms. This could alternatively explain the lower mention frequency of the parties as the party leader is mentioned instead. With respect to Fig. 6, the odd one out is Marijnissen, although her party (SP) has the same amount of seats as Ploumen's PvdA, she is mentioned less overall.

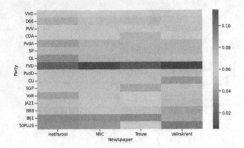
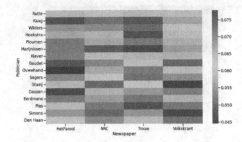

Fig. 7. Relative party-newspaper coverage

Fig. 8. Relative politician-newspaper coverage

Furthermore, the relatively high coverage of Segers (CU) could be attributed to the fact that his party was part of the government.

With an increased contrast, the Relative Normalised Mention Frequency, is depicted in Figs. 7 and 8. With respect to parties, no large differences in coverage are seen, except for the FVD which is mentioned significantly more in NRC and less in Het Parool, Trouw and Volkskrant. Apart from Mark Rutte (VVD and prime minister) who is covered fairly consistently over all sources, the contrasts in politician coverage are more prevalent. Kaag (D'66) for example, does relatively well in Het Parool and Trouw. Hoekstra (CDA) and van der Plas (BBB) are relatively prominent in Trouw and Simons in Volkskrant.

In conclusion, the results for the Log Normalised Frequency and Relative Normalised Frequency show disproportionate coverage of certain politicians and parties. Which indicates a certain bias in news coverage.

5   General and Source Specific Political Discourse

To investigate to what extent shared political topics are discernible (SQ2), as well as source specific topics (SQ3), Latent Dirichlet Allocation (LDA) [3], a modern topic modelling technique is used. LDA is a generative probabilistic model of a corpus [13].

5.1   Topic Modelling

To prepare the text data specifically for the topic modelling punctuation and special characters are removed and the text is lowercased. An NLTK stop word list is used to remove non-significant words. This list is extended manually to remove remaining HTML tags. In addition to the preprocessing of the text, a subset of the total article collection is used to construct the LDA model. As the purpose of this research is to distinguish political topics, the political subset as mentioned in Sect. 3 is used.

The LDA model is analysed using the pyLDAvis package. This depicts the Intertopic Distance Map and the top-30 most relevant terms for a topic. A relevance metric of $\lambda = 0.3$ is used to balance the word probability under a topic relative to its lift [26]. Each topic is interpreted manually based on the top-30 most relevant terms for the topic.

The number of topics is setup consistent with the number of topics that provides the most distinguishable topics over the general data on a manual basis. Some experiments with various numbers of topics were performed ranging from 5–20. Here the clearest topics were present with the number of topics set to 10. This number is kept consistent for each of the specific sources in order to compare a set of the same size.

5.2   Experiments and Results

The results of the LDA topic modelling in the political subset are described in Table 2. The assigned topics are ordered in marginal topic distribution. This can be interpreted as the importance of a topic with respect to the corpus.

The most prominent topic is national politics and corona policy. Furthermore, topics consisting of far right/left, EU, and international politics are distinguished. Finally, thematic topics on family life, law and order, economy, elections and personal assets/debt are present. One of the topics has not generalised to an interpretable topic or theme and thus is left blank. The first four clearly political topics are the most prominent; it is interesting to see which additional politically related topics arise. These themes can give insight into the topics discussed in a political context. Thus, illustrating the agenda setting in general political discourse.

The source specific topic modelling is analysed with regards to the topic modelling results on the general political discourse based on the complete collection of articles. The topics or themes that arise in the modelling of articles from a particular source are considered a subset of the general political discourse. National politics is the only topic consistently found for all the sources. Thus, a limited overlap of political topics is present based on this analysis.

5.3   Word Embeddings

Another approach to comparing the general and source-specific discourse is to represent the text data in vector space and visualise the respective embeddings of parties and politicians in a lower-dimensional space. In the embedding space words that are similar and appear in the same context have a similar vector. Visualising these vectors can therefore show what parties or politicians are discussed in a similar context. This offers a spatial projection of the parties and politicians based on how newspapers write about them as an alternative to the Horseshoe model as introduced in Sect. 1. That model is based on the ideological position of a party or politician while this projection is based on newspaper coverage and the position in political discourse.

Table 2. LDA topic modelling (translated into English)

	General	NRC	Trouw	Het parool	Volkskrant
1	Domestic policy, Corona policy	Domestic policy, Corona policy	Domestic policy	Domestic policy	Domestic policy
2	Far right/left	Far right/left, purchasing power	-	-	Corona policy
3	EU politics	(Distrust) Domestic politics	Coalition formation	Domestic policy	Life
4	Foreign politics	Family matters/ housing/living	-	Far right/left	Far right
5	Family matters	'Wappies' (corona conspiracy)	-	-	(Distrust) Domestic politics
6	Safety and Law enforcement	-	Domestic policy/Corona policy	-	(Far) left
7	-	Corona/AZC (refugee centers)	Domestic policy	Amsterdam politics	Culture
8	Economy	(Distrust) Domestic politics	Domestic policy	-	Housing and work
9	Elections	-	(Distrust) Domestic politics	-	Safety and Law enforcement
10	Wealth/Debt management	-	Domestic policy	Amsterdam politics	-

First, a gensim Word2Vec model is trained on the corpus of the political subset to cover general political discourse and a political subset of a newspaper to cover specific political discourse. Words representing the same party or politician are drawn together. For example, "GroenLinks" and "GL". Second, the dimensionality of the word vectors in the model is reduced with t-SNE. Third, this reduced word representation is extracted for parties and politicians and visualised. Representing the textual data in vector space and visualising the respective embeddings of parties and politicians in a lower-dimensional space gives an intuition to how is written about parties or politicians in general or source-specific.

5.4 Experiments and Results

The text data is preprocessed by removing punctuation and special characters as well as lowercasing the text.

The general political discourse is visualised in Fig. 9. The grouping of the parties that end up in government in 2022 is distinguished at the bottom left. VVD, CDA, D66 and CU. GL, PvdA and SP are also in the vicinity which may be explained by their efforts to be part of the formation. The farthest away from this governing party group we find the FVD and PVV in the top right. These parties are both considered far right and therefore may profile themselves opposing the established parties. The remaining parties can be described as the moderate opposition.

The source-specific political discourse is visualised in Fig. 10. Concerning the NRC figure, a similar grouping of governing parties is present in the bottom left of the figure along with GL, PvdA and SP in the vicinity. The CU is located far away at the top of the figure. The NRC mentions the CU in a relative distant context from the governing parties. Moderate opposition parties are found on

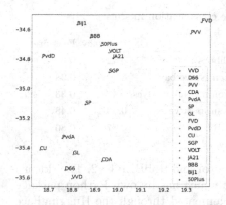

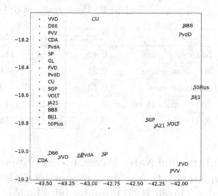

Fig. 9. Word2Vec + tSNE: parties in general

Fig. 10. Word2Vec + tSNE: parties in NRC

the middle right. Compared to the general political discourse visualised in Fig. 9, the most distant parties from the governing parties are now BBB and PvdD in the upper right. The far-right parties FVD and PVV, located on the bottom right, are relatively close to the governing and moderate opposition parties.

In conclusion, these results do not show a consistent shape of the parties in the embedding space. This is an indication against the presence of a generally shared political discourse.

6 Discriminating Newspapers by Article Texts

The fourth sub-question is approached by training classifier models to distinguish political articles by source and analysing the features the classifier uses to discriminate. The input of the models consists of the political subset of the data set labelled with the respective source. First, the models are tuned and compared with respect to performance. The models and classifications are then interpreted and analysed.

Determining the source identifiability is an approach to analyse the style coherence of a source. The features a model uses to distinguish sources can inform us on the major differences between sources. Furthermore, the complexity of this task says something about the depth of these difference. For example, if distinction is manageable for a simple model this would mean there is a big difference in superficial aspects of the textual data like specific words. Alternatively, if distinction is only manageable for a complex model this would mean that the difference are more nuanced for example based on writing style.

Preprocessing of the textual data in the political articles is performed by removing punctuation, special characters and stop words. Furthermore, the text is converted to lowercase. Thereafter, for the non-transformer models, TF-IDF features are extracted using sklearn's TfidfVectorizer. A minimum document frequency of 30 is used to eliminate infrequent words to improve performance.

Experimentation is performed using various modelling techniques: Decision Tree, RBF Support Vector, XGBoost, KNeighbors, Gaussian Naive Bayes,

Table 3. Performance of source classification models

Model	Accuracy	F1-score	Model	Accuracy	F1-score
Majority class	0.41	0.14	KNeighbors	0.42	0.35
Random guess	0.24	0.23	Gaussian Naive bayes	0.40	0.38
Decision tree	0.43	0.27	Multinomial Naïve bayes	0.47	0.33
RBF support vector	0.55	0.46	Linear support vector	0.53	0.48
XGBoost	0.51	0.41	RobBERT	0.87	0.86

Multinomial Naïve Bayes, Linear Support Vector and RobBERT v2. The sklearn implementation is used except for XGBoost which has its own Python package and a Dutch BERT model [8] which is implemented through the HuggingFace Transformers package. From the political subset of articles 80% is used as training set and 20% as test set. The performance of the models is compared in terms of macro F1-score. For each of the non-transformer models, default parameters were used. For RobBERT v2 the parameters that were used are a learning rate of 1e–5, batch size 16, 3 training epochs and weight decay of 0.01.

6.1 Experiments and Results

For the non-transformer models TF-IDF features are extracted using sklearn's TfidfVectorizer. A minimum document frequency of 30 is used to eliminate infrequent words to improve performance. This results in a vocabulary of 11804 words. This minimum document frequency is used to prevent the vocabulary from having a unmanageable size.

The performance of each of the models applied to the source classification task is given in table 3. When comparing the simpler models (Decision Tree, KNeighbors, Gaussian Naive Bayes, Multinomial Naive Bayes) with the Majority Class classifier only a small improvement in accuracy is seen, though the F1-score does get improved significantly. Runner up are the RBF Support Vector, Linear Support Vector and XGBoost models. They show a significant improvement in F1-score and an accuracy of >50%. The best performance is found with the most advanced model, RobBERT.

With respect to the linear SVC model the importance of features can be interpreted by analysing the size of the coefficients of the one-vs-one classifiers. For two class combinations, the top ten positive and negative predictors are visualised. With respect to Parool-NRC, Fig. 11, it is logical to see 'amsterdam' as a strong positive feature and 'nrc' as a strong negative. With respect to Parool-Trouw in Fig. 12, it is interesting to see 'mark' a strong predictor for Parool in contrast with 'premier' for Trouw.

7 Article Generation

Modern transformer models enable automatic natural language generation. It is possible to fine-tune these on specific source material to generate text in the

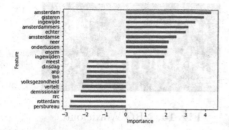

Fig. 11. Parool vs NRC

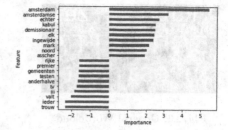

Fig. 12. Parool vs Trouw

style of an author or news medium. For sports articles automatic generation is already in use [18]. Inversely, this technique could be used to analyse the general writing style or bias of an author or news medium. These models are a form of extrapolation of writing. Therefore, this analysis is limited by its assumption that this extrapolation is an accurate representation of how the author or news medium writes.

With respect to sub question 5, we fine-tune generative natural language models for each newspaper separately and analyse and compare generated articles based on a common prompt. A pre-trained Dutch version of GPT-2 is utilised, GroNLP's small Dutch model [30]. This model recycles the original English GPT-2 model [22]. The recycling means retraining the lexical embeddings of the originally English model for Dutch alternatives while fixing the transformer layers. This retraining of the lexical embeddings is performed with a dataset consisting of Wikipedia (2.8 GB), newspaper articles (2.9 GB) from 2007, books (6.5 GB) and articles from various Dutch news websites (2.1 GB). The model can be fine-tuned on a specific textual data set. In the experiments we use GroNLP's small Dutch model zero-shot. Furthermore, the model is fine-tuned on the NRC, Volkskrant, Trouw and Het Parool political subset as well as these collectively, which is described as the general model.

This analysis using generative AI offers advantages over analysing the source data. First, experiments can be performed very specifically due to the text being generated on the basis of a prompt. Second, as the textual data are generated using a language model, the samples can be considered a general collective style or writing angle of the complete source. For example, a single author from a newspaper may have a different style than all the writers in the newspaper combined.

7.1 Experiments and Results

The divergence in text generation of these models is compared through initiation of the different model versions with a neutral prompt. The model is implemented using the Huggingface's transformer package. The following sub-packages are used: AutoTokenizer, TextDataset, DataCollatorForLanguageModeling, Trainer, TrainingArguments and AutoModelWithLMHead. The model is

Fig. 13. General Wordcloud

Fig. 14. NRC Wordcloud

fine-tuned using the full collection of articles as described in Sect. 3. A maximal sequence length of 128 tokens was used with truncation, a batch size of 32, prediction loss only and a warm up of 500 steps for the learning rate scheduler.

To analyse the generative models with a neutral prompt, sampling is performed based on: "X houdt een toespraak" ("X gives a speech"). A set of 1000 samples is produced with maximal sequence length set to 30. From these texts, word clouds are produced where the most prominent terms are displayed scaled to their occurrence using the Wordcloud python package, with prompt words removed. One of the generated samples is (translated from Dutch): "X is giving a speech on the developments around the corona virus in his capital, The Hague. On social media, he has criticised politicians who do not get themselves investigated together whether they can use corona vaccinations to prevent that".

As can be seen from this example, the specific capital mentioned is not correct. Still, the usage of terms and coverage of topics can provide insight. The word cloud based on the general text generator model, Fig. 13, prominently contains two names of politicians, Rutte and de Jonge. During the corona crisis they gave speeches together informing the public of corona measures. Considering the NRC-word cloud, Rutte and D66 are very prominent and the other words in the cloud cover corona measures and infections. These results show a significant divergence in topics resulting from a neutral prompt. We have carried out a range of other generative experiments that have been omitted here for brevity, for full details see [5] (Fig. 14).

8 Discussion

Concerning SQ1, on political bias, some results stand out. A low coverage in relation to the number of seats of far right parties is present in three newspapers. With respect to the politicians there are four that receive an unexpected amount of coverage either too high or low, including the far right. This indicates that there is a bias present in Dutch newspapers in terms of coverage.

Concerning SQ2, on general political discourse, a set of clear topics is distinguished in the collective of newspapers through LDA visualisation analysis. Furthermore, representation of the political articles in vector space results in a structured clustering of political parties in government, opposition and far right.

Concerning SQ3, on political discourse, national politics is the most prominent topic across all newspapers. However, other topics differ significantly.

Regarding the vector space representation of newspaper-specific political discourse, the structure of the parties is comparable to the general political discourse cluster-wise: governing, far right and moderate opposition. However, how these clusters are located in the space is considerably different. Taking into account topic modelling and vector representation analysis, the newspaper-specific political discourse differs considerably from the general political discourse.

Concerning SQ4, on the identification of a newspaper given an article, this task was very manageable for the advanced RobBERT model. For simpler methods only moderate accuracy was reached. Thus, identifying the newspaper for which an article was written is a complex but achievable task.

Concerning SQ5, on the divergence of text generation models trained on specific newspapers, each of the fine-tuned models takes its own direction when prompted neutrally. These are just very simple initial experiments for illustrative purposes, but in our view already demonstrates that generative models can be interesting tools in this context, though one needs to consider that this type of research is more speculative as it based on generated, synthetic data (see [5] for more results).

9 Research Limitations and Future Work

The analysis in this paper rely on the dataset of articles that have been collected. Due to some newspaper websites disallowing crawling or scraping activities they could not be added to the research data set. It would have been interesting to incorporate a tabloid newspaper like the Telegraaf, a financial oriented newspaper like Financieel Dagblad and AD which characterises itself as politically and religiously neutral. Furthermore, the data used for this paper is limited to the year 2021 and temporal effects are not analysed. For example, it would be interesting to train generative AI on data for each year from 2012 up to 2022 and analyse the sentiment divergence towards a politician or party.

10 Conclusion

In this paper, we have analysed the extent to which the ideology of a newspaper is reflected in their writing. This subject was approached from several angles: measuring coverage bias, comparing general- and source specific discourse, performing classification of articles and analysing generative models trained on articles. The results showed several indications of political tendencies: disproportionate coverage of politicians and parties, limited overlap of political discourse, classifiable article source and divergence of generated text. Even though it is generally known that newspapers write from an ideological and political point of view, solely perceiving their writing on a left-to-right scale is inadequate as the political tendencies of newspaper are intricate. One should consider this when consuming media, and as in our new analysis, use a multitude of tools to analyse the data from multiple perspectives.

References

1. Abduljaber, M.: The dimensionality, type, and structure of political ideology on the political party level in the *arab* world. Chin. Polit. Sci. Rev. **3**(4), 464–494 (2018)
2. Abuhamad, M., Rhim, J., AbuHmed, T., Ullah, S., Kang, S., Nyang, D.: Code authorship identification using convolutional neural networks. Futur. Gener. Comput. Syst. **95**, 104–115 (2019)
3. Blei, D.M., Ng, A.Y., Jordan, M.I.: Latent Dirichlet allocation. J. Mach. Learn. Res. **3**, 993–1022 (2003)
4. Brown, T., et al.: Language models are few-shot learners. Adv. Neural. Inf. Process. Syst. **33**, 1877–1901 (2020)
5. Congleton, C.: Tracing Political Positioning. Master's thesis, Leiden University, July 2022
6. Coppock, A., et al.: The long-lasting effects of newspaper op-eds on public opinion. Q. J. Polit. Sci. **13**(1), 59–87 (2018)
7. Dallmann, A., Lemmerich, F., Zoller, D., Hotho, A.: Media bias in German online newspapers. In: Proceedings of the 26th ACM Conference on Hypertext & Social Media, pp. 133–137 (2015)
8. Delobelle, P., Winters, T., Berendt, B.: RobBERT: a Dutch RoBERTa-based language model. In: Findings of the Association for Computational Linguistics: EMNLP 2020, pp. 3255–3265. Association for Computational Linguistics, November 2020. https://doi.org/10.18653/v1/2020.findings-emnlp.292
9. Eberl, J.M., Wagner, M., Boomgaarden, H.G.: Are perceptions of candidate traits shaped by the media? The effects of three types of media bias. Int. J. Press/Polit. **22**(1), 111–132 (2017)
10. Enevoldsen, K.C., Hansen, L.: Analysing political biases in Danish newspapers using sentiment analysis. J. Lang. Works-Sprogvidenskabeligt Studentertidsskrift **2**(2), 87–98 (2017)
11. Gatt, A., Krahmer, E.: Survey of the state of the art in natural language generation: core tasks, applications and evaluation. J. Artif. Intell. Res. **61**, 65–170 (2018)
12. Hassell, H.J., Miles, M.R., Reuning, K.: Does the ideology of the newsroom affect the provision of media slant? Polit. Commun. **39**(2), 184–201 (2022)
13. Jelodar, H., et al.: Latent Dirichlet allocation (LDA) and topic modeling: models, applications, a survey. Multimed. Tools App. **78**(11), 15169–15211 (2019)
14. Kang, H., Yang, J.: Quantifying perceived political bias of newspapers through a document classification technique. J. Quant. Linguist. **29**, 1–24 (2020)
15. Kats, T., van der Putten, P., Schelling, J.: Distinguishing commercial from editorial content in news. In: Preproceedings 33rd Benelux Conference on Artificial Intelligence and the 30th Belgian Dutch Conference on Machine Learning (BNAIC/BENELEARN 2021), Luxembourg, 10–12 November 2021 (2021)
16. Kawintiranon, K., Singh, L.: PoliBERTweet: a pre-trained language model for analyzing political content on twitter. In: Proceedings of the 13th Conference on Language Resources and Evaluation (LREC 2022) (2022)
17. Kirk, H.R., et al.: Bias out-of-the-box: an empirical analysis of intersectional occupational biases in popular generative language models. Adv. Neural. Inf. Process. Syst. **34**, 2611–2624 (2021)
18. Kunert, J.: Automation in sports reporting: strategies of data providers, software providers, and media outlets. Med. Commun. **8**(3), 5–15 (2020)

19. Lewenberg, Y., Bachrach, Y., Bordeaux, L., Kohli, P.: Political dimensionality estimation using a probabilistic graphical model. In: Proceedings of the Thirty-Second Conference on Uncertainty in Artificial Intelligence, pp. 447–456. UAI 2016, AUAI Press, Arlington, Virginia, USA (2016)
20. Liu, R., Jia, C., Wei, J., Xu, G., Vosoughi, S.: Quantifying and alleviating political bias in language models. Artif. Intell. **304**, 103654 (2022)
21. Radford, A., et al.: Improving language understanding by generative pre-training (2018)
22. Radford, A., et al.: Language models are unsupervised multitask learners. OpenAI Blog **1**(8), 9 (2019)
23. Ressmeyer, R., Masling, S., Liao, M.: "Deep faking" political twitter using transfer learning and GPT-2 (2019)
24. Romanov, A., Kurtukova, A., Shelupanov, A., Fedotova, A., Goncharov, V.: Authorship identification of a Russian-language text using support vector machine and deep neural networks. Futur. Internet J. **13**(1), 3 (2020)
25. Schelling, J., van Eekelen, N., van Veelen, I., van Hees, M., van der Putten, P.: Bursting the bubble (extended abstract). In: MISDOOM 2020, p. 72, October 2020
26. Sievert, C., Shirley, K.: LDAvis: a method for visualizing and interpreting topics. In: Proceedings of the Workshop on Interactive Language Learning, Visualization, and Interfaces, pp. 63–70 (2014)
27. Susánszky, P., Kopper, Á., Zsigó, F.T.: Media framing of political protests-reporting bias and the discrediting of political activism. Post-Soviet Affairs. 1–17 (2022)
28. Tangian, A.: Visualizing the political spectrum of Germany by contiguously ordering the party policy profiles. Data Anal. App 2. Util. Results Eur. Top. **3**, 193–208 (2019)
29. Vaswani, A., et al.: Attention is all you need. Adv. Neural Inf. Process. Syst. **30**, 1–11 (2017)
30. de Vries, W., Nissim, M.: As good as new. How to successfully recycle English GPT-2 to make models for other languages. CoRR abs/2012.05628, pp. 836–864 (2020). https://arxiv.org/abs/2012.05628

Digital Information Seeking and Sharing Behaviour During the COVID-19 Pandemic in Pakistan

Mehk Fatima[1,2], Aimal Rextin[1,5], Mehwish Nasim[3,4,6(✉)],
and Osman Yusuf[1]

[1] Asthma and Allergy Institute Pakistan, Islamabad, Pakistan
[2] University of Chenab, Gujrat, Pakistan
[3] The University of Western Australia, Perth, Australia
`mehwish.nasim@uwa.edu.au`
[4] Flinders University, Adelaide, Australia
[5] National University of Sciences and Technology, Islamabad, Pakistan
[6] The University of Adelaide, Adelaide, Australia

Abstract. Studies on digital interaction in emergent users' population are rare. We analyse the electronic data generated by users from Pakistan on Google Search Engine and WhatsApp to understand their information-seeking behaviour during the first wave of the Covid-19 pandemic. We study how the Pakistani public developed their understanding about the disease, (its origin, cures, and preventive measures to name a few) through digital media. Understanding this *information seeking behaviour* will allow corrective actions to be taken by health policymakers to better inform the public in future health crises through electronic media, as well as the digital media platforms and search engines to address misinformation among the users in the emergent markets.

Keywords: Digital information · Covid-19 · Google trends · WhatsApp · Misinformation

1 Introduction

The first wave of COVID-19 pandemic tested the health care systems and economies around the world. A key point noted in Pakistan was the lack of understanding about the causes, symptoms, and preventive measures of COVID-19. That frequently led to lax attitude towards social distancing protocols [45] or widespread adoption of pseudo-medicinal remedies that are known be ineffective or to have dangerous side effects [8].

In October 2020, Gallup Pakistan released a survey report that described the public's behaviour on COVID-19, just before the increase in the number of new infections during second wave in Pakistan. According to that report, almost 75% of the population thought that COVID-19 was under control and the need for continued precautions was no longer necessary. Whereas, nearly 70% of the public thought that the threat of the SARS-CoV-2 virus was exaggerated, 46% consider COVID-19 as a foreign conspiracy, and 45% public thought that it was a laboratory-made virus. Hence, according to the survey, the public underestimated the threat posed by this disease and many even considered it unreal [1]. Conveying correct medical information to the public is extremely important in a country like Pakistan with limited medical resources, and the high prevalence of pseudo-medicine and quackery in order to ensure that the information seekers have been provided with correct and reliable information. The aim of this paper is to understand how the Pakistani public developed its understanding of this disease, its origin, cures, and preventive measures. Understanding this *information seeking behaviour* will allow corrective actions to be taken by health policymakers to better inform the public for possible future waves of this pandemic, especially through electronic channels.

2 Relevant Literature

Online search trends can be very helpful in digital surveillance and prediction of an infectious disease. Relative search volume regarding COVID-19 increased during the early period of the pandemic and there was a positive correlation between daily new cases and relative search volume [22, 42]. A study found a strong correlation between COVID-19 related Google trends and daily new cases in the US, with R value around 0.80 [26]. Similarly, a sharp hike in Google trends happened in searches related to COVID-19 after the detection of the first case in Taiwan [23]. This strong correlation between the daily confirmed cases and related Google search trends worldwide can be used to predict the trends of outbreak [4, 26]. The rapid increase in web searches on COVID-19 and related topics also created an infodemic like situation and caused the worldwide spread of misinformation on disease [5, 35, 36]. Effective strategies are needed by governments and public health organizations to better manage such infodemic and strengthen the public awareness on the outbreak [22]. Educating the public to use websites of official public health forums can be helpful in this regard [21]. Social media played a key role in propagating health-related misconceptions and poses a big challenge to practitioners and policymakers [20]. The main reason for this challenge is that many people are not clear about the relationship between science, policy-making and media [34], and they tend to rely more on nonscientific but more definitive advice. For example, misinformation circulating during the 2014 Ebola outbreak challenged the efforts of health workers to control the epidemic [11]. Even in countries like Germany, Italy, US and UK, social media movements incited people to resist getting measles vaccination [12, 17]. Similarly, another study analysed 2691 tweets about the treatments and preventive measures of gynecologic cancer and found 30% of them to contain misinformation [10]. While another study found that 40% of links shared on health-related forums contained fake news and were shared more than 450, 000 times between 2012–2017 [44]. Psychological and cognitive biases greatly influence how we react in a pandemic. People anticipated that the SARS-CoV2 virus cases would grow linearly, and they underestimated the possibility of an exponential growth [14]. This lack of understanding and failure of public health messaging had disastrous results even in developed countries [37]. Conspiracy theories and myths pose another serious threat to public health and affect the behavioural responses of people [31] that can dangerously affect the situation in a pandemic. Pseudo-medicinal information and conspiracy theories about COVID-19 circulated through social media traveled faster than the virus itself [15]. Many websites containing unproven claims about COVID-19 are widely visited by the public. They also shared on social media sometimes due to naivety and surprisingly sometimes intentionally to share inaccurate information [32]. This lack of accurate health information on COVID-19 also severely affected the psychological condition of the general public during the pandemic [43].

Google search trends, search queries, and social media debates can be used to analyse the public interests on a specific topic. This data can be specifically helpful during international crises and epidemics. A few studies tried to predict the spread of epidemics in a specific geographical location by performing analysis on search engine queries and Google trends in that region [18,33,39]. Search query analysis also showed that the public immediately started searching about the pandemic but they started searching for prevention and protection e.g. social distancing in the initial stages of the COVID-19 pandemic [6]. Similarly, studies indicated that social media can also be a useful way for early detection of epidemics [25,40].

3   Methodology

In this section we will present our methodology to understand the digital information seeking behaviour of Pakistani users during the first wave of COVID-19. Pakistani users are considered an emergent users group when it comes to technology use [7,24]. Although digital information can take many forms like text, images, and videos, we focused on analysing text data due to ease of availability and simplicity of analysis. There is a plethora of literature on studying the spread of information or misinformation in text based digital data on online social networking sites such as Twitter [27,38]. However, we took an alternative route and chose the following two other sources of digital information:

1. We studied how information was searched on **Google search engine** for COVID-19 related searches through Google Trends related to pseudo-medicinal information on COVID-19. We then compared these search trends with real world circumstances like changing government SoPS, the number of cases, and number of deaths etc., to understand the information trajectory in Pakistan during the COVID-19 crises.
2. WhatsApp is a popular way of communication in Pakistan. According to a mobile ranking forum, WhatsApp is the second most used mobile application in the country. Owing to the popularity of this communication medium, we identified a public **WhatsApp group** focused on COVID-19. We then exported the conversations in the form of textual data from that group. In an

automated way, we replaced all names and phone numbers with unique identifiers and we then stored the data as a *.csv* file with the following columns: Time and *Date, User Identifier, Text Message*. We then analysed the data to understand the mood and content of the messages.

We selected keywords so the data can be mined more easily. It was obvious to use corona, covid etc., but it was not clear which pseudo-medicinal treatment we should use as keywords.

3.1 Pseudo-medicinal Treatments

We observed the following non-scientific treatments of COVID-19 were popular on social media platforms during the first wave of the pandemic in Pakistan:

1. **Herbs and Spices** such as garlic, ginger tea, lemon tea, olive leaf and senna makki (a laxative). Albeit some of these are harmless, *senna makki*, being a laxative, can cause dehydration and in extreme cases deaths in patients.
2. **Homeopathic drugs** such as Arsenicum album received publicity as a powerful immunity booster and were thought to help in preventing COVID-19. While the drug by itself may not have any serious side effects but people consider themselves immune to COVID-19 and as consequence took lesser preventive measures.
3. **Medicines** such as Chloroquine (also marketed with brand name Resochin) and Hydroxychloroquine are antimalarial drugs that gained a lot of attention on social and traditional media without any solid scientific backing and sometimes can be dangerous. Further this medicine is also used for rheumatoid arthritis patients and over-the counter availability of this drug created a shortage in the market for the patient in need.
4. **Convalescent Plasma** therapy was a popular treatment in Pakistan[1] and worldwide including U.S. despite many concerns on its effectiveness and possible adverse effects in some cases [29].

The above list of unproven treatments of COVID-19 acted as keywords for our textual analysis. However, it was not clear whether the general Pakistani public was aware of those terms and hence used them for in their online search queries and conversations. We tried to confirm the suitability of using these keywords through a *small non-representative sample* of users. We electronically sent our consent form and questionnaire to potential participants and then proceeded with only those who indicated their consent electronically. The questionnaire listed misinformation on social media (as listed above) as keywords and asked the participant to tick the boxes which they recognized. The targeted population of this survey was the general Pakistani public and we tried to get the representation from different areas of the country. A total of 40 participants (18 Males and 22 Females) filled this online survey. The participants were geographically distributed in 19 locations around Pakistan from residents of small towns to those living in big cities.

---

[1] https://p.dw.com/p/3eeAj.

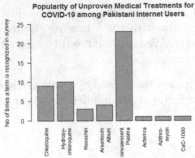
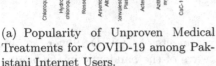
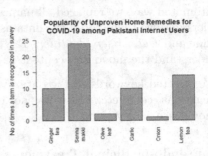

(a) Popularity of Unproven Medical Treatments for COVID-19 among Pakistani Internet Users.

(b) Popularity of Unproven Home Remedies for COVID-19 among Pakistani Internet Users.

Fig. 1. Popularity of Unproven treatments identified on different social and electronic media forums among Pakistani internet users. We can see that the most popular home treatment was Senna Makki, followed by Lemon Tea, Ginger Tea, and Garlic. On the other hand, plasma therapy was a very popular medicinal treatment followed by Hydroxychloroquine and Chloroquine

All home remedies identified by our research team were validated through this survey. As shown in Fig. 1(a), the most popular home treatment was Senna Makki, followed by Lemon Tea, Ginger Tea, and Garlic. Figure 1(b) shows the popularity of unproven medical treatments for COVID-19 in Pakistan, which shows that a lot of interest was shown by internet users in plasma therapy as a possible treatment for COVID-19 plasma therapy followed by Hydroxychloroquine and Chloroquine.

4 Analysis 1: Search Trends During COVID-19 Pandemic

We performed a systematic analysis to evaluate the relationship between Google search trends on various non-scientific treatments on pseudo-medicinal information and the changing situation of COVID-19 pandemic in Pakistan.

4.1 Dataset

Google Trends represents the popularity of a specific search term on Google during a specific duration. For a specific search term, Google Trends shows the daily relative popularity of the search term during this duration. It returns a number n ranging between 0 and 100, where $n = 100$ on the day when the search term was most popular and $n = 0$ when it was least popular. This allows the analysis of search interests of users in specific regions as well as around the globe. It also provides the comparison of search trends on multiple search terms by similarly normalizing them between 0 and 100. This allows us to compare the relative popularity of multiple search terms, giving us insight to public interests and concerns at a specific time.

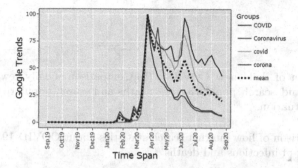

Fig. 2. Comparison of Google trends on Coronavirus search terms during pandemic in Pakistan. The dashed line shows the mean popularity of COVID-19 related searches.

We first performed a comparative analysis of Google Trends on different terms that can be alternatively used for searching details about COVID-19 in Pakistan. We choose 4 generic terms that are commonly used in Pakistan: COVID-19, Coronavirus, Covid, and Corona. As shown in Fig. 2, all these terms started to appear in Google Trends during the 3rd week of January 2020 and they all reached their peak in 3rd Week of March 2020. A sudden rise appeared in search trends during the second Week of March as the government implemented various spread control measures including nationwide lockdown. We also calculated their mean popularity on Google Trends and in the remainder of this paper, we will only use the mean of the various terms used to search for Coronavirus as shown in Fig. 2.

We also checked whether the quick spread of COVID-19 in the region and the rising number of infections and deaths resulted in increased searches in COVID-19 by the public. Here our assumption is that the increased number of searches indicate increased public concern about the pandemic. We explored this by comparing the day to day statistical data of COVID-19 cases in Pakistan with the popularity of COVID-19 searches using data from Google Trends. We computed the correlation of search popularity of COVID-19 searches with daily new infections and found that it has a value of just 0.27. Similarly, the correlation of popularity of COVID-19 searches with daily deaths came out to be 0.23. We can see that these are very small values, indicating that the search popularity was insignificantly influenced by the spread of the pandemic. Figure 3(a) shows how search popularity change with rising number of new infections and similarly Fig. 3(b) shows how search popularity change with daily deaths. It is surprising as well concerning that people seem to be searching very little even at the peak of the pandemic and it seems that Google searches about COVID-19 was

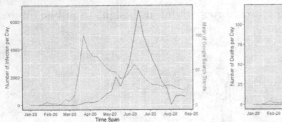 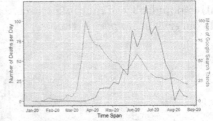

(a) Comparison of daily new COVID-19 infections and search popularity of Coronavirus situation.

(b) Comparison of daily new COVID-19 deaths and search popularity.

Fig. 3. A comparison of how internet search statistics about COVID-19 changed with changing number of infections and deaths.

fuelled more because of the initial total lack of knowledge about the virus and the resulting disease.

4.2 Search Interest Regarding Treatment and Prevention of COVID-19

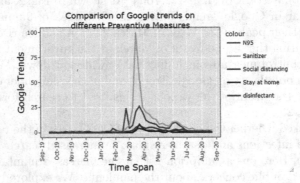

Fig. 4. Comparison of Google trends on preventive measures during Pandemic in Pakistan.

We also performed a comparative analysis of Google trends in Pakistan on different preventive measures suggested by WHO for COVID-19. We choose 5 popular terms that were commonly used in Pakistan: N95 mask, Sanitizer, Social distancing, stay at home, disinfectant. Figure 4 shows the comparison and it is clear that "Sanitizer" is clearly the most popular of these terms during the first wave of the pandemic in Pakistan. We used the top trending term "Sanitizer" for further analysis to evaluate the relationship between these trends and peaks of trends on different pseudo-medicinal information search terms.

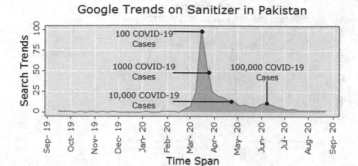

Fig. 5. Comparison of Google trends on Sanitizer during March-August 2020.

Figure 5 shows the pattern of how the popularity of the search term *sanitizer* varies over time. We can see that this search term experienced a sudden rise in popularity immediately after the first patient was detected, this was when the whole country was experiencing previously unknown levels of fear and uncertainty. At this time, many items essential for the pandemic like sanitizers, masks, and other hygiene related items experienced a sudden increase in demand. This was probably when the public was searching if sanitizers were available online or if they are available at cheaper price. However, very soon private businesses started to fill this newly created demand and as a result the search term "sanitizer" quickly dropped in popularity However, it still remained more popular than pre-pandemic time. We also investigated the Google Trends to check the popularity of "Chloroquine" and "Hydroxychloroquine" in Pakistan after Trump's endorsement of these drugs and found a pattern very similar to that in the US. As presented in Fig. 6, there was a sudden hike in Google searches on both medicinal terms in the last week of March, 2020 and they remain popular till 3rd week of April, 2020. This indicates that the backing of a popular personality drives the public interests and increases the trustworthiness of a piece of information.

In summary, the results presented suggests that people in Pakistan actively search COVID-19 related information during the early stages of the first wave of the outbreak but later the public interest seemed to have waned.

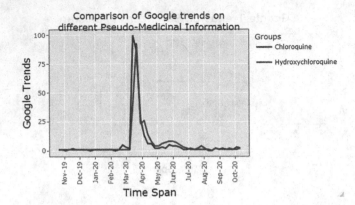

Fig. 6. Comparison of Google trends on Chloroquine and Hydroxychloroquine in Pakistan.

5   Analysis 2: WhatsApp Public Group Data

Now, we present an analysis of data from a public WhatsApp group and also explore the popularity of the pseudo-medicinal information in the discussions during the first wave of COVID-19.

After careful scrutiny, we focused on one public WhatsApp group specifically created in response to the COVID-19 pandemic called `Understanding COVID-19`. The group was created to understand the causes and potential cures of this novel disease and its members actively discussed various issues about the pandemic, especially in the start of the pandemic when limited information about this disease was available. The group was created in the middle of March 2020, when the number of daily infections and deaths started to grow. This group had 53 members, all of whom were Pakistani residents and most of them living in different major cities of Pakistan. Moreover, almost all members were literate and with basic healthcare knowledge and some of them were even medical doctors. The complete record of the WhatsApp group was exported till the 3rd week of August as a CSV file for text analysis in R. Since most of the discussion on this group was in English with Urdu being used only occasionally, the text analysis was done only on text messages in English. Careful pre-processing was performed to clean the data while making sure that important information was not lost.

The time series visualized in Fig. 7 represents the frequency of messages per day and the points indicate important events during the first wave of the COVID-19 pandemic in Pakistan. We can see in Fig. 7, the group remains mostly active between March and July 2020, the period when COVID-19 cases were at its peak. An increase in the number of messages in a day can be seen after two important events, the day the first patient died and the day when the national lockdown was initiated.

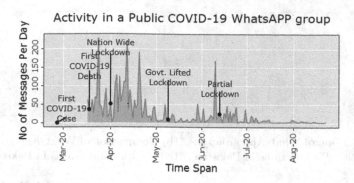

Fig. 7. A representation of message frequency per day in COVID-19 public group with important events in Pakistan. An increase in the number of messages in a day can be seen after two important events, the day the first patient died and the day with the national lock.

We then wanted to get an idea of the discussion in this WhatsApp group. We plotted a word cloud as it gives a good idea of the most frequent words used and hence the discussions between the group members. We performed the below pre-processing steps so our plot can be more meaningful.

– We converted all text to lower case.
– We removed all punctuation marks.
– We then performed stemming i.e. reduced all words to their root form.

These pre-processing steps were completed through the `stm` package of R. The most commonly used words in their discussions. The words show that there were discussions on patients, clinics, hospitals, medics, and also various possible treatments.

To check whether the number of infections/deaths was related to increase in discussions on the WhatsApp group, we first computed the correlation, which came out to be 0.0006 for daily new infections and −0.0135 for the daily new deaths respectively. It indicates that the discussion was not correlated at all with how fast the pandemic is spreading, in fact in case of new deaths it seems that in some cases higher number of deaths seem to have resulted in lower number of messages on the WhatsApp group. We hence compared how the time series of daily number of messages exchanged on the group changes the time series for the daily number of infections and daily number of deaths respectively. Figure 8(a) compares the number of messages per day with the number of new COVID-19 number of cases per day in Pakistan, while Fig. 8(b)compares it with daily deaths due to COVID-19. This patterns shows the concern of the public at the very start of the pandemic and as the number of infections and deaths increased. However, very soon with the increasing number of infections and deaths in Pakistan. It can be seen from both figures that the group was more active in earlier

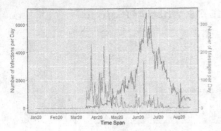 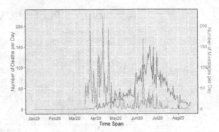

(a) Comparison of WhatsApp group ac-   (b) Comparison of WhatsApp group activity with daily infections in Pakistan.   tivity with daily deaths in Pakistan.

Fig. 8. Comparison of WhatsApp group activity with daily reported COVID-19 numbers in Pakistan. Please note that the peaks in Fig. 8(b) look larger because the number of deaths are significantly less than the number of infections. The 4 peaks in the WhatsApp messages count seem to influenced more by coverage in traditional news media and initial fear among the public.

phases of the COVID-19 (i.e., March-July 2020) and later the public seemed to be less concerned about the pandemic and possible dangers from it. The 4 peaks in the WhatsApp messages count seem to influenced more by coverage in traditional news media and initial fear among the public. More specifically, the first peak was around the time soon after the government implement country wide complete lockdown, the second peak came because there was a lot discussion about possible treatments and sharing individual experiences; the 3rd peak came because of there was a lot of discussion about psychological issues resulting from the pandemic and sharing views on how to cope with this new reality; while the 4th peak in mid June was because this was when the total number of infections in Pakistan crossed 100, 000.

We also explored communication related to the two anti-malarial drugs Chloroquine and Hydroxychloroquine, and found that both started to be discussed immediately after the endorsement of President Trump and Elon Musk. They remain in regular discussion till July 2020 as can be seen in Fig. 9. This was despite of the fatality reported on March 22, 2020 [28].

Lastly, we applied thematic analysis to extract main topics in the WhatsApp group. We started by applying an algorithmic technique called Latent Dirichlet Allocation but did not find the results to be satisfactory. As a result, we followed the 6-step process suggested by Braun and Clarke for thematic analysis [9]. We note here that *thematic analysis* studies are suited for studies that are of exploratory nature and to generate hypotheses that can be later tested from a representative sample. After initial scanning of the messages for getting a high-level idea of about the issues being discussed in this group, the first author went through each message and identified 11 categories labeling each message accordingly. This labeling was done to uncover the repeated patterns of behaviour i.e. *themes* in the data. The second author then reviewed this categorization by going through the file and reviewing 40% messages and their associated labels

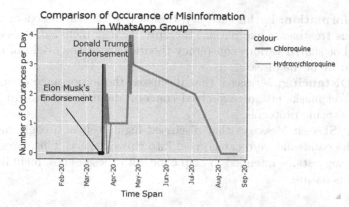

Fig. 9. Chloroquine and Hydroxychloroquine started being discussed immediately after the endorsement of the high profile personalities and remained in discussion till July 2020.

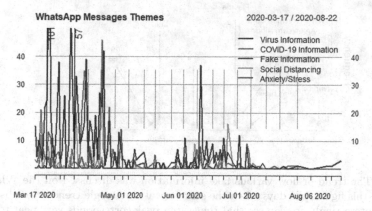

Fig. 10. Themes observed in the discussion on the public WhatsApp group. We can see that there was a lot of interest at the start of the pandemic and gradually interest reduced. Interestingly, we observed that all themes tend to be discussed more or less together with most of the discussion being focused on either information about the virus or information about the disease.

and suggested merging some categories and also recategorized some other messages. After this recategorization, we ended up with 6 categorizes. The categories and their brief explanation is given below:

1. **General Conversation:** General conversations messages such as hellos, goodbyes, greetings, etc.
2. **Virus Information:** Messages that sought and shared information about the SARS-CoV-2 virus, its origin, how it spreads etc.
3. **COVID-19 Information:** In this category, the participants discussed the disease its risks, possible treatments and shared information that can be helpful to the patients of COVID-19.

4. **Fake Information:** In this category, the participants discussed various fake or dubious treatments like plasma therapy. We also included messages that discussed or shared various conspiracy theories about the origin of the virus or the nature of the disease.
5. **Social Distancing:** Messages that discussed the importance of social distancing and masks etc. or expressed concern about the non-compliance of social distancing protocols.
6. **Anxiety/Stress:** Messages that discussed high levels of anxiety and stress due to the pandemic were categorized into this category. This category also included suggestions intended to help cope with these issues, including those of religious nature.

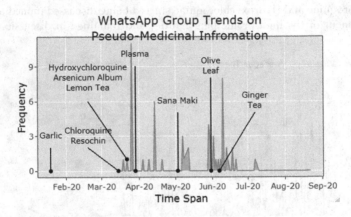

Fig. 11. The trend of how various fake information was discussed on the WhatsApp group. In this figure, the days when the search peak on Google trends was observed is labeled. Interestingly, we can see that the search peak corresponds very near to a peak in the WhatsApp discussion about some fake information.

The variation of these themes with time is shown in Fig. 10. We did not include the category of general conversation in the interest of clarity of the figure. Moreover, the plot does not show two very high peaks, but their values are written where the peak is truncated. We can see from the figure that discussions in this group started as soon as it was created and the initial discussions revolved around basic information about the virus, its origin, the disease, and social distancing other preventive measures. In about a week's time, the discussion also started to have significant messages on fake information and also anxiety/stress issues. A large number of messages were exchanged for about 2 months till about May 2020 and when the volume of messages in all themes dropped. However, all themes started being discussed again with renewed interest in the middle of June, but the level of interest was lesser than the initial weeks of the pandemic and it dropped to insignificant levels within a few weeks. Recall that mid-June was the time when the total number of infections in Pakistan crossed 100,000.

Interestingly, we observed that all themes tend to be discussed more or less together with most of the discussion being focused on either information about the virus or information about the disease.

We plotted the trend of how discussions on fake and pseudo-medicinal remedies identified in Sect. 3 varied with time. We can see from Fig. 11 that this discussion seems to be bursty and the peaks seem to fall very close to the time with the peak of pseudo-medicinal treatment on Google Trends. This indicates that both the WhatsApp discussion as well as the search peak seem to be related.

6 Conclusion

In this paper, we investigated the information-seeking behaviour of the Pakistani public during the first wave of the COVID-19 pandemic in Pakistan. We decided to focus on online resources and social media as they were a major source of health-related information during the COVID-19 pandemic. The major contributions of this paper are the following:

1. We investigated how the public searched the web for various COVID-19 related information as the pandemic progressed. We used data from Google Trends for this purpose. Interestingly, our analysis seems to indicate that although the number of infections and number of deaths due to COVID-19 was increasing, the general public was searching lesser for COVID-19 related information. Analysis of search trend of COVID-19 related treatments and prevention also indicated that search volume seems to be influenced more by external factors like Donald Trump and Elon Musk endorsing a drug; sanitizer not being available in the market, or the psychological effect and media coverage when the number of patients crossed 100,000.
2. For a high-level semantic understanding about the information sought during the first wave, we analysed data from a public WhatsApp group that was created to share information about COVID-19. Similar to search trends, the group members shared more information during the early weeks of the pandemic and gradually the number of messages decreased despite the pandemic becoming more widespread. Like search trends, discussion in this group seemed to be sparked by external factors and associated media coverage. For example, a sudden increase in the volume of messages was observed when the COVID-19 patient died; when government-imposed countrywide complete lockdown; and when the number of infected persons crossed the 100,000 threshold.

The results discussed in Sect. 4 and Sect. 5 seem to indicate that the public was very concerned at the start of the pandemic, however with time their level of concern gradually reduced. Their level of concern and interest then seem to rise occasionally when an event that they perceived as occurred. This seems to indicate habituation, here *habituation* is psychological behaviour found in all living things and it informally means the reduction of a particular response after repeated exposure of the same stimulus [19]. A number of studies have been conducted to establish the causality of repeated exposure of the same stimulus and resulting decrease in response [13,30]. In case our paper, the stimulus is the daily pandemic-related news that everyone heard or read at various places and the response was their level of concern and resulting online behaviour that we tried to observe. Habituation is also found to be *stimulus specific* [41], hence the response can be returned to previous levels when an individual who is already habituated to one stimulus is presented with a novel stimulus [16].

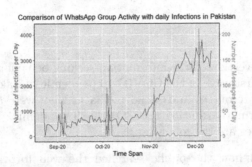

Fig. 12. Number of Messages on the Whatsapp group in the second wave compared to number of infections.

We conjecture that in the case of the COVID-19 pandemic, the public habituated after daily exposure of warnings and worrying news on traditional media as well as on social media. They were, however, 'dishabituated' when the stimulus changed, for example when news of the number of infections crossing 100,000. We check this conjecture by plotting the number of messages exchanged on the WhatsApp group in the second wave as shown in Fig. 12. Note this plot only shows till December 2020 as the WhatsApp group was deactivated soon after it. We can see that very few messages were exchanged, however, the number of messages on the group experienced sudden and short peaks. On further investigating, they all seem to be a result of something unusual or different, explained as follows:

1. **First Peak:** (September 04, 2020) At this time, the public was concerned about the likely effect of government's decision to open schools.
2. **Second Peak:** (October 06, 2020) A famous newspaper Dawn publishes a gloomy article [3] about second wave and how deadly it can be. There was a lot of discussion about this article.
3. **Third Peak:** (November 04, 2020) There was discussion about the news [2] that the government ruling out lockdown again.
4. **Fourth Peak:** (December 04, 2020) Clinical trials of the COVID-19 vaccine starts in Pakistan and it was discussed a lot in the group.

A similar pattern can be seen for the search results data from Google Trends (Fig. 6). The keywords chosen in Sect. 4 were very frequent from March 2020 till about July 2020 probably due to initial scare and confusion. After the initial scare, at the height of the first wave, they dropped to almost pre-pandemic times. Hence supporting our conjecture (Fig. 13).

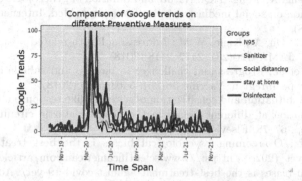

Fig. 13. Figure showing Google trends data of keywords selected in Sect. 4 were only very high from March 2020 till about July 2020 probably due to initial scare and lack of information.

Further work is needed to confirm whether there is a causal relationship between online activity and external factors. It also needs to be investigated how governments, health agencies, digital media platforms should communicate with the general public so habituation can either be avoided or reduced in future pandemics, specifically for the emergent user communities.

References

1. Coronavirus attitude tracker survey report - wave 8 (2020). https://gallup.com.pk/wp/wp-content/uploads/2020/10/Gallup-Pakistan-Coronavirus-Attitude-Tracker-Survey-Wave-8-.pdf
2. NCC rules out comlete lockdown (2020). https://www.dawn.com/news/1588511. Accessed 11 Nov 2021
3. Second wave (2020). https://www.dawn.com/news/1583507/second-wave. Accessed 11 Nov 2021
4. Ayyoubzadeh, S.M., Ayyoubzadeh, S.M., Zahedi, H., Ahmadi, M., Kalhori, S.R.N.: Predicting COVID-19 incidence through analysis of google trends data in Iran: data mining and deep learning pilot study. JMIR Public Health Surveill. **6**(2), e18828 (2020)
5. Badell-Grau, R.A., Cuff, J.P., Kelly, B.P., Waller-Evans, H., Lloyd-Evans, E.: Investigating the prevalence of reactive online searching in the COVID-19 pandemic: infoveillance study. J. Med. Internet Res. **22**(10), e19791 (2020)
6. Bento, A.I., Nguyen, T., Wing, C., Lozano-Rojas, F., Ahn, Y.Y., Simon, K.: Evidence from internet search data shows information-seeking responses to news of local COVID-19 cases. Proc. Natl. Acad. Sci. **117**(21), 11220–11222 (2020)
7. Bilal, A., Rextin, A., Kakakhel, A., Nasim, M.: Analyzing emergent users' text messages data and exploring its benefits. IEEE Access **7**, 2870–2879 (2018)

8. Blandizzi, C., Scarpignato, C.: Gastrointestinal drugs. In: Side Effects of Drugs Annual, vol. 33, pp. 741–767. Elsevier (2011)
9. Braun, V., Clarke, V.: Using thematic analysis in psychology. Qual. Res. Psychol. **3**(2), 77–101 (2006)
10. Chen, L., Wang, X., Peng, T.Q.: Nature and diffusion of gynecologic cancer-related misinformation on social media: analysis of tweets. J. Med. Internet Res. **20**(10), e11515 (2018)
11. Chou, W.Y.S., Oh, A., Klein, W.M.: Addressing health-related misinformation on social media. JAMA **320**(23), 2417–2418 (2018)
12. Datta, S.S., et al.: Progress and challenges in measles and rubella elimination in the who European region. Vaccine **36**(36), 5408–5415 (2018)
13. Davis, M.: Habituation and sensitization of a startle-like response elicited by electrical stimulation at different points in the acoustic startle circuit. In: Sensory Functions, pp. 67–78. Elsevier (1981)
14. Denworth, L.: Overcoming psychological biases is the best treatment against COVID-19 yet (2020). https://www.scientificamerican.com/article/overcoming-psychological-biases-is-the-best-treatment-against-covid-19-yet/. Accessed 11 Nov 2021
15. Depoux, A., Martin, S., Karafillakis, E., Preet, R., Wilder-Smith, A., Larson, H.: The pandemic of social media panic travels faster than the COVID-19 outbreak (2020)
16. Dewsbury, D.A.: Effects of novelty of copulatory behavior: the coolidge effect and related phenomena. Psychol. Bull. **89**(3), 464 (1981)
17. Filia, A., Bella, A., Del Manso, M., Baggieri, M., Magurano, F., Rota, M.C.: Ongoing outbreak with well over 4,000 measles cases in Italy from January to end August 2017 - what is making elimination so difficult? Eurosurveillance **22**(37), 30614 (2017)
18. Ginsberg, J., Mohebbi, M.H., Patel, R.S., Brammer, L., Smolinski, M.S., Brilliant, L.: Detecting influenza epidemics using search engine query data. Nature **457**(7232), 1012–1014 (2009)
19. Gluck, M.A., Mercado, E., Myers, C.E.: Learning and Memory: From Brain to Behavior. Worth Publishers, New York (2008)
20. Gupta, L., Gasparyan, A.Y., Misra, D.P., Agarwal, V., Zimba, O., Yessirkepov, M.: Information and misinformation on COVID-19: a cross-sectional survey study. J. Korean Med. Sci. **35**(27) (2020)
21. Hernández-García, I., Giménez-Júlvez, T.: Assessment of health information about COVID-19 prevention on the internet: infodemiological study. JMIR Public Health Surveill. **6**(2), e18717 (2020)
22. Hu, D., et al.: More effective strategies are required to strengthen public awareness of COVID-19: evidence from google trends. J. Global Health **10**(1) (2020)
23. Husnayain, A., Fuad, A., Su, E.C.Y.: Applications of google search trends for risk communication in infectious disease management: a case study of COVID-19 outbreak in Taiwan. Int. J. Infect. Dis. **95**, 221–223 (2020)
24. Joshi, A.: Technology adoption by 'emergent' users: the user-usage model. In: Proceedings of the 11th Asia Pacific Conference on Computer Human Interaction, pp. 28–38 (2013)
25. Kim, K.D., Hossain, L.: Towards early detection of influenza epidemics by using social media analytics. In: DSS, pp. 36–41 (2014)
26. Kurian, S.J., et al.: Correlations between COVID-19 cases and google trends data in the united states: a state-by-state analysis. In: Mayo Clinic Proceedings, pp. 2370–2381. Elsevier (2020)

27. Kušen, E., Strembeck, M.: Politics, sentiments, and misinformation: an analysis of the twitter discussion on the 2016 Austrian presidential elections. Online Soc. Netw. Media **5**, 37–50 (2018)
28. Liu, M., Caputi, T.L., Dredze, M., Kesselheim, A.S., Ayers, J.W.: Internet searches for unproven COVID-19 therapies in the United States. JAMA Internal Med. **180**(8), 1116–1118 (2020)
29. Malani, A.N., Sherbeck, J.P., Malani, P.N.: Convalescent plasma and COVID-19. JAMA **324**(5), 524 (2020)
30. Malcuit, G., Bastien, C., Pomerleau, A.: Habituation of the orienting response to stimuli of different functional values in 4-month-old infants. J. Exp. Child Psychol. **62**(2), 272–291 (1996)
31. Moyer, M.W.: People drawn to conspiracy theories share a cluster of psychological features (2019). https://www.scientificamerican.com/article/people-drawn-to-conspiracy-theories-share-a-cluster-of-psychological-features/. Accessed 11 Nov 2021
32. Pennycook, G., McPhetres, J., Zhang, Y., Lu, J.G., Rand, D.G.: Fighting COVID-19 misinformation on social media: experimental evidence for a scalable accuracy-nudge intervention. Psychol. Sci. **31**(7), 770–780 (2020)
33. Polgreen, P.M., Chen, Y., Pennock, D.M., Nelson, F.D., Weinstein, R.A.: Using internet searches for influenza surveillance. Clin. Infect. Dis. **47**(11), 1443–1448 (2008)
34. Post, S., Bienzeisler, N., Lohöfener, M.: A desire for authoritative science? How citizens' informational needs and epistemic beliefs shaped their views of science, news, and policymaking in the COVID-19 pandemic. Public Underst. Sci. **30**(5), 496–514 (2021). https://doi.org/10.1177/09636625211005334
35. Rathore, F.A., Farooq, F.: Information overload and infodemic in the COVID-19 pandemic. JPMA J. Pak. Med. Assoc. **70**(5), S162–S165 (2020)
36. Rovetta, A., Bhagavathula, A.S.: COVID-19-related web search behaviors and infodemic attitudes in Italy: infodemiological study. JMIR Public Health Surveill. **6**(2), e19374 (2020)
37. Shah, M.: The failure of public health messaging about COVID-19 (2020. https://www.scientificamerican.com/article/the-failure-of-public-health-messaging-about-covid-19/. Accessed 11 Nov 2021
38. Sharma, K., Seo, S., Meng, C., Rambhatla, S., Dua, A., Liu, Y.: Coronavirus on social media: analyzing misinformation in twitter conversations. arXiv preprint arXiv:2003.12309 (2020)
39. Teng, Y., et al.: Dynamic forecasting of zika epidemics using google trends. PLoS ONE **12**(1), e0165085 (2017)
40. Thapen, N., Simmie, D., Hankin, C., Gillard, J.: Defender: detecting and forecasting epidemics using novel data-analytics for enhanced response. PLoS ONE **11**(5), e0155417 (2016)
41. Thompson, R.F., Spencer, W.A.: Habituation: a model phenomenon for the study of neuronal substrates of behavior. Psychol. Rev. **73**(1), 16 (1966)
42. Walker, A., Hopkins, C., Surda, P.: The use of google trends to investigate the loss of smell related searches during COVID-19 outbreak. In: International Forum of Allergy & Rhinology. Wiley Online Library (2020)
43. Wang, C., et al.: Immediate psychological responses and associated factors during the initial stage of the 2019 coronavirus disease (COVID-19) epidemic among the general population in china. Int. J. Environ. Res. Public Health **17**(5), 1729 (2020)

44. Waszak, P.M., Kasprzycka-Waszak, W., Kubanek, A.: The spread of medical fake news in social media-the pilot quantitative study. Health Policy Technol. **7**(2), 115–118 (2018)
45. Wolf, M.S., et al.: Awareness, attitudes, and actions related to COVID-19 among adults with chronic conditions at the onset of the us outbreak: a cross-sectional survey. Ann. Internal Med. **173**(2), 100–109 (2020)

Investigating the Validity of Botometer-Based Social Bot Studies

Florian Gallwitz[1]([⊠]) and Michael Kreil[2]

[1] Nuremberg Institute of Technology, Kesslerplatz 12, 90489 Nuremberg, Germany
`florian.gallwitz@th-nuernberg.de`
[2] SWRdata, Hans-Bredow-Strasse 9, 76530 Baden-Baden, Germany
`contact1@michael-kreil.de`

Abstract. The idea that social media platforms like Twitter are inhabited by vast numbers of social bots has become widely accepted in recent years. Social bots are assumed to be automated social media accounts operated by malicious actors with the goal of manipulating public opinion. They are credited with the ability to produce content autonomously and to interact with human users. Social bot activity has been reported in many different political contexts, including the U.S. presidential elections, discussions about migration, climate change, and COVID-19. However, the relevant publications either use crude and questionable heuristics to discriminate between supposed social bots and humans or—in the vast majority of the cases—fully rely on the output of automatic bot detection tools, most commonly *Botometer*. In this paper, we point out a fundamental theoretical flaw in the widely-used study design for estimating the prevalence of social bots. Furthermore, we empirically investigate the validity of peer-reviewed *Botometer*-based studies by closely and systematically inspecting hundreds of accounts that had been counted as social bots. We were unable to find a single social bot. Instead, we found mostly accounts undoubtedly operated by human users, the vast majority of them using Twitter in an inconspicuous and unremarkable fashion without the slightest traces of automation. We conclude that studies claiming to investigate the prevalence, properties, or influence of social bots based on *Botometer* have, in reality, just investigated false positives and artifacts of this approach.

Keywords: Social bots · Bot detection · Botometer · False positives

1 Introduction

Social bot or not? An extensive amount of research has been published in recent years suggesting that social media platform like Twitter are inhabited by vast numbers of social bots. These are supposed to be accounts pretending to be human users but which are operated automatically by malicious actors with the goal of manipulating public opinion. The supposed influence of social bots in political discussions has raised significant concerns, particularly given their alleged potential to adversely impact democratic outcomes.

F. Spezzano et al. (Eds.): MISDOOM 2022, LNCS 13545, pp. 63–78, 2022.
https://doi.org/10.1007/978-3-031-18253-2_5

The idea of social bot armies has been widely and frequently covered by media outlets across the world, with new reports of supposed social bot activity appearing almost on a weekly basis for the last couple of years, in the context of a wide variety of different topics. Discussions that have reportedly been attacked by social bot activity include the Brexit referendum, elections and political unrests in various countries, climate change, immigration, racial unrest, cannabis, vaping, COVID-19, vaccines, and even celebrity gossip. As a consequence, political countermeasures against the supposed dangers of social bot activity have been discussed and legal regulations have been implemented, for example California's Bot Disclosure Law (2019) or Germany's 'Medienstaatsvertrag' (2020).

Many of these news reports and also most scientific publications about social bots from research groups around the world are based on *Botometer* (originally called *BotOrNot*), which has often been referred to as the "state-of-the-art bot detection method". A Google Scholar search in May 2022 using the query `"BotOrNot" OR "Botometer"` returns 1,720 results.

A typical definition of a social bot is given in [1]: *"Social bots are automated accounts that use artificial intelligence to steer discussions and promote specific ideas or products on social media such as Twitter and Facebook. To typical social media users browsing their feeds, social bots may go unnoticed as they are designed to resemble the appearance of human users (e.g., showing a profile photo and listing a name or location) and behave online in a manner similar to humans (e.g., 'retweeting' or quoting others' posts and 'liking' or endorsing others tweets)."*

However, as has been pointed out by Rauchfleisch and Kaiser [15], there is some confusion as to what exactly "social bot" researchers or tools like *Botometer* are trying to find. Authors in this field often use the terms 'social bot', 'bot', 'social media bot', or 'automated account' more or less interchangeably, even though—according to the above definition—automation is a necessary but not a sufficient condition for a social bot. A deeper discussion of these issues can be found in [6]. For the purposes of this paper, however, the exact definition of these terms will not matter. In particular, we will demonstrate that the vast majority of the accounts that are flagged as "bots" by *Botometer* are real people and do not involve any automation at all. In the rare occasions where we found partly automated accounts, e.g. automated retweets or accounts that automatically cross-posted content from other social media platforms on Twitter, we will point this out explicitly.

This paper is structured as follows: In Sect. 2, we discuss theoretical and methodological limitations of automatic bot-detection tools like *Botometer*. We point out a fundamental theoretical flaw of the commonly used approach of estimating the level of social bot activity. In Sect. 3, we evaluate the performance of *Botometer* empirically using various samples of Twitter accounts and discuss related research that used a similar approach. When using *Botometer* on accounts of known humans, the false-positive rate turns out to be significant. In Sect. 4, we describe our experiments to evaluate the validity of *Botometer* scores in real-world scenarios. To our knowledge, a systematic evaluation of this type has never been reported before. Our results are devastating for the whole body of *Botometer*-based research: Nearly all accounts that are labeled as "bots" based on *Botometer* scores are false positives. Many of these accounts are operated by people with impressive academic and professional credentials. Not a single one of the hundreds of accounts we inspected—each of which had been flagged by *Botometer*—was a "social bot" according to the above definition. In Sect. 5, we discuss recent research that is related to our study. In Sect. 6, we present our conclusions.

2 Theoretical and Methodological Limitations of Botometer-Based Social Bot Detection

Botometer is an automated tool designed to discriminate social bots from human users. It is built on a supervised machine learning approach. To discriminate between the two classes, a random forest classifier is trained on two samples of user accounts, one labeled "human" and one labeled "bot". The classification is based on more that 1,000 features which, according to [2], include statistical features of retweet networks, meta-data, such as account creation time, the median number of followers of an accounts social contacts, the tweet rate, and features based on part-of-speech tagging and sentiment analysis.

The training of *Botometer* is based on a publicly available dataset[1] where (in 2019) 57,155 accounts were labeled "bot" and 30,853 were labeled "human" [19] The accounts come from a variety of different sources and many of the labels seem at least questionable. The largest subset of "bots" comes from a sample of spammy or promotional accounts from the early days of Twitter (2009–2010). The study where these accounts were collected referred to them as "content polluters" and did not claim that these accounts were automated or bots [13]. Many of the accounts from other sources were apparently labeled manually by laypersons with little understanding of the state-of-the-art in human-machine interaction and the difficulty of evading Twitter's detection of nefarious platform use, and based on a naïve understanding of what constitutes a "bot" (possibly based on questionable clues like a high amount of retweets, a small or large number of followers, missing profile picture, digits in the Twitter handle, or, as empirically validated in [17], opposing political views). Some accounts in the "bot repository" were explicitly labeled as "bots" because they appeared to have participated in "follow trains", a technique used by human political activists on Twitter to rapidly increase their follower count. Clearly, the lack of reliable ground truth data is the first glaring methodological problem of *Botometer*. It seems far from obvious that training a classifier on a rather arbitrary selection of account samples which are based on vastly different ideas of what constitutes a "bot" will result in a useful tool.

Botometer is available both over an API and over a web interface. It provides a score between 0 and 1 for individual Twitter accounts which is calculated by

---

[1] https://botometer.osome.iu.edu/bot-repository/datasets.html.

calibrating the raw score provided by the random forest classifier. Higher scores are associated with a higher "bot likelihood" on accounts that are labeled "bot" in the bot repository. This "bot likelihood" is linearly rescaled to a scale from 0 to 5 and presented on the website. Additionally, a "complete automation probability" (CAP) is provided since version 3. The CAP is based on a non-linear rescaling of the bot score according to the Bayes rule and is supposed to be interpreted as the posterior probability that an account is a bot. According to [19], the CAP is based on the assumption that the prior probability of observing a bot is 0.15 and provides "generally more conservative" scores than the original bot score. That is, the rescaled "bot likelihood" is based on the assumption that roughly 50% of the accounts encountered by *Botometer* are bots, whereas the CAP is based on the assumption that 15% of these accounts are bots.[2]

Now consider the typical methodology of most disinformation studies which employ *Botometer* (or similar tools). Two of many such studies will be discussed in detail in Sect. 4:

1. A large sample of tweets or user accounts is collected related to a certain topic, for example, all followers of certain accounts or all tweets that contain certain hashtags or keywords, e.g. 'political issue'.
2. The list of accounts is fed into *Botometer* and the resulting "bot scores" are stored in a file.
3. The study authors take a look at the histogram of the "bot scores". On this basis, a suitable threshold is selected in some obscure or arbitrary manner. This step is often skipped and instead, a threshold of 50% (2.5 out of 5) is employed.
4. The amount of "bots" and "bot-generated" tweets is calculated based on this threshold, resulting in headlines like *"30% of the Twitter users who tweet about 'political issue' are bots"*, or *"half of the tweets about 'political issue' are generated by bots"*.

Even under the optimistic assumption that there is a significant correlation between the "bot score" and the true nature of the account, this approach is fundamentally flawed. By adjusting the threshold, almost any amount of "bots" between 0% and 100% that is desired or expected by the authors can be produced as a result (see Fig. 3). Researchers expecting a large number of social bots will choose a low threshold, while researchers expecting a low number of social bots will choose a high threshold.[3] On the other hand, if the threshold is not adjusted, the implicit assumption is that the relative number of bots in the real-world sample is the same as in the training and/or validation data used to optimize *Botometer*. In either case, using this approach to estimate the prevalence of "bots" is a textbook example of circular reasoning. The prevalence of

---

[2] Notably, this 15% estimate was obtained using an earlier version of *Botometer* as a classifier and without manually verifying those results [16].

[3] This resembles a technique of adjusting a bedridden patient's blood pressure reading by heavily tilting the bed, as described in Samuel Shem's satirical novel *House of God*: *"You can get any blood pressure you want out of your gomer"*.

social bots desired or expected by the researchers directly affects the prevalence that will be "measured".

The problem can also be pointed out in a probabilistic framework. An optimal classifier for "bots" vs. "humans" will follow the Bayes decision rule which minimizes the number of errors. Therefore, based on a feature vector x, it will make a decision for the class Bot if and only if

$$p(Bot) \cdot p(x|Bot) > (1 - p(Bot)) \cdot p(x|Human). \qquad (1)$$

$Botometer$, like any other classifier, incorporates an estimate of the prior probability $p(Bot)$, explicitly or implicitly. As discussed above, the calibrated "bot score" is based on the assumption that $p(Bot)$ is roughly 50%, whereas the CAP is based on the assumption that $p(Bot)$ is 15%. Adjusting the "bot score" threshold is equivalent to modifying the prior probability $p(Bot)$. However, $p(Bot)$ is nothing but the prevalence of social bots that researchers are trying to measure in the first place. This is a circular dependency: In order to classify accounts into "bots" and "humans" with the goal of using the relative frequency of "bots" as an estimate for $p(Bot)$, we already need to know $p(Bot)$ beforehand.

Using a classifier like $Botometer$ to obtain a reliable estimate of $p(Bot)$ by counting unvalidated classification results would require probability density functions $p(x|Bot)$ and $p(x|Human)$ with virtually no overlap. Only then, the impact of the unknown probability $p(Bot)$ on the classification result could reasonably be neglected. However, looking at actual "bot score" distributions and given the consistent failure of $Botometer$ in our experiments, this is clearly not the case.[4]

These considerations leave little hope that $Botometer$ or similar tools might be of any value for estimating the prevalence of "bots".

3   Evaluating Botometer on Samples of Known Humans

The problem that $Botometer$ produces enormous amounts of false positives and that it should never be trusted without manual verification has been pointed out for years [5,10–12,15].

Different methods have been used to demonstrate the problem. A simple and effective way is to use $Botometer$ to classify accounts that are without doubt operated by humans. When we tested $Botometer$ in April 2018, nearly half of U.S. Congress members present on Twitter were misclassified as bots (47%),

---

[4] A similar problem arises when human labelers are instructed to rate accounts as "bots" or "humans". The ratings will typically be based on unrealistically high expectations of the bot prevalence $p(Bot)$ (fueled by $Botometer$-based publications and media coverage), a limited understanding of the state of the art in artificial intelligence combined with misconceptions of what features might be "bot-like" (i.e. a bad estimate of $p(x|Bot)$), as well as false and narrow expectations of what a "normal" human behavior on Twitter might be (i.e. a bad estimate of $p(x|Human)$). As a result, many accounts that are clearly not automated but were rated "bots" by human labelers can be found in the "bot repository" used to train $Botometer$.

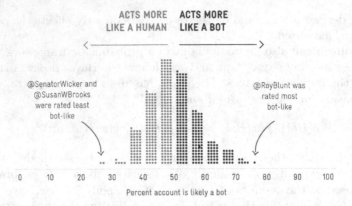

Fig. 1. Distribution of the *Botometer* "bot scores" for the members of the U.S. Congress who were present on Twitter (April 2018)

using the most commonly used "bot score" threshold of 50% (or 2.5 on a scale from 0 to 5), see Fig. 1.[5]

In similar experiments in May 2019 [5,11,12], we found that

- 10.5% of NASA-related accounts are misclassified as bots.
- 12% of Nobel Prize Laureates are misclassified as bots.
- 14% of female directors are misclassified as bots.
- 17.7% of Reuters journalists are misclassified as bots.
- 21.9% of staff members of UN Women are misclassified as bots.
- 35.9% of the staff of German news agency "dpa" are misclassified as bots.

Clearly, *Botometer*'s glaring false positive problem has still not been solved with the current version. In January 2021, even the Twitter account @POTUS of the newly elected president of the United States, Joe Biden, was classified as a "bot", with a "bot score" of 3.2, see Fig. 2. In May 2022, both presidential accounts @POTUS and @JoeBiden received "bot scores" of 3.8.

The lack of reliability goes both ways. When we tested *Botometer* with real, automated Twitter bots in May 2019, we found that

- 36% of known bots by New Scientist are misclassified as humans.
- 60.7% of the bots collected by Botwiki are misclassified as humans.

A similar, but more systematic approach to evaluate the ability of *Botometer* to discriminate between automated accounts and humans was chosen by [15]. The authors performed experiments on five datasets of verified bots and verified humans. Although the datasets had been partly used to train *Botometer*, the

---

[5] Surprisingly, in May 2019, *Botometer* performed dramatically better on the members of Congress; the false positive rate dropped from 47% to 0.4%. Possibly, these accounts had been added to the *Botometer* training data as examples of human users in the meantime.

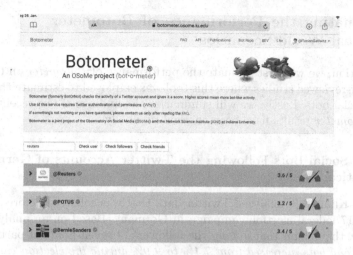

Fig. 2. Screenshot of *Botometer*'s web interface showing the "bot scores" of the verified Twitter accounts @Reuters, @POTUS, and @BernieSanders, each being misclassified as a bot (January 2021)

authors find that *"the Botometer scores are imprecise when it comes to estimating bots. [...] This has immediate consequences for academic research as most studies using the tool will unknowingly count a high number of human users as bots and vice versa."*

Although they clearly demonstrate severe limitations of *Botometer*, evaluations on manually selected lists of accounts do not allow for an estimate of *Botometer*'s reliability in a real-world setting. In a real-world scenario, an enormous variety of human user behaviors may occur which might not be included in manually constructed test samples. Also, it seems unlikely that actual malicious "social bots" would behave in the same manner as the bots employed in these experiments. Therefore, the only way to get a realistic impression of *Botometer*'s performance in real-world scenarios is to take a closer look at the accounts that are classified as bots in a specific setting. Unfortunately, it turns out that authors of studies of this type are extremely reluctant to share their lists of "bots". In our impression, most of the study authors we contacted were fully aware that the lion's share or even all of the accounts they counted as "bots" were, in fact, humans.

This reluctance to share data motivated us to replicate one study of this type about alleged social bots among the followers of German political parties [9]. In only one case, we were able to obtain the relevant raw data from the authors of a peer-reviewed *Botometer*-based study. We are grateful that Dunn et al. [4] shared their list of "bots" with us to allow us to take a closer look.

4   Evaluating the Performance of Botometer in Real-World Scenarios

In this section, we will first evaluate the performance of *Botometer* on the basis of two peer-reviewed studies where this tool was employed to estimate the prevalence of social bots. Lastly, we will summarize the findings of two recent studies where *Botometer* results have been checked manually.

4.1   Are Social Bots Following the Twitter Accounts of German Political Parties?

Keller and Klinger [9] analyzed Twitter data that was collected before and during the 2017 federal election campaign in Germany. Based on an analysis with *Botometer*, they claim that among the followers of seven political parties, *"the share of social bots increased from 7.1% to 9.9% during the election campaign"*. The total numbers of Twitter followers they analyzed during the election campaign was 838,026, which, assuming the claimed social bot prevalence of 9.9%, would correspond to roughly 83k social bots. However, the paper does not provide any examples of social bot accounts and the raw data was not shared. When we contacted the authors, they were unable to provide us with a single credible example of a "social bot".

In order to verify the validity of these results, we tried to replicate Keller's and Klinger's approach in May 2019. Although we expected some changes in the follower lists of the political parties over the 20 month period between September 2017 to May 2019, we see no reason for (or evidence of) a fundamental change.

When we downloaded the followers of the seven political parties using the Twitter API, we found a total of 521,991 different accounts that had at least tweeted once (*Botometer* is not able to provide scores for accounts without tweets). To classify these accounts into "bots" and "humans", we used the *Botometer* API to determine the "bot score" for each of the accounts and used the same, unusually high "bot score" threshold that Keller and Klinger had chosen for their study: 76%, or 3.8 on a scale from 0 to 5.

Surprisingly, the amount of social bots appeared to have increased dramatically since the elections. We found a total of 270,572 accounts that exceeded the "bot score" threshold of 3.8. This corresponds to a social bot prevalence of 51.8%. Mysteriously, the amount of social bots among the followers of German political parties appeared to have increased fivefold in the 20 months since the election, while the total number of followers had decreased. The commonly used threshold of 50% or 2.5 would have resulted in a "social bot" prevalence of 67%, see Fig. 3.

In order to understand what was really going on, we chose to take a closer look at the list of social bots. Obviously, it is not feasible to manually analyze 270k Twitter accounts. In order to assess the true nature of these accounts, we decided to select a sample of slightly more than 100 of the alleged "social bot" accounts. While random sampling might have been feasible, we preferred a

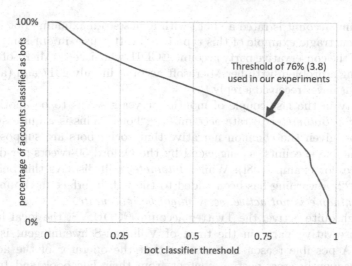

Fig. 3. Cumulative distribution of the *Botometer* "bot scores" for the Twitter accounts following the accounts of the largest German political parties in May, 2019. The threshold of 76% (3.8 out of 5) which was defined by [9] and reused in our replication attempt is highlighted.

deterministic strategy to make our results reproducible. At the same time, the approach should guarantee a representative sample. For this purpose, we sorted the 270k "bot" accounts in descending order of their "bot score". Within that list, accounts with the same "bot score" were sorted in descending alphabetical order according to their Twitter handle. From the resulting list, we selected all accounts in lines where *linenumber* mod $2,500 = 1$, i.e. the 1st, 2501st, 5001st, ... account. This selection procedure resulted in a list of 109 alleged social bots covering the range of "bot scores" from 3.857 to 4.931.

Each of the 109 accounts was closely analyzed manually, using tools like https://accountanalysis.app to check for unusual timing patterns and to retrieve the Twitter clients that were used for recent tweets and retweets. Most importantly, we closely inspected the tweets and retweets as well as the interactions with other users to search for traces of potential automation.

The complete list of accounts with the "bot score" assigned by *Botometer*, the Twitter handle, the follower number, and a short comment about distinctive characteristics of the account can be found in the Supplemental Materials, Section A.[6] Here, we want to give some examples of such accounts. We will also speculate about potential reasons why these accounts might have been misclassified as "bots".

– More than 20% of the accounts that were misclassified as "bots" only tweeted a single tweet after the account was created. We found this to be a reproducible behavior of *Botometer*: After creating a new account and tweeting a single

---

[6] https://www.in.th-nuernberg.de/Professors/Gallwitz/gk-md22-suppl.pdf.

tweet, any account is rated a "bot" with a close-to-maximum "bot score". A somewhat tragic example of this type is a Twitter user in our sample, a follower of the conservative party account @CDU, who asked @Microsoft for help regarding a problem with her Microsoft account in July 2017 and (as of May 2022) has never received a reply.

- Inactivity in the last couple of months or years seems to be another main reason for *Botometer* to rate accounts as "bots". This is a quite surprising behavior, given the common narrative that social bots are supposed to be highly active accounts, as suggested by the Oxford 50-tweets-per-day criterion (see, for example, [8]). While *Botometer* still displays this behavior in May 2022, a warning has been added to the web interface in the meantime: *@accountname is not active, score might be inaccurate.*
- Although quite active, the Twitter account @CDU_VS, the local branch of the conservative party in the town of Villingen-Schwenningen, is rated a "bot". A possible reason seems to be that the operator of the account is quite frequently cross-posting content from their Facebook and Instagram pages directly through the "Tweet" button on these platforms. However, this is a perfectly normal, frequent and acceptable way of sending tweets and has nothing to do with the concept of a social bot. User @hoockstar, for example, also might have turned himself into a "bot" by posting a couple of Instagram links in this manner.
- A similar issue might have turned six other Twitter users in our sample into "bots". Each of them sent at least one tweet through a game app, such as "8 ball pool" or "ClumsyNinja". Tweeting your progress in games like these is often honored with a reward in some kind of in-game currency, while the tweet serves as an ad for the creators of the game.

To summarize the result, not a single one of the accounts in the list was a "bot" in any meaningful sense of the word, certainly not a social bot according to the definition given in the Introduction. In other words, every single "bot" in our sample was a false alarm. Assuming that *Botometer* does not perform *worse* than a random number generator on the followers of German political parties (as we did not check the accounts rated as human), we can also conclude that the best guess for the number of social bots following the political parties in Germany is not 83,000, as claimed by Keller and Klinger, but zero.

4.2   Are Social Bots Attempting to Spread Vaccine-Critical Information?

The second study we used as a basis for evaluating *Botometer* in a real-life scenario investigates the influence of "bots" in the spread of vaccine-critical information [4]. The authors examined a study population of 53,188 U.S. Twitter users who were selected independently of whether they were exposed to or shared vaccine-related tweets or not. Additionally, about 21m vaccine-related tweets coming from approx. 5m accounts had been identified based on keyword filtering. The study examined whether and how the users of the study population interacted with vaccine-related tweets, and whether the vaccine-related tweets users were exposed to came from "bots".

In order to determine if a Twitter account was a bot, *Botometer* was employed, using the usual threshold of 50% (2.5 out of 5). A total of 5,124,906 accounts was scored, resulting in 197,971 "bots", which corresponds to a "bot" prevalence of 3,8%.

Although the study concluded that the exposure to bot-generated content was limited—which seemed highly plausible to us—we were skeptical about the true nature of the accounts that had been counted as "bots".

The authors kindly provided us with the list of Twitter UserIDs that were counted as "bots", as well as the corresponding *Botometer* scores. The scenario differs from the German party follower study in important aspects which should help to avoid two main causes of false positives:

- The sample of 5m accounts was selected based on active tweets that contain vaccine-relevant keywords. Therefore, inactive accounts (which, as we have seen, are commonly misclassified as "bots" by *Botometer*) could not become part of the sample.
- Given that every account in the sample had to post at least one tweet with a vaccine-related keyword, it was highly unlikely (though, as it turned out, not impossible) that accounts which had only produced a single tweet in their lifetime could become part of the sample. (Accounts like these, as we have seen, are commonly—if not always—misclassified as "bots" by *Botometer*.)

Therefore, the dramatically lower prevalence of "bots" in this sample (3.8% vs. 67% on the basis of the 50% threshold) is not surprising.

Again, we wanted to select a suitable, representative subset of the 197,971 "bot" accounts in a deterministic manner which would undergo manual analysis. The list provided to us by [4] included unique numerical user IDs, not the alphanumeric Twitter handles we had used in the party follower scenario. For deleted or suspended accounts, we could not reconstruct the alphanumeric Twitter handles. Also, Twitter handles may change over time. Therefore, in order to keep our approach reproducible, we used a selection strategy which was directly based on the numerical user IDs: We sorted the list of accounts numerically in increasing order according to their unique Twitter UserID and selected all accounts in lines where *linenumber* mod $1,500 = 1$, i.e. the 1st, 1,501st, 3,001st, ... account. This resulted in a list of 132 alleged social bots covering the range of "bot scores" from 2.557 to 4.871.

Of these 132 accounts, 11 had been deleted since the data had been collected (2017–2019). On the basis of the numerical Twitter UserID alone, without access to the Twitter handle, an investigation through the Internet Archive was not successful. This left us with 121 "bot" accounts that we could analyze.

We used tools like https://accountanalysis.app to check for unusual timing patterns and to retrieve the Twitter clients that had been used for recent tweets and retweets. Most importantly, we closely inspected the tweets and retweets as well as the interactions with other users to search for traces of potential automation. We put a significant amount of effort into establishing the true identity of the persons behind the accounts wherever possible, using Google Search, Facebook, LinkedIn, photo comparisons, homepages of physicians and scientific institutions, as well as various other information sources available on the internet.

The complete list of accounts with the "bot score" assigned by *Botometer*, the Twitter handle, the follower number, and a short comment about distinctive characteristics of the account can be found in the Supplemental Materials, Section B.[7]

A surprisingly high number of the 121 alleged "bots" in our sample are in reality individuals with academic or professional credentials, many of them directly related to the topic of vaccines. Each of them used their real name in their Twitter bio. The list included (in the order of User ID) a medical intern and researcher from Saudi Arabia, an International Development and Public Health professional at the University of London, a pediatric nurse practitioner in New York, a senior lecturer at the School of Business at the Örebro University, a Technical Manager at a health products company in Nigeria, an IT professional in Tohana, India, a former Pediatrician who is now working at the Embassy Medical Centres of HOPE Worldwide in Cambodia, a human resource professional in Michigan, a specialist in trauma surgery at Oscar G Johnson Veterans Admin. Hospital, the former Director of WHO's Prevention of Noncommunicable Diseases who holds multiple academic degrees and titles, a pediatrician in Loma Linda, California, a medical student at the University of Rwanda, a postdoctoral researcher at the Institut de Recherche en Infectiologie de Montpellier, a junior researcher working in the area of infectious diseases at the University Medical Center Rotterdam, an Associate Professor at the University of Texas Southwestern Medical Center and a Senior Economist at the RAND Corporation, a student in the Master's program Health Studies at the Athabasca University in Canada, and a Public Health Officer from Kampala University.

A number of the 121 alleged "bots" are, in reality, the official Twitter accounts of health-related organizations:

- @THEWAML, The World Association for Medical Law
- @CdnAcadHistPhm, The Canadian Academy of the History of Pharmacy
- @Infprevention, The Infection Prevention and Control Conference IPCC
- @jubileetanzania, The Jubilee Insurance Company of Tanzania Ltd.
- @JFoundation_, The Jamachiz foundation in Lagos which supports the improvement of basic human welfare.
- @UNMCkidney, The University of Nebraska Medical Center Division of Nephrology

Animals are commonly vaccinated as well. This contributed to the fact that some of the alleged "vaccine bots" are, in reality, Twitter accounts related to agricultural topics and pets:

- @agriview, "Wisconsin's Leading Agriculture Newspaper"

---

[7] https://www.in.th-nuernberg.de/Professors/Gallwitz/gk-md22-suppl.pdf.

David McKeag hat retweetet
ten @tentrixbanares · 22.04.18

LOOKING FOR BLOOD DONORS for our Golden Retriever. 🐶 We need dog donors at least 27kg and above 🐶, complete with vaccinations. Please RT and help us find a donor for Sansa. 💜

Fig. 4. Viral tweet about a dog in need of a canine blood donor. As it contains the keyword 'vaccinations', thousands of users who had retweeted this tweet and were misclassified as "bots" by *Botometer* were counted as "vaccine bots" in [4].

- @top5stories, Links to stories and videos about pitbulls, e.g. americanbully-daily.com
- @Thinkagro, Thinkagro Co Ltd., a China-based provider for agricultural products and solutions
- At least two of the accounts ended up as "vaccine bots" because, like 177k other users, they had retweeted a tweet about a seriously ill Golden Retriever in need of a canine blood donor. The tweet included the keyword 'vaccinations', see Fig. 4.
- @anonymousinapp1 tweeted only a single tweet with a joke that contained the word 'vaccines' and got one like for it.

Some of the accounts in the list use a certain degree of automation, none of which has anything to do with attempts to spread vaccine-critical information:

- A hospital doctor used the RoundTeam Twitter content management platform to tweet about hospital-related topics. The commercial service claims that it *"enables you to grow your presence on Twitter"*. (The doctor who used this service for a year acquired a total of 11 followers—highlighting how difficult it is to acquire followers even for a real and reputed person if their tweets remain generic and impersonal.)
- @Onderzoekers is the automated Twitter feed of a Dutch website which offers job openings in science and research.
- @top5stories uses the web-based automation tool IFTTT to automatically posts links to newly published articles on a some pitbull related sites.
- @vectorborg is a hashtag retweet bot with 1k followers that retweets tweets which contain the hashtag #GreenEnergy. Retweet bots of this type were

fairly common in the early days of Twitter. For example, a list of *"77 Useful Twitter Retweet Bots"*, including dozens of bots dedicated to retweeting tweets that mention a German city from #Aachen to #Wuerzburg, was presented by [3]. However, retweet bots give spammers easy access to the timeline of the followers of these bots, simply by including hashtags or keywords in unrelated tweets. As of May 2022, most retweet bots—including the ones in the list—have been deactivated or suspended by Twitter.

– @LoydGailpg is an account with 6 followers that used IFTTT to retweet links to newly published airline and travel related articles.

To summarize, in a representative sample of 121 of the almost 198k accounts that were counted as "bots" in [4], we found 116 human-operated accounts with no signs of automation. We can therefore estimate that approx. 190k human accounts were falsely counted as "bots" in this study. Many of these Twitter users have impressive academic and professional credentials. Consider that approx. 1,500 scientists and experts with similar credentials have been misclassified as social bots for each of the scientists and experts in our sample. Only 5 of the accounts in our sample might be considered (unmalicious) bots. Not a single one of these accounts had anything to do with automated attempts at spreading vaccine-critical information or disinformation.

Again, we could not find a single account that fits the usual definition of a social bot as cited in the Introduction.

5   Related Work

Our devastating findings about *Botometer*'s lack of reliability in real-world scenarios are consistent with findings in two recently published studies.

In [7], the Twitter debate around mask-wearing during the COVID-19 pandemic was analyzed, focusing on U.S.-based tweets. Like so many disinformation researchers before them, the authors used *Botometer* to detect the "social bots" in their sample of Twitter accounts. However, they followed the recommendations in [15] and manually labeled a random sample of 500 distinct users to check the reliability of *Botometer*'s results. Similar to our approach, they took a look at user profiles, tweeting histories, and interactions with other users in order to determine whether they were dealing with a social bot or not.

They did not find a single bot in their sample of 500 accounts. *Botometer*, however, labeled 29 (or 5.8%) of these accounts as "bots".

The authors decided to ignore the *Botometer* results: *"[...] based on manual review, many of these users were simply hyper-active tweeters. Their online activities did exhibit the normal behavior of human users, e.g. the content they posted did not appear to be automatically authored and they participated in active interactions with other Twitter users."*

In [14], the vaccine-related stance of English-language Twitter users during the COVID-19 pandemic was investigated. As the authors wanted to focus on human users, they tried to exclude bots using *Botometer*. In their sample of 675 accounts, 68 received a score (presumably the CAP) of 0.5 or higher. However, the authors also followed the recommendations in [15] and manually checked these accounts. They found only one of these accounts to be automated, an account that shared articles from a personal blog on Twitter. The other 67 accounts were human users, i.e. false alarms.

In a recent preprint by the research group that created *Botometer* [18], the authors speculate that *Botometer* might work more reliably on English language accounts than on non-English accounts. However, our results do not seem to confirm this hypothesis. Only one of the four real-world studies discussed in our paper involves mainly non-English language accounts. Nevertheless, in all four studies, between 96% and 100% of the accounts rated as "bots" on the basis of *Botometer* turned out to be false positives. Not a single one of them was a social bot according to the definition cited in the Introduction.

6   Conclusion

The field of social bot research is fundamentally flawed. While social bot researchers have received an enormous amount of public attention, the vast majority of their findings fully rely on the accuracy of *Botometer*. Many researchers simply refer to all accounts in their studies as "bots" or even as "social bots" as long as they exceed some arbitrarily chosen *Botometer* threshold. However, this approach is highly questionable from a theoretical point of view. And, as we have demonstrated empirically, Botometer fails miserably and consistently when evaluated under real-world conditions. Studies claiming to investigate the prevalence, properties, or influence of social bots based on *Botometer* have, in reality, just investigated false positives and artifacts of this approach.

While automated Twitter accounts exist, we have yet to see a single credible example of a malicious social bot, i.e. an account that pretends to be a human user and is operated by some sinister actor to manipulate public opinion.

In our impression, a prevailing culture of intransparency is a major factor that has enabled an entire field of research to rely on deeply flawed methods. Publishing or sharing raw data, as it is common practice in many other fields of science, would have helped to identify and highlight the fundamental methodological problems much earlier.

We conclude that all past and future claims about the prevalence or influence of social bots that are not accompanied by lists of account IDs are highly questionable and should be ignored. In those cases where actual social bot accounts are named, we recommend an in-depth analysis of these accounts to verify whether these are not simply human beings—made of flesh and blood—who have been misclassified as social bots like hundreds of thousands of Twitter users before them.

Acknowledgements. We are grateful to Adam Dunn for sharing with us the relevant raw data we used in Sect. 4.2. We sincerely appreciate the valuable comments and suggestions by Adrian Rauchfleisch, Darius Kazemi, and Jürgen Hermes, which helped us to improve the quality of the manuscript.

References

1. Allem, J.P., Ferrara, E.: Could social bots pose a threat to public health? Am. J. Public Health **108**(8), 1005 (2018)
2. Davis, C.A., Varol, O., Ferrara, E., Flammini, A., Menczer, F.: Botornot: a system to evaluate social bots. In: Proceedings of the 25th International Conference Companion on World Wide Web, pp. 273–274 (2016)
3. Dreißel, J.: 77 nützliche Twitter Retweet Bots. Onlinelupe.de, 11 July 2010 (2010). https://www.onlinelupe.de/online-marketing/77-nutzliche-twitter-retweet-bots/
4. Dunn, A.G., et al.: Limited role of bots in spreading vaccine-critical information among active twitter users in the United States: 2017–2019. Am. J. Public Health **110**(S3), S319–S325 (2020)
5. Gallwitz, F., Kreil, M.: The Social Bot Fairy Tale. Tagesspiegel Background, 3 June 2019 (2019). https://background.tagesspiegel.de/digitalisierung/the-social-bot-fairy-tale
6. Gorwa, R., Guilbeault, D.: Unpacking the social media bot: a typology to guide research and policy. Policy Internet **12**(2), 225–248 (2020)
7. He, L., et al.: Why do people oppose mask wearing? A comprehensive analysis of us tweets during the COVID-19 pandemic. J. Am. Med. Inform. Assoc. **28**(7), 1564–1573 (2021)
8. Howard, P.N., Kollanyi, B., Woolley, S.: Bots and Automation over Twitter during the US Election. Technical report, Oxford Internet Institute (2016)
9. Keller, T.R., Klinger, U.: Social bots in election campaigns: theoretical, empirical, and methodological implications. Polit. Commun. **36**(1), 171–189 (2019)
10. Kreil, M.: Social Bots, Fake News und Filterblasen. 34th Chaos Comminication Congress (34C3), December 2017 (2017). https://media.ccc.de/v/34c3-9268-social_bots_fake_news_und_filterblasen
11. Kreil, M.: The army that never existed: the failure of social bots research. OpenFest Conference, November 2019 (2019). https://michaelkreil.github.io/openbots/
12. Kreil, M.: People are not bots. 13th HOPE Conference, July 2020 (2020). https://archive.org/details/hopeconf2020/20200726_2000_People_Are_Not_Bots.mp4
13. Lee, K., Eoff, B., Caverlee, J.: Seven months with the devils: a long-term study of content polluters on twitter. In: Proceedings of the International AAAI Conference on Web and Social Media, vol. 5, pp. 185–192 (2011)
14. Poddar, S., Mondal, M., Misra, J., Ganguly, N., Ghosh, S.: Winds of Change: Impact of COVID-19 on Vaccine-related Opinions of Twitter users. arXiv preprint arXiv:2111.10667 (2021)
15. Rauchfleisch, A., Kaiser, J.: The False positive problem of automatic bot detection in social science research. PLoS ONE **15**(10), e0241045 (2020)
16. Varol, O., Ferrara, E., Davis, C., Menczer, F., Flammini, A.: Online human-bot interactions: detection, estimation, and characterization. In: Proceedings of the International AAAI Conference on Web and Social Media, vol. 11 (2017)
17. Wischnewski, M., Bernemann, R., Ngo, T., Krämer, N.: Disagree? You must be a bot! How beliefs shape twitter profile perceptions. In: Proceedings of the 2021 CHI Conference on Human Factors in Computing Systems, pp. 1–11 (2021)
18. Yang, K.C., Ferrara, E., Menczer, F.: Botometer 101: social bot practicum for computational social scientists. arXiv preprint arXiv:2201.01608 (2022)
19. Yang, K., Varol, O., Davis, C., Ferrara, E., Flammini, A., Menczer, F.: Arming the public with artificial intelligence to counter social bots. Hum. Behav. Emerg. Technol. **1**(1), 48–61 (2019)

New Automation for Social Bots: From Trivial Behavior to AI-Powered Communication

Christian Grimme[1]([✉])[iD], Janina Pohl[1][iD], Stefano Cresci[2][iD], Ralf Lüling[3], and Mike Preuss[4][iD]

[1] University of Münster, Münster, Germany
{christian.grimme,janina.pohl}@uni-muenster.de
[2] IIT-CNR, Pisa, Italy
s.cresci@iit.cnr.it
[3] Aleph Alpha, Heidelberg, Germany
ralf.lueling@aleph-alpha.de
[4] LIACS, Universiteit Leiden, Leiden, The Netherlands
mpreuss@liacs.leidenuniv.nl

Abstract. Today, implications of automation in social media, specifically whether social bots can be used to manipulate people's thoughts and behaviors are discussed. Some believe that social bots are simple tools that amplify human-created content, while others claim that social bots do not exist at all and that the research surrounding them is a conspiracy theory. This paper discusses the potential of automation in online media and the challenges that may arise as technological advances continue. The authors believe that automation in social media exists, but acknowledge that there is room for improvement in current scientific methodology for investigating this phenomenon. They focus on the evolution of social bots, the state-of-the-art content generation technologies, and the perspective of content generation in games. They provide a background discussion on the human perception of content in computer-mediated communication and describe a new automation level, from which they derive interdisciplinary challenges.

Keywords: Social media · Automation · Bots · Artificial intelligence · Content generation

1 Introduction

Automation[1] in social media has become a central point of discussion in computational social science, computer science, psychology, political science, journalism, and related domains. The central questions are *whether*, *to what extent*, *how*

---

[1] In the most general sense, we understand automation to mean technically controlled processes that ensure a specified target achievement largely without human intervention. In closed-loop systems, target achievement is controlled by feedback mechanisms and through self-regulating control mechanisms. In open-loop systems, no feedback mechanism is implemented [31].

F. Spezzano et al. (Eds.): MISDOOM 2022, LNCS 13545, pp. 79–99, 2022.
https://doi.org/10.1007/978-3-031-18253-2_6

convincingly, and *with what effects* automation is used. In the online and social media ecosystem, automation usually relates to the (partly or completely) self-regulating mechanization of communication by algorithms, either with a wider public (one-to-many) or individuals (one-to-one). Today, an almost classic subject of discussion is the social bot – a type of automaton in online media that (also temporarily) hides behind (possibly real) online accounts to interfere with human communication [14, 30]. Those bots are often described as tools that act autonomously, behave or respond intelligently to others, and even manipulate people's minds, e.g., to influence elections [8]. Others describe social bots and automation as simple tools, performing simple tasks like amplifying predefined content designed by humans [6]. Still others narrow their view to the assumed intelligent and autonomous automata, find that social bots do not exist at all, and claim that contemporary research on this topic is a huge conspiracy theory by greedy scientists aiming for funding [27]. Regardless of how social bots are defined and understood (as simple spammers or as super-smart and autonomous actors), we ask the question whether automation is already mature enough to produce textual and pictorial content systematically, autonomously, and convincingly[2] so that people can be manipulated by their means?

This work addresses the context of automation in online media with a broad perspective. It refrains from finding definitions of social bots, deficiencies in methodology, or participating in the non-targeted discussion of conspiracy beliefs. On the contrary, it focuses on exploring the potential of automation in the online media ecosystem based on current technologies and preconditions and discusses potential threats and challenges that may arise as these technologies are combined or advance further. Clearly, the authors are convinced of the existence of automation in social media. However, they acknowledge (and have contributed to) the discussion on shortcomings of current scientific methodology in investigating this phenomenon (e.g. in detection methods, [7, 29, 30]).

The presented results and discussion partly stem from a theme development workshop titled "AI: Mitigating Bias and Disinformation", held in May 2022, which also addressed the topic of "Automation in Online Media". The authors of this paper are a subset of experts and participants of the workshop, approaching communication automation from different angles by integrating the evolution of social bots, state-of-the-art content generation technologies, and the perspective of content generation in games. In the remainder of this work, we provide a background discussion on the human perception of content in computer-mediated communication. After that, we describe a new automation level and derive interdisciplinary challenges from it. Overall, we present this paper as an initial perspective on mid-term and future challenges and research questions regarding possible new aspects of automation.

---

[2] "Convincingly" in the sense that social media users are not aware of messaging with an automaton or consuming artificially generated content. This does not relate to direct change of opinion.

2 Background and Context of Computer-Mediated Communication

Although the context of automation in online media is about communication, the infrastructural and technical conditions of social media platforms provide a unique and, in contrast to direct human communication, often limited form of communication. Consequently, communication behavior, content, and reception deviate, influencing the requirements for the automation of communication. Over the years, several theoretical frameworks have been developed that may illuminate aspects of human-computer communication and interaction patterns.

A basic model of computer-mediated communication (CMC) developed by Walther [76] states that computer interfaces enable humans to communicate with less bias. Due to the reduced number of cues (e.g., absence of ambient noise or gestures), fewer social responses are triggered that blur the transmitted message. However, recent works show that the number of social media cues increased dramatically, e.g., due to the introduction of emojis [78]. These shall provide rich information, e.g., to judge whether someone else is a fake account [34].

Nass et al. developed the computers are social actors (CASA) model [49]. CASA states that cues emitted by a machine can trigger users to apply the same social heuristics used for human-to-human interactions [59]. Studies prove CASA's validity in the social media context: Ho et al. [33] showed that chatbots and humans could be equally effective in achieving positive conversation outcomes. Similarly, bots posting informational content on Twitter are perceived as trustworthy, although human curators were assessed as being more credible [22,23,66].

The Uncanny Valley, introduced as a theoretical (and partly speculative) model by Mori [47], is defined as the low point of a qualitative function representing human affinity toward technology. Generally, affinity increases the more human-like machines become. This, however, only works until their real nature is unclear to a human observer, which then provokes a feeling of eerie. The brain triggers this effect when incoherent behavior is detected, i.e., when the expectation of seeing a machine is not met by reality [62]. In line with CASA, participants in a study by Skjuve et al. [65] reacted similarly to a bot as to a human conversation partner, as long as bots were able to carry the conversation. In several other studies, people reacted more positively to a chatbot without an avatar or were more likely to befriend another user with a comic-like rather than a hyper-realistic virtual avatar [5,13,63].

Sundar's MAIN model [68] defines cues that are used mindlessly by humans to rate digital media's credibility: Modality, Agency, Interactivity, and Navigability. Intuitively, an audio-visual mode has more credibility than text-only media. However, presumably because of the Uncanny Valley effect, people trust multimodal media, including text and images, although audio-visual media are closer to real conversations. Agency is defined as the source of information, i.e., the more social presence the source has, the more trustworthy it is. Interactivity addresses the response behavior of digital media. The faster and more adapted the response to the ongoing conversation is, the more trust is granted. Navigability features the design of a digital medium, i.e., information structured according to human expectations is more credible. Using the MAIN model, researchers showed that humans perceive chatbots as being credible [66], while bots on Twitter found with automated detection methods like Botometer [80] are considered less credible [4]. Nevertheless, since Botometer was shown to detect only unsophisticated bots [15,29], the limited cues given by them (e.g., text-only, no variation of actions) may lead to the reduced credibility assessment.

Already before the COVID-19 pandemic and Facebook announced its transformation into Meta Platforms [45], the Metaverse has been considered as digital future of social interaction [39]. The term was coined in a science-fiction novel from 1992 [67] to describe a virtual world next to the physical world in which users interact with each other and services via avatars. It combines elements from virtual and extended reality (VR and XR, respectively) but is not adequately defined yet due to the use of the word for different marketing purposes [57]. First steps towards a Metaverse have been taken in products of the gaming industry such as Second Life or online role play games [40]. Recently, Facebook published its first version of a Metaverse in which humans can create avatars and socialize with friends while wearing VR headsets [53]. Due to the resurgence of the topic, little contemporary research has been published until now. Jeon [36], for example, studies how users designing their perfect self in a Metaverse react to advertisements emotionally, while others explored the security and privacy risks of the Metaverse [20].

The development of theories about how humans perceive the digital world and act in it happened in line with the advancement of technologies. Due to various social cues transmitted via social media but also due to known restrictions and the human ability to bridge perception gaps with social scripts (anthropomorphization), humans may perceive the online ecosystem as similar to the real world, especially if no unexpected behavior occurs.

3   Three Perspectives

To illuminate the current state and future perspectives of (automatic) communication on social media, we discuss three different viewpoints: social bots as actors, content generation models as tools, and games and artificial intelligence as references for content generation in virtual worlds. Especially the interplay and interference of these three perspectives provide a multifaceted basis for identifying current unresolved issues and future challenges.

3.1   Evolution of Social Bots

The paramount example of automation in social media is the social bot – an account that is at least partially automated to perform a set of predefined tasks. Since the very emergence of social media, their support for anonymity and the possibility of setting up programmatic interactions via APIs resulted in the rapid development and diffusion of social bots [26]. Despite the existence of neutral or even benign bots that contribute to answering the information needs of social media users, a large number of bots have shady purposes. Because of this, and in parallel to the rise of social bots, platform administrators and scholars devoted significant efforts to the development of bot detection techniques [14,44].

Through time, the characteristics of social bots have changed much. Bots developed in the early 2010s were very simple accounts characterized by limited personal information, few social (i.e., friend/follower) relationships, and repetitive posting activity. On the one hand, their simplicity allowed bot developers to create many such accounts in a short time. On the other hand, however, it also made detecting those bots a relatively easy task [79]. For this reason, subsequent social bots were more sophisticated, featured detailed – yet obviously fake – profile information (e.g., credible profile picture, short bio or account description, birthday), and had human-comparable social relationships and diversified activity. These characteristics made the sophisticated social bots much harder to be distinguished from human-operated accounts, as empirically demonstrated by the increased difficulty of both social media users and machine learning-based bot detectors at spotting newer bots with respect to older (and simpler) ones [15]. In fact, the development of sophisticated social bots started an arms race between bot developers and bot detectors that continues these days [16].

The burden of creating carefully engineered and thus credible bots were on the shoulders of the bot developers. In other words, all of the detailed information required to disguise social bots had to be manually inserted, which implies that significant effort and time were required to create a large number of sophisticated bots. Similarly, the behavior of social bots was rule-based, meaning that bot developers typically created simple sets of rules to determine their actions and activities. These could drive the bots to reshare all content posted by certain accounts, post messages at predefined times, or even automatically follow a set of target accounts. Overall, until recently, social bots featured limited "intelligence", independently of their complexity and degree of resemblance to human-operated accounts [6]. However, this scenario is about to change due to the recent advances in AI that provide unprecedented opportunities for creating more intelligent and human-like social bots. For example, generative adversarial networks (GANs) demonstrated exceptional capabilities at artificially creating realistic-looking pictures of men and women of all ages,[3] among other things.[4] These could very well be used as credible profile pictures of fake accounts, as it already happened on Facebook and Instagram.[5] Similarly, recent advances in natural language generation (e.g., OpenAI's GPT 3) opened up the possibility to create artificial texts on any given topic,[6] even mimicking the writing style of a target character, or adopting a peculiar one. New bots could (and already do) exploit these techniques to craft more effective and credible messages before posting them on social media [25,52]. Finally, AI has also been used to generate

---

[3] https://thispersondoesnotexist.com/.
[4] https://thisxdoesnotexist.com/.
[5] https://www.wired.com/story/facebook-removes-accounts-ai-generated-photos/.
[6] https://openai.com/blog/better-language-models/.

artificial online behaviors (i.e., sequences of actions) to trick detectors of malicious accounts into misclassifying AI-driven accounts as benign ones [32]. These figures paint a worrying picture of the capabilities that future bots could exhibit.

3.2 Multimodal Artificial Content Generation

The advent of transformers-based language models like BERT [18] or GPT [54] changed the status-quo of natural language generation (NLG). In contrast to previous approaches like convolutional neural networks, transformers draw global dependencies between input tokens, allowing the connection of coherent words that do not appear in consecutive order [75]. Additionally, by using as many unlabeled, cross-domain, and multilingual texts as possible during an extensive pre-training, transformers gain a good understanding of language and implicitly learn a variety of potential sub-tasks. Thus, few- or even zero-shot learning is possible, where the model either receives only a few examples as input or even fulfills the task spontaneously [11].

The current state-of-the-art in text-only generation is GPT-3 [11], which can be used to generate texts that are indistinguishable from human-written ones, especially if they are short [35]. The mean human accuracy at detecting five hundred word articles written by GPT-3 was 52% [11][7]. Although a BERT model trained to detect GPT-generated texts performed slightly better, finding a reliable way to detect these artificial texts remains an open task [1]. Fagni et al. [25] demonstrate this problem based on fake accounts that use artificial tweets generated with GPT-2, amongst others. They evaluated thirteen supervised detectors, like various BERT variants, assessing several accounts and tweet features. Accounts backed-up with GPT-2 generated tweets were hardest to detect for these trained models, with a mean accuracy of 75%.

However, in the context of the automated production of information, not only the text is relevant, but also the associated visualizations in the form of images, drawings, and avoidably scientific diagrams to underline the statements to be conveyed. Large language models can help generate natural language treatises to generate the associated visualizations and then describe them depending on the situation. A good way to generate images from text is Dall-E, a 12 billion parameter version of GPT-3 that is trained to generate images from text descriptions using a data set of text-image pairs [55]. Extensive pre-training is fast becoming the norm in Vision Language (VL) modeling. However, the prevailing VL approaches are limited by the need for labeled data and the use of complex multi-level pre-training targets. It is a simple method for enriching generative language models with additional modalities using adaptor-based fine-tuning. For example, building on Frozen [74], the Aleph Alpha model MAGMA [24] trains a set of VL models that autoregressively generate text from any combination

---

[7] The readers may ask themselves whether they can judge who wrote the abstract of this paper - the authors or GPT-3. In fact, the abstract has been generated automatically by GPT-3 using only the introduction chapter of this paper as input. No editing has been done by the authors.

of visual and textual inputs. The pre-training is fully end-to-end and uses a single language modeling objective, which simplifies optimization compared to previous approaches. Notably, the language model weights remain unchanged during training, allowing for the transfer of encyclopedic knowledge and contextual learning skills from language pre-training.

3.3   Perception of Content in Games and Social Media

Games are at the forefront of AI research and have recently been a testbed for many new algorithmic developments, which have led to seminal papers. Deep Reinforcement Learning was first shown to be successful on the Atari Learning Environment [46], and the more abstract (board game) Go problem was first successfully tackled on and beyond the human grandmaster level using AlphaGo [64]. Many improvements followed, as summarized in [61]. Togelius [71] explains why this direction is going to continue to be prominent in AI, especially if we want our methods to further develop in the direction of *artificial general intelligence* (AGI). As of May 2022, the last current step may be Gato [58], an agent that can deal with hundreds of tasks, including many games successfully, but also handle natural language problems. In this case, solving a problem often means to *create* an answer that matches the expectations of humans. Whereas Gato can e.g. create speech that matches the context as, e.g., GPT-3 [11] does, Dall-E2 [55] generates stunning pictures from text prompts.

Generation of content has some tradition in the computer game field; it has been one of the most vital research areas in this realm at least since around 2013 [72] and is usually subsumed under the term *Procedural Content Generation* (PCG). There are early examples of generative methods for maps/levels in games already employed in the 1980s, notably Elite which featured a vast science fiction universe that could by no means have been stored in the memory of available computers. The generation method basically relied on controlled randomness, however, more recent methods use randomness only as variational effect to prevent too strong similarities in the provided content which would create an "artificial" impression. As a main driving force, they use explicit optimization (according to a measurable criterion) or a model that implicitly stores knowledge about content in a machine learning fashion, usually a (deep) artificial neural network. Nowadays, there is basically no type of game content that is not semi-automatically or fully automatically generated to some extent, including whole non-player characters (NPCs), missions or full plots, graphical components, music up to almost complete game creation. Notable examples here are *No Man's Sky*[8] (2016, as of 2022 still extended several times every year), and Ultima Ratio Regum [38][9] (started in 2012, still in beta). Content creation may also be personalized to the expectations of users according to the Experience-Driven PCG paradigm [81].

From this viewpoint of users, and especially if seen from an automated generation perspective, computer games share a lot with social media:

---

[8] https://www.nomanssky.com/.
[9] https://www.markrjohnsongames.com/games/ultima-ratio-regum/.

interactivity: whereas most of the content has to be perceived by the user, interaction is not only possible in contrast to other media (e.g., movies, newspapers), but a vital component of the setting;

immersion: games, as well as social media providers, aim to catch and hold the attention of users as long as possible;

believability: it is not necessary to understand the content or use it with a specific plan or intention, but it must be made in a way that appears to be meaningful and believable.

One crucial difference, especially concerning believability, may be that in computer games, users apply the *suspension of disbelief* because they know that they are in a game's context and still *want to believe* in the content they see. In other words, they know that they will be tricked but want to be tricked well enough to ignore that thought. In social media, users usually expect to be confronted with believable content because it is real, produced by other users with some intention. It seems necessary to make quite big mistakes to raise the user's suspicion that the observed content may be generated, which, of course, simplifies betraying users by inserting (semi-) automatically created content and making them believe it is from real users. Thus users do not expect to be tricked, and therefore the level at which small mistakes go unnoticed is relatively high.

In games and social media, being successful requires achieving emotional attachment to provoke reactions. However, and this is another difference, the attachment must be at least partly positive in games. It can be challenging, but players will simply churn and play another game if it is more negative than positive. This is not the same for social media users who are also engaged by negative attachment (e.g., shit storms). Additionally, social media content is consumed at a much higher frequency, user attention is much more fluent, and several threads can be worked on in a minute. Therefore, believability may be more effortless to achieve as the amount of content a user sees before, e.g., accepting or setting up a friendship request or supporting an existing statement, is relatively small.

In consequence, we can presume that making believable content in social media, especially for fast-paced media like Twitter (where lengthy statements are rare), is probably easier than for games, where the problem of computationally generating narrative is still only working in specific contexts and on a small scale [2]. Additionally, considering that some human social media actors (e.g., from the Alt-Right scene) use distortion and confusion as means of communication, it seems even easier to produce believable postings automatically. Generating nonsensical, out-of-context, or arbitrary statements is certainly possible already now with the available generation algorithms, as GPT-3 [11]. Despite these advances in generation, putting different media types together is undoubtedly more challenging. In game AI, this is known as facet orchestration [41] with the overall goal of generating full games, and there are only a few examples of doing it only with two facets (e.g., graphics and audio) successfully, none of which goes into a completely automated direction. A certain amount of human coordination is always necessary to obtain a good result. Using techniques such as Dall-E2 or MAGMA would not help here, as they would just try to express the same content in another facet (from text to graphics or vice versa), but in games and media, text and pictures used in the text are not totally congruent but rather synergetic.

Riedl already argued in 2016 [60] that being able to generate meaningful computational narrative is necessary for interaction with humans. This leads towards the probably most important current research direction in AI, which deals with the cooperation of AI agents and humans. It comes under different labels, human-computer interaction, hybrid intelligence, team AI [48], computer-supported cooperative work, but eventually means that machines have to interact in a meaningful way with humans and other machines even if an out-of-distribution event (something they have not been trained for) happens. Thorough research in this direction has just started and presumably, will keep us busy for a long time. In the meantime, interaction with the AI that controls a bot will be the only (fairly) safe way for a human user to find out if there is a machine on the other side, as was suggested for games some time ago [43]. Needless to say, Turing-testing is itself hard to automatize, making it a cure for experienced users but not for automated bot-finding.

4   New Automation

In the previous sections of this paper, we presented various developments, research results, models, and insights regarding the current state of automation in online media, the generation of artificial content, and the perception of content and communication in various technical environments (social media to game worlds). At this point, we draw new conclusions from these observations and point out what seems to be a realistic perspective toward a new level of automation. New Automation creates challenges that go far beyond previous research questions and will need to be addressed by the research community and society in the future.

Automation in social media is currently, in most cases, still limited to the technical implementation and imitation of human behavior at a rudimentary level. Besides the massive content duplication, only simple reactive actions are usually performed on other users (repetition of content, signaling approval/disapproval). In this context, the simulation of human-like behavior does not primarily serve to increase the credibility of automated actors vis-á-vis human communication partners but rather to avoid detection and sanctioning by monitoring mechanisms of social platforms. Similarly, massively repetitive content and automated approval or disapproval do not aim at human communication partners. They target the recommendation mechanisms that decide which content and topics users see as important in their timelines [69].

This status quo may now change permanently under the new circumstances of the development of content-generating technologies. While it was previously challenging to generate thematically appropriate content without human intervention, transformers-based neural networks and even multimodal advancements of these technologies now represent a step in the direction of (partially) autonomous and reactive systems for direct communication. Thus, the technological base of behavioral imitation can now be complemented by a substantive building block of automation in content generation (see Fig. 1). Specifically, automata can now be developed so that they not only behave in a human-like manner (i.e., follow a regular daily routine, simulate human reaction speed) but also generate creative-seeming but indeed variable content. Textual content is not only variable at the word level; it can also be preset to views and opinions to a limited extent (few-shot learning). For this purpose, content from other users can be used as preset content to configure an opinion of the automaton to simulate a contextual response. The generation of multimodal content can increase this aspect – and the credibility of the content according to the MAIN model.

However, the content's credibility depends not only on the quality of the generated content. Although today's systems often generate convincing artifacts that are no longer identifiable as artificial even to humans, they do not always function flawlessly and convincingly. Still, this is less of a problem than we would assume in a classic communication situation (face-to-face) for several reasons:

First, as presented before, it is essential to consider the environment and the lack of external influences during communication in social media while at the same time including human scripts to deal with this type of communication. Content generated by automata is not presented entirely to a single user, but distributed to multiple users, so that no single user can see the whole picture of a campaign. Spelling mistakes in single messages could be perceived as simple slips and nonsensical posts, as human trolling, or misunderstanding from the receiver's side. Humans are programmed to understand messages sent by a communication partner not only by content but also by interpreting social cues like facial expressions or gestures. Consequently, communication with no or reduced social cues leads to misunderstandings since it is abstract and less intuitive. An exciting field of self-experience of this phenomenon has undoubtedly been text-based communication during the pandemic: the restricted environment of a chat platform may lead to frequent misunderstandings. Even using additional cues, such as emojis or stickers, is insufficient to solve this problem since they sometimes may even increase misunderstandings if a meaning of an emoji is ambiguous. An automaton must only act similar as humans would with all their errors and deviations to disguise its true identity from the message receiver.

Second, as mentioned in the perspective of content generation in games and social media, users believe that the things they are confronted with on social media are real. In contrast to gaming, where gamers are in a clearly virtual setting and pushed to the content and action to reach a suspension of disbelief, social media users belief in a real social setting and seemingly often do not want to scrutinize the origin of the information. Partly this may be the case since it is laborious to review every source in such a broad ecosystem like social media (similar to the situation of real social interaction scenarios). Additionally, tedious fact checking would pop the bubble on their social media platforms, where they can see personalized content which correspond to their world view. Especially in

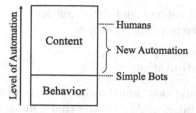

Fig. 1. Visualization of the gap between simple automatons and human communication that must be closed by New Automation techniques.

times of events like the pandemic, users rely on their social interactions via social media, making it very painful to disintegrate the reliability of these platforms for every single user. Thus, only strong cues that irritate users seem to be strong enough to make users question the validity of the information.

However, most of the limited cues transmitted via social media are enough to trigger humans' socialization scripts (e.g., as in the CASA model [49]) for ensuring believable communication. This offers two new levels of individual influence: (1) Cues can be reduced in a way that messages become more ambiguous (e.g., the use of fewer emojis will lead to uncertainty regarding the intent of the message and may leave a communication partner being insecure and occupied with deciphering the reduced message). Here, automation can easily be applied since it only needs to be sophisticated enough to provide enough cues such that users are not entirely sure whether their communication partner is an automaton or a human being. (2) Cues can be inserted to trigger specific social scripts for causing specific reactions. This is certainly more difficult and directly correlates to the sophistication of the applied content generation technology. Still, the auto-generated text has only been adjusted to the situation and should be good enough to fulfill human expectations, but not better so as to avoid triggering the Uncanny Valley.

As shown in Fig. 1 for the application of persuasive automation in online media, the challenge is not to accurately replicate interpersonal communication. It is to properly control cues and content in the setting of feature-poor communication in technical environments for creating sufficient uncertainty in the communication partner about the actual nature of an actor behind an account or avatar. New Automation has to close the gap between only simulating human behavior by producing content for completing the human appearance of an account or avatar in the restricted scenario of online media.

5   Future Challenges Implied by New Automation

The recent advancements to the tools and techniques capable of generating artificial content and driving the next generation of automated accounts pose opportunities, questions, and dire challenges. Among them are the challenges related to detecting AI-powered social bots, assessing the effects of New Automation, measuring the quality of content and detecting low-quality one, designing and applying corrective interventions, and ethics.

5.1   Detection of Automation

AI-powered accounts could post multimedia content with human-like patterns by combining the capabilities of AI systems that generate realistic and credible behaviors, photos, videos, and texts. An account with these characteristics and whose behavior is decided by an AI to minimize its detectability while maximizing its impact inevitably poses much increased challenges than those faced by bot detectors up to now. This observation raises an important question as to whether *it will even be possible to distinguish such bots from human-operated accounts* in the future. In more than a decade of research on social bot detection, we witnessed countless efforts aimed at developing detectors capable of effectively spotting the majority of existing bots. This considerable effort led to the development of literally hundreds of different bot detectors [14]. Unfortunately, existing benchmark studies demonstrated the inherent difficulty of this task, which, as of now, still stands as largely unsolved [15, 21, 52, 56]. The unsatisfactory results obtained against unresourceful bots cast a shadow on our capacity to detect future intelligent bots. To turn the tide in the fight against automated and other malicious accounts, some scholars proposed alternative approaches, such as those aimed at detecting coordinated behaviors rather than automated ones [50, 77], or those that take into account the presence of adversaries by design [16]. Others, however, deemed the task too difficult and recommended policy, legal, and normative interventions to curb the many possible malicious applications of automation and AI in online media [10]. New Automation thus introduces a conundrum within this context: Detecting the next generation of social bots might prove simply too tricky or outright impossible, but leaving them be would make us vulnerable to their manipulations.

5.2   Measurement of Content Quality

An interesting and undoubtedly complex challenge in the context of New Automation is measuring content quality concerning a given context. Here, different measures were developed in the past, focusing on assessing the adequacy, fluency, diversity and factuality of the automatically generated texts [12]. Besides the complexity of finding suitable proxies for assessing these criteria in the multimodal domain [3], it is also a double-edged sword. On the one hand, assessing content under investigation needs to examine it for coherence with the broader context. On the other hand, using such a measure would be easy to identify incoherent content and poor combinations of multimodal constructs (e.g., image and text). At the same time, these measures would also be suitable to be used as optimization criteria for generating processes and thus for their improvement.

However, currently, there are no such combined measures available. Although some indicators for text quality exist, they do not measure what needs to be measured to judge artificially generated content in more than one dimension. While the so-called BLEU Score [51] and its successors were initially being developed for evaluating machine translations (the closer translation to professional human translation, the better), the ROUGE score [42] was developed based on BLEU for text summarization. It compares the summary with the original text and implements different score versions (e.g., based on the longest common sub-strings or different numbers of n-grams as a basis). At least the BERT-Score [82] calculates (in contrast to BLEU and ROUGE) a semantic similarity score for each token in a candidate sentence with each token in a reference sentence. However, (a) all measures need a reference to compare with; (b) they cannot evaluate whether a text represents a specific opinion or a whether the text makes any sense in specific content, and (c) they only measure one specific aspect of the text's quality instead of providing an overall picture.

The only currently available option to check for the quality of the generated text is the evaluation by humans. As we have seen from the discussion of the New Automation paradigm in social media, this may not necessarily influence the applicability of the automation side but certainly the detection side. While humans may activate their social scripts to integrate artificial content into the current context, detection methods will fail to notice discrepancies objectively.

5.3 Effects of Automation

The effects derived from New Automation can be either positive or negative, depending on the use case, context and intentions. Positive effects may be derived from the increased communication efficiency. For example, if suitable methods have been designed that can detect the spread of fake news, content moderators may intervene early in the distribution process. Further, in particular situations like natural disasters, information can spread faster and be targeted more directly to the affected people. Additionally, although research may not be able to detect social bots anymore, it will maybe focus on mitigating the effects of their actions. Thus, the final goal – making social media an uninfluenced platform for the free exchange of opinions – may be achieved nevertheless.

However, the dark side of New Automation includes the scenario of information warfare [19]. If social bots and disinformation cannot be detected reliably, moderators or other concerned parties may use other methods like pre- or debunking to counteract these developments. This would increase the amount of content on social media, possibly one half in favor and the other half against a particular opinion. Overall, this polarized situation would decrease users' trust and reliance on social media. Especially in times of a pandemic, where many people are socially isolated, this may have severe psychological consequences. Lastly, if more and more content is posted online (and the creation of this content is not effortful anymore), communication itself may become arbitrary. Like industrialization decreased the efforts to create objects, making them more expendable, will the automation of word generation make conversations less valuable? Artificial content may eventually even dominate social interaction. If such data is used as input for training language generating models (as it is done currently on large corpora of text from the web), a self-enforcing cycle of stereotype language generation may result. Whatever effects materialize, it seems to be certain that the nature and the intention of communication but maybe also New Automation itself will be affected by New Automation.

5.4   Moderation Interventions and New Platforms

A significant challenge in the face of New Automation is content moderation and moderation interventions – i.e., taking action directly and in a timely manner in ongoing events to stop abuses [28]. Simple regulation is not enough; automatic methods for detecting and contrasting automation, low-quality content and misbehavior must be implemented. At the level of the platform operators, this would mean permanent monitoring of data and content, which indeed harbors its dangers (for example, the censorship regulations of platform operators may damage their public image). Nevertheless, if one wants to take this path, the methodological gap in evaluating and classifying content exists, as described above. Then, in addition to simply detecting problematic content and behavior, effective content moderation also implies the deployment of adequate corrective actions (i.e., moderation interventions) [37,73]. The ultimate goal of moderation interventions is that of persuading users to drop harmful or otherwise problematic behavior (e.g., posting offensive or fake content). As such, applying moderation interventions automatically brings us back to the challenges of computer-mediated communication and of creating convincing AI-generated interventions (e.g., messages [9,70]). The design, (automated) deployment and evaluation of moderation interventions is still a relatively little explored area of research [17], and even more so in relation to New Automation.

At the same time, the human scripts and behaviors described above may provide a starting point in the long term for shifting attention away from these (instinctive) scripts and toward a critical approach to the content consumed. A first step could be to make it clear to users through the virtual environment design that social media are not a reflection of natural social interaction. Another step may be to warn users more often and openly about the difficulties of detecting, for example, social bots. An opposite trend will undoubtedly be the merging of virtual environments and social media in the next few years [20]. The so-called Metaverse could play an essential role in this. Users are undoubtedly aware that they are in a parallel, virtual world in this environment. It would be conceivable that in such an environment, the game world's rules dominate, creating a decoupling of virtual (and very global) reality and genuine social (often local) interaction. This makes it more challenging to transfer narratives and deception from the virtual world (including so-called extended reality) to the real world.

5.5   Ethical Implications

Finally, we want to briefly address several ethical issues that arise with research in the mentioned challenges but also with this paper itself. Any advancement in technology can be used for the prevention of malicious actions or applied in the context of malicious use (e.g., as part of the manipulation of disinformation campaigns). This is true for measures of content quality, detection mechanisms and contrasting actions [17]. If misuse can be detected, countermeasures can be evaluated with these detectors. As such, automation and bot detection is in a continuous arms race with malicious actors that try to avoid detection [16].

However, this work not only contributes to a multifaceted perspective of possible near- and midterm developments in automated communication in online media but can also be understood as an invitation or idea provider for malicious actors to increase focus on human perception and new technologies as an effective entity in the context of New Automation. Nevertheless, we think it is more important to highlight the challenges and possible upcoming technology leaps implied by New Automation than to ignore the possibilities or even dismiss them as a conspiracy and hope for the best.

6 Conclusion

In this work, we have theoretically explored the topic of AI-driven New Automation of communication in social media under the use of modern generation technologies at the content level. To this end, three relevant perspectives have been incorporated: the research on automated (often very simple) communication in social media, the technological perspective on automated content generation, and the facet of automated content generation in games. Placement in existing models such as computer-mediated communication (CMC), computers are social actors (CASA), Uncanny Valley, and the Modality, Agency, Interactivity, and Navigability model (MAIN) allow us to predict that already current AI-based content generation technologies (such as GPT, DALL-E, or MAGMA) have sufficient capabilities to deceive human actors when communicating with automata (which hide behind abstract social media accounts). On the one hand, this deception is based on the very specific environment of social media - a very restricted environment in which important cues of human interaction are missing to make a confident statement about the counterpart. On the other hand, the very deliberate setting of cues can sow uncertainty about the nature of the counterpart, activating human interaction scripts and thus supporting a humanization of automata and with it also the acceptance of generated content.

The present work is theoretical in nature and is based on an analysis of existing current technologies which, at least according to the literature and the authors' state of knowledge, are not yet in widespread use. Therefore, there seems to be no need to speculate about coming technology leaps and their effects, as long as already the presented New Automation brings a large amount of challenges: Challenges in detecting advanced automation, measuring content quality, exploring the effects of New Automation, and the possibilities of corrective interventions by platforms.

References

1. Adelani, D.I., Mai, H., Fang, F., Nguyen, H.H., Yamagishi, J., Echizen, I.: Generating sentiment-preserving fake online reviews using neural language models and their human- and machine-based detection. In: Barolli, L., Amato, F., Moscato, F., Enokido, T., Takizawa, M. (eds.) AINA 2020. AISC, vol. 1151, pp. 1341–1354. Springer, Cham (2020). https://doi.org/10.1007/978-3-030-44041-1_114
2. Alabdulkarim, A., Li, S., Peng, X.: Automatic story generation: challenges and attempts (2021). https://doi.org/10.48550/ARXIV.2102.12634. https://arxiv.org/abs/2102.12634
3. Alam, F., et al.: A survey on multimodal disinformation detection. In: The 29th International Conference on Computational Linguistics (COLING 2022). ACL (2022)
4. Alhayan, F., Pennington, D.R., Ruthven, I.: "She seems more human": understanding twitter users' credibility assessments of dementia-related information. In: Smits, M. (ed.) Information for a Better World: Shaping the Global Future. LNCS, vol. 13193, pp. 292–313. Springer, Cham (2022). https://doi.org/10.1007/978-3-030-96960-8_20
5. Arsenyan, J., Mirowska, A.: Almost human? A comparative case study on the social media presence of virtual influencers. Int. J. Hum. Comput. Stud. **155**, 102694 (2021). https://doi.org/10.1016/j.ijhcs.2021.102694
6. Assenmacher, D., Clever, L., Frischlich, L., Quandt, T., Trautmann, H., Grimme, C.: Demystifying social bots: on the intelligence of automated social media actors. Soc. Media + Soc. **6**(3) (2020). https://doi.org/10.1177/2056305120939264
7. Assenmacher, D., et al.: Benchmarking crisis in social media analytics: a solution for the data-sharing problem. Soc. Sci. Comput. Rev. (2021). https://doi.org/10.1177/08944393211012268
8. Bessi, A., Ferrara, E.: Social bots distort the 2016 U.S. Presidential election online discussion. First Monday **21**(11) (2016). https://doi.org/10.5210/fm.v21i11.7090. https://firstmonday.org/ojs/index.php/fm/article/view/7090
9. Bilewicz, M., et al.: Artificial intelligence against hate: intervention reducing verbal aggression in the social network environment. Aggress. Behav. **47**(3), 260–266 (2021)
10. Boneh, D., Grotto, A.J., McDaniel, P., Papernot, N.: How relevant is the Turing test in the age of sophisbots? IEEE Secur. Priv. **17**(6), 64–71 (2019)
11. Brown, T., et al.: Language models are few-shot learners. In: Larochelle, H., Ranzato, M., Hadsell, R., Balcan, M.F., Lin, H. (eds.) Advances in Neural Information Processing Systems, vol. 33, pp. 1877–1901. Curran Associates, Inc. (2020)
12. Chen, D., Dolan, W.: Collecting highly parallel data for paraphrase evaluation. In: Proceedings of the 49th Annual Meeting of the Association for Computational Linguistics: Human Language Technologies, Portland, Oregon, USA, pp. 190–200. Association for Computational Linguistics (2011). https://aclanthology.org/P11-1020
13. Ciechanowski, L., Przegalinska, A., Magnuski, M., Gloor, P.: In the shades of the uncanny valley: an experimental study of human-chatbot interaction. Futur. Gener. Comput. Syst. **92**, 539–548 (2019). https://doi.org/10.1016/j.future.2018.01.055
14. Cresci, S.: A decade of social bot detection. Commun. ACM **63**(10), 72–83 (2020)
15. Cresci, S., Di Pietro, R., Petrocchi, M., Spognardi, A., Tesconi, M.: The paradigm-shift of social spambots: evidence, theories, and tools for the arms race. In: The 26th International Conference on World Wide Web Companion (WWW 2017), pp. 963–972 (2017)

16. Cresci, S., Petrocchi, M., Spognardi, A., Tognazzi, S.: The coming age of adversarial social bot detection. First Monday **26**(7) (2021)

17. Cresci, S., Trujillo, A., Fagni, T.: Personalized interventions for online moderation. In: The 33rd ACM Conference on Hypertext and Social Media (HT 2022), pp. 248–251. ACM (2022)

18. Devlin, J., Chang, M.W., Lee, K., Toutanova, K.: BERT: pre-training of deep bidirectional transformers for language understanding. In: Proceedings of the 2019 Conference of the North American Chapter of the Association for Computational Linguistics: Human Language Technologies, Volume 1 (Long and Short Papers), Minneapolis, Minnesota, pp. 4171–4186. Association for Computational Linguistics (2019). https://doi.org/10.18653/v1/N19-1423

19. Di Pietro, R., Caprolu, M., Raponi, S., Cresci, S.: New Dimensions of Information Warfare. Advances in Information Security, vol. 84. Springer, Cham (2021). https://doi.org/10.1007/978-3-030-60618-3

20. Di Pietro, R., Cresci, S.: Metaverse: security and privacy issues. In: The 3rd IEEE International Conference on Trust, Privacy and Security in Intelligent Systems, and Applications (TPS 2021), pp. 281–288. IEEE (2021)

21. Echeverría, J., De Cristofaro, E., Kourtellis, N., Leontiadis, I., Stringhini, G., Zhou, S.: LOBO: evaluation of generalization deficiencies in Twitter bot classifiers. In: The 34th Annual Computer Security Applications Conference (ACSAC 2018), pp. 137–146 (2018)

22. Edwards, C., Beattie, A.J., Edwards, A., Spence, P.R.: Differences in perceptions of communication quality between a twitterbot and human agent for information seeking and learning. Comput. Hum. Behav. **65**, 666–671 (2016). https://doi.org/10.1016/j.chb.2016.07.003

23. Edwards, C., Edwards, A., Spence, P.R., Shelton, A.K.: Is that a bot running the social media feed? Testing the differences in perceptions of communication quality for a human agent and a bot agent on twitter. Comput. Hum. Behav. **33**, 372–376 (2014). https://doi.org/10.1016/j.chb.2013.08.013

24. Eichenberg, C., Black, S., Weinbach, S., Parcalabescu, L., Frank, A.: Magma-multimodal augmentation of generative models through adapter-based finetuning. arXiv preprint arXiv:2112.05253 (2021). https://doi.org/10.48550/arXiv.2112.05253

25. Fagni, T., Falchi, F., Gambini, M., Martella, A., Tesconi, M.: TweepFake: about detecting deepfake tweets. PLoS ONE **16**(5), e0251415 (2021)

26. Ferrara, E., Varol, O., Davis, C., Menczer, F., Flammini, A.: The rise of social bots. Commun. ACM **59**(7), 96–104 (2016)

27. Gallwitz, F., Kreil, M.: The rise and fall of 'social bot' research. SSRN 3814191 (2021). https://ssrn.com/abstract=3814191

28. Gillespie, T.: Custodians of the Internet: Platforms, Content Moderation, and the Hidden Decisions That Shape Social Media. Yale University Press, New Haven (2018)

29. Grimme, C., Assenmacher, D., Adam, L.: Changing perspectives: is it sufficient to detect social bots? In: Meiselwitz, G. (ed.) SCSM 2018. LNCS, vol. 10913, pp. 445–461. Springer, Cham (2018). https://doi.org/10.1007/978-3-319-91521-0_32

30. Grimme, C., Preuss, M., Adam, L., Trautmann, H.: Social bots: human-like by means of human control? Big Data **5**(4), 279–293 (2017). https://doi.org/10.1089/big.2017.0044

31. Groover, M.: Fundamentals of Modern Manufacturing: Materials, Processes, and Systems. Wiley, Hoboken (2010)

32. He, B., Ahamad, M., Kumar, S.: PETGEN: personalized text generation attack on deep sequence embedding-based classification models. In: The 27th ACM SIGKDD Conference on Knowledge Discovery & Data Mining (KDD 2021), pp. 575–584 (2021)

33. Ho, A., Hancock, J., Miner, A.S.: Psychological, relational, and emotional effects of self-disclosure after conversations with a chatbot. J. Commun. **68**(4), 712–733 (2018). https://doi.org/10.1093/joc/jqy026

34. Im, J., Tandon, S., Chandrasekharan, E., Denby, T., Gilbert, E.: Synthesized social signals: computationally-derived social signals from account histories. In: Proceedings of the 2020 CHI Conference on Human Factors in Computing Systems, Honolulu, HI, USA. ACM (2020). https://doi.org/10.1145/3313831.3376383

35. Ippolito, D., Duckworth, D., Callison-Burch, C., Eck, D.: Automatic detection of generated text is easiest when humans are fooled. In: Proceedings of the 58th Annual Meeting of the ACL, pp. 1808–1822. ACL (2020). https://doi.org/10.18653/v1/2020.acl-main.164

36. Jeon, Y.A.: Reading social media marketing messages as simulated self within a metaverse: an analysis of gaze and social media engagement behaviors within a metaverse platform. In: 2022 IEEE Conference on Virtual Reality and 3D User Interfaces Abstracts and Workshops (VRW), pp. 301–303 (2022). https://doi.org/10.1109/VRW55335.2022.00068

37. Jhaver, S., Boylston, C., Yang, D., Bruckman, A.: Evaluating the effectiveness of deplatforming as a moderation strategy on Twitter. In: The 24th ACM Conference On Computer-Supported Cooperative Work And Social Computing (CSCW 2021). ACM (2021)

38. Johnson, M.R.: Collecting highly parallel data for paraphrase evaluation. In: Proceedings of the 6th Workshop on Procedural Content Generation. Dundee, Scotland, UK (2016). https://www.pcgworkshop.com

39. Knox, J.: The metaverse, or the serious business of tech frontiers. Postdigit. Sci. Educ. **4**(2), 207–215 (2022). https://doi.org/10.1007/s42438-022-00300-9

40. Lee, L.H., et al.: All One Needs to Know about Metaverse: A Complete Survey on Technological Singularity, Virtual Ecosystem, and Research Agenda (2021). arXiv Preprint. https://doi.org/10.48550/ARXIV.2110.05352

41. Liapis, A., Yannakakis, G.N., Nelson, M.J., Preuss, M., Bidarra, R.: Orchestrating game generation. IEEE Trans. Games **11**(1), 48–68 (2019). https://doi.org/10.1109/TG.2018.2870876

42. Lin, C.Y.: ROUGE: a package for automatic evaluation of summaries. In: Text Summarization Branches Out, Barcelona, Spain, pp. 74–81. ACL (2004). https://aclanthology.org/W04-1013

43. Livingstone, D.: Turing's test and believable AI in games. Comput. Entertain. **4**(1), 6 (2006). https://doi.org/10.1145/1111293.1111303

44. Mendoza, M., Tesconi, M., Cresci, S.: Bots in social and interaction networks: detection and impact estimation. ACM Trans. Inf. Syst. **39**(1), 1–32 (2020)

45. Meta Platforms: The Facebook Company Is Now Meta (2021). https://about.fb.com/news/2021/10/facebook-company-is-now-meta/. Accessed 22 May 2022

46. Mnih, V., et al.: Human-level control through deep reinforcement learning. Nature **518**(7540), 529–533 (2015). https://doi.org/10.1038/nature14236

47. Mori, M.: The uncanny valley. Energy **7**(4), 33–35 (1970). https://doi.org/10.1109/MRA.2012.2192811

48. Mozgovoy, M., Preuss, M., Bidarra, R.: Guest editorial special issue on team AI in games. IEEE Trans. Games **13**(4), 327–329 (2021). https://doi.org/10.1109/TG.2021.3127967

49. Nass, C., Steuer, J., Tauber, E.R.: Computers are social actors. In: Conference Companion on Human Factors in Computing Systems, Boston, MA, USA, CHI 1994, p. 204. Association for Computing Machinery (1994). https://doi.org/10.1145/259963.260288

50. Nizzoli, L., Tardelli, S., Avvenuti, M., Cresci, S., Tesconi, M.: Coordinated behavior on social media in 2019 UK general election. In: The 15th International AAAI Conference on Web and Social Media (ICWSM 2021), pp. 443–454. AAAI (2021)

51. Papineni, K., Roukos, S., Ward, T., Zhu, W.J.: BLEU: a method for automatic evaluation of machine translation. In: Proceedings of the 40th Annual Meeting on Association for Computational Linguistics - ACL 2002, Philadelphia, Pennsylvania, p. 311. Association for Computational Linguistics (2001). https://doi.org/10.3115/1073083.1073135

52. Pohl, J.S., Assenmacher, D., Seiler, M.V., Trautmann, H., Grimme, C.: Artificial social media campaign creation for benchmarking and challenging detection approaches. In: Proceedings of the 16th International Conference on Web and Social Media. NEATCLasS, Association for the Advancement of Artificial Intelligence (AAI), Hybrid: Atlanta, Georgia, US and Online (2022)

53. Rabkin, M.: Connect 2021 Recap: Horizon Home, the Future of Work, Presence Platform, and More (2021). https://www.oculus.com/blog/connect-2021-recap-horizon-home-the-future-of-work-presence-platform-and-more/. Accessed 22 May 2022

54. Radford, A., Narasimhan, K., Salimans, T., Sutskever, I.: Improving language understanding by generative pre-training. Technical report, OpenAI (2018)

55. Ramesh, A., Dhariwal, P., Nichol, A., Chu, C., Chen, M.: Hierarchical text-conditional image generation with clip latents. arXiv preprint arXiv:2204.06125 (2022). https://doi.org/10.48550/ARXIV.2204.06125

56. Rauchfleisch, A., Kaiser, J.: The false positive problem of automatic bot detection in social science research. PLoS ONE 15(10), e0241045 (2020)

57. Rauschnabel, P.A., Felix, R., Hinsch, C., Shahab, H., Alt, F.: What is XR? Towards a framework for augmented and virtual reality. Comput. Hum. Behav. 133, 107289 (2022). https://doi.org/10.1016/j.chb.2022.107289

58. Reed, S., et al.: A generalist agent (2022). https://doi.org/10.48550/ARXIV.2205.06175. https://arxiv.org/abs/2205.06175

59. Reeves, B., Nass, C.: The Media Equation: How People Treat Computers, Television, and New Media Like Real People and Pla. Bibliovault OAI Repository, the University of Chicago Press (1996)

60. Riedl, M.O.: Computational narrative intelligence: a human-centered goal for artificial intelligence. arXiv preprint arXiv:1602.06484 (2016)

61. Risi, S., Preuss, M.: From chess and atari to StarCraft and beyond: how game AI is driving the world of AI. KI - Künstliche Intelligenz 34(1), 7–17 (2020). https://doi.org/10.1007/s13218-020-00647-w

62. Saygin, A.P., Chaminade, T., Ishiguro, H., Driver, J., Frith, C.: The thing that should not be: predictive coding and the uncanny valley in perceiving human and humanoid robot actions. Soc. Cogn. Affect. Neurosci. 7(4), 413–422 (2012). https://doi.org/10.1093/scan/nsr025

63. Shin, M., Song, S.W., Chock, T.M.: Uncanny valley effects on friendship decisions in virtual social networking service. Cyberpsychol. Behav. Soc. Netw. 22(11), 700–705 (2019). https://doi.org/10.1089/cyber.2019.0122

64. Silver, D., et al.: Mastering the game of go with deep neural networks and tree search. Nature 529(7587), 484–489 (2016). https://doi.org/10.1038/nature16961

65. Skjuve, M., Haugstveit, I., Følstad, A., Brandtzaeg, P.: Help! Is my chatbot falling into the uncanny valley? An empirical study of user experience in human-chatbot interaction. Hum. Technol. **15**, 30–54 (2019). https://doi.org/10.17011/ht/urn. 201902201607

66. Spence, P.R., Edwards, A., Edwards, C., Jin, X.: 'The bot predicted rain, grab an umbrella': few perceived differences in communication quality of a weather twitterbot versus professional and amateur meteorologists. Behav. Inf. Technol. **38**(1), 101–109 (2019). https://doi.org/10.1080/0144929X.2018.1514425

67. Stephenson, N.: Snow Crash. Metropolis Media (1992)

68. Sundar, S.S.: The MAIN Model: A Heuristic Approach to Understanding Technology Effects on Credibility. Digital Media, p. 29 (2008)

69. Tardelli, S., Avvenuti, M., Tesconi, M., Cresci, S.: Characterizing social bots spreading financial disinformation. In: Meiselwitz, G. (ed.) HCII 2020. LNCS, vol. 12194, pp. 376–392. Springer, Cham (2020). https://doi.org/10.1007/978-3-030-49570-1_26

70. Tekiroglu, S., Bonaldi, H., Fanton, M., Guerini, M.: Using pre-trained language models for producing counter narratives against hate speech: a comparative study. In: Findings of the Association for Computational Linguistics (ACL 2022), pp. 3099–3114. ACL (2022)

71. Togelius, J.: We tried learning AI from games. How about learning from players? (2022). https://modl.ai/learning-ai-from-players. modl.ai blog

72. Togelius, J., et al.: Procedural content generation: goals, challenges and actionable steps. In: Lucas, S.M., Mateas, M., Preuss, M., Spronck, P., Togelius, J. (eds.) Artificial and Computational Intelligence in Games, Dagstuhl Follow-Ups, vol. 6, pp. 61–75. Schloss Dagstuhl-Leibniz-Zentrum fuer Informatik, Dagstuhl, Germany (2013). https://doi.org/10.4230/DFU.Vol6.12191.61. http://drops.dagstuhl.de/opus/volltexte/2013/4336

73. Trujillo, A., Cresci, S.: Make reddit great again: assessing community effects of moderation interventions on r/The_Donald. In: The 25th ACM Conference On Computer-Supported Cooperative Work And Social Computing (CSCW 2022). ACM (2022)

74. Tsimpoukelli, M., Menick, J., Cabi, S., Eslami, S.M.A., Vinyals, O., Hill, F.: Multimodal few-shot learning with frozen language models. In: Beygelzimer, A., Dauphin, Y., Liang, P., Vaughan, J.W. (eds.) Advances in Neural Information Processing Systems (2021)

75. Vaswani, A., et al.: Attention is all you need. In: Proceedings of the 31st International Conference on Neural Information Processing Systems, NIPS 2017, pp. 6000–6010. Curran Associates Inc., Red Hook (2017)

76. Walther, J.B.: Computer-mediated communication: impersonal, interpersonal, and hyperpersonal interaction. Commun. Res. **23**(1), 3–43 (1996). https://doi.org/10.1177/009365096023001001

77. Weber, D., Neumann, F.: Amplifying influence through coordinated behaviour in social networks. Soc. Netw. Anal. Min. **11**(1), 1–42 (2021). https://doi.org/10.1007/s13278-021-00815-2

78. Xu, K., Liao, T.: Explicating cues: a typology for understanding emerging media technologies. J. Comput.-Mediat. Commun. **25**(1), 32–43 (2020). https://doi.org/10.1093/jcmc/zmz023

79. Yang, C., Harkreader, R., Gu, G.: Empirical evaluation and new design for fighting evolving Twitter spammers. IEEE Trans. Inf. Forensics Secur. **8**(8), 1280–1293 (2013)

80. Yang, K.C., Varol, O., Hui, P.M., Menczer, F.: Scalable and generalizable social bot detection through data selection. In: Proceedings of the AAAI Conference on Artificial Intelligence, New York, NY, USA, vol. 34 (2020). https://doi.org/10.1609/aaai.v34i01.5460
81. Yannakakis, G.N., Togelius, J.: Experience-driven procedural content generation. IEEE Trans. Affect. Comput. **2**(3), 147–161 (2011). https://doi.org/10.1109/T-AFFC.2011.6
82. Zhang, T., Kishore, V., Wu, F., Weinberger, K.Q., Artzi, Y.: BERTScore: evaluating text generation with BERT. arXiv preprint arXiv:1904.09675 (2019)

Moderating the Good, the Bad, and the Hateful: Moderators' Attitudes Towards ML-based Comment Moderation Support Systems

Holger Koelmann[1]([✉])[iD], Kilian Müller[1][iD], Marco Niemann[1][iD],
and Dennis M. Riehle[2][iD]

[1] University of Münster - ERCIS, Münster, Germany
{holger.koelmann,kilian.mueller,marco.niemann}@ercis.uni-muenster.de
[2] University of Koblenz-Landau, Koblenz, Germany
riehle@uni-koblenz.de

Abstract. Comment sections have established themselves as essential elements of the public discourse. However, they put considerable pressure on the hosting organizations to keep them clean of hateful and abusive comments. This is necessary to prevent violating legal regulations and to avoid appalling their readers. With commenting being a typically free feature and anonymity encouraging increasingly daunting comments, many newspapers struggle to operate economically viable comment sections. Hence, throughout the last decade, researchers set forth to develop machine learning (ML) models to automate this work. With increasingly sophisticated algorithms, research is starting on comment moderation support systems that integrate ML models to relieve moderators from parts of their workload. Our research sets forth to assess the attitudes of moderators towards such systems to provide guidance for future developments. This paper presents the findings from three conducted expert interviews, which also included tool usage observations.

Keywords: Community management · Machine learning · Content moderation · Comment moderation support system · Digital work

1 Introduction

You are a community manager for the online presence of a large newspaper. Your area of work should include tasks like user engagement, participating in discussions, and researching the validity of discussion points. However, you are often tasked with reviewing and deciding on publishing or withholding user-generated content. How did we get to this point?

Social media in general and user comments in particular have seen a remarkable rise over the last decades. While formerly, letters to the editors of newspapers were a comparatively rare phenomenon, nowadays, readers can engage with

F. Spezzano et al. (Eds.): MISDOOM 2022, LNCS 13545, pp. 100–113, 2022.
https://doi.org/10.1007/978-3-031-18253-2_7

the editorial team much easier on the website, using discussion fora and comment sections [19,28,31]. While bad behavior on the internet has a long tradition [4], the number of comments that readers, i.e., users visiting the newspaper's website, publish has increased massively (e.g., the New York Times received about 9,000 comments per day in 2015 [16]), leading to an increased reader engagement and yields positive effects on the economic sustainability of newspaper organizations [19].

With the rise of comments, the amount of problematic comments has risen as well. The digital feel-good society has—in parts—turned into a more unjoyful society, where hate, incitement, oppression, and discrimination exist. Hate speech [37,41,53] and other malicious content, like misinformation [30,60] or cyberbullying [29,61], are disrupting the online discourse and keep increasing in volume [58]. Studies estimate abusive user-generated content somewhere between 2% and 80% [3,10,19,25,35,42], which is an inaccurate estimate but shows that the problem of critical user comments exists and is relevant. As hateful or insulting comments can cause legal consequences [44], newspapers tend to and are, to a certain extent, forced to keep these toxic comments off their platforms by moderating incoming comments [2].

A moderation process, in whatever form it might take place, requires resources, most often human resources; as a consequence, newspapers locked their comment sections either for highly debated topics or, in some cases, even for all topics [3,27,44,56]. Therefore, community managers, who normally would foster a healthy discussion culture and interact with the readers, are forced to fill the roles of content cleaners [3]. The only other option would be to close the discussion sections completely, an action some newspapers have already taken [9,32,38]. Thus, community managers are in need of support.

One idea to ease the burden of community managers, allowing them to perform their indented tasks, is the use of machine learning (ML) embedded in (semi-)automated comment moderation support systems (CMSS) [21,23,27]. These systems can either act as a decision support system (DSS) flagging comments for the moderators to review or as an automated system that accepts or rejects comments. The (automated) moderation of user-generated comments is a complex issue, as aside from legal restrictions of publishable comments, most free, democratic states also guarantee "freedom of speech"; therefore, these systems have to be handled with care; both by the developers as well as by the community managers [23]. As the community managers are the ones already walking this narrow ridge, we want to find out how to best support them in their current work. Are CMSS already a viable option for moderators, and if not, what factors could lead to a possible adoption of CMSS to support moderators in their daily business?

Therefore, with this study, we aim to provide insights into the general possibility of (semi-)automated content moderation, how community managers have already adopted it, and which requirements still need to be fulfilled to reach a reasonable amount of productivity. Therefore, we aim to answer our main research question **RQ**: *What are the attitudes of community managers towards (semi-)automated comment moderation support systems?* Subsequently, we address the following sub-research questions: *SRQ-1: What is the current state of digital comment moderation, and which systems are already utilized by community managers?*, *SRQ-2: How well do the requirements for CMSS derived from literature reflect the needs of community managers?*, and *SRQ-3: Which factors may lead to the adoption or non-adoption of (semi-)automated comment moderation support systems by community managers of news outlets?*

To tackle these research questions, we interviewed community managers from different newspapers. Therefore, we conducted a series of interviews with representatives from the community management field of some of the major newspapers in Germany. Within these interviews, we are evaluating community managers' experiences with CMSS, how such systems might already be used in practice, and which improvements have to be made in the future. In order to construct an interview guideline that encompasses the relevant aspects, we reviewed the already existing literature. An excerpt of our findings from the literature is presented in Sect. 2. Section 3 details our research approach while Sect. 4 presents the results from our interviews. Finally, Sect. 5 concludes the paper.

2   Theoretical Background

Regarding the comment moderation process, two scenarios are possible: A *post-moderation* refers to a process where each received comment is published. If the newspaper receives complaints about a comment or if the comment is reported, the comment will be read by a moderator, evaluated, and, if necessary, blocked or deleted. In contrast, a *pre-moderation* refers to a process where each comment is moderated before it is published online. While both approaches have pros and cons, the most notable downside of a post-moderation is that newspapers might run into legal issues with criminal comments published, while for pre-moderation, a large amount of human resources is required [44,46].

A solution that is suitable both from an economic (less human resources required), as well as legal (do not publish hate comments) perspective can be the inclusion of ML as part of the moderation process [47]. Here, comment moderation can be seen as a two-stepped process. On the first level, an ML algorithm scans incoming comments and puts them into different categories like critical and uncritical. On a second level, only a subset of all comments is moderated by humans. For instance, only comments in the category "critical" might be manually moderated, while comments in the category "uncritical" could be published immediately without human interaction.

Abusive speech and the challenges of moderation endeavors are a long-standing problem—one that in Europe, and especially in Germany, reached a culmination point in the wake of the refugee crisis in 2015/2016 [27,48]. Up to 50% of the newspapers in Germany decided to give up their comment sections back then [54]—a trend that could also be observed elsewhere [14,32,45]. However, the last years indicate that comment sections are not dead and still desirable for newspapers [15]. Evidence for this assumption can be found in recent studies indicating that a substantial number of newspapers are still operating comment sections—especially the small and medium-sized ones [40]. Furthermore, solutions such as the Coral Talk project are still actively maintained and developed, indicating a need for specialized commenting software [11,26]. Beyond these approaches, newspapers added further protective measures such as upfront registrations and rule sets [40].

So far, all these adjustments are still based primarily on human efforts. In addition, academia and practice started to work on automation more than a decade ago [41,62]. Till today no conclusive approach to automatically detect abusive language has been found [18,24,34,51,63]. However, the same research indicates that considerable progress is made on this classification task. With the increased efficacy of ML algorithms in detecting abusive language, initial research is coming up that seeks to design systems to integrate such algorithms in a moderation interface [7,33]. While the approaches differ in the specific goals and pathways, they all aim to leverage the ML capabilities to reduce the community managers' and moderators' workload—not to replace them. Some follow a more punitive strategy [7], whereas others aim at rewarding creators of quality comments [33,43]. One consistent notion is the goal to provide decision support instead of decisions—sometimes phrased implicitly [33] and sometimes explicitly [7]. This does not necessarily preclude partial automation [7]; however, it typically then connects back to the decision support idea by giving moderators the power for corrective actions, which can be *used as learning input for future algorithm generations* [33].

Given the complexity of many modern ML approaches as well as the *typical black box nature of their decision processes* [50], and with most community managers being no ML experts, transparency is becoming an important aspect [7]. This aligns with legal regulations that recommend—partially even mandate—being able to explain automated (or semi-automated) decisions [17,22,57]. Despite the increased focus on ML tools for comment moderation, support systems are often conceptualized to include "non-ML" capabilities that should provide additional guidance to users. This can range from the provision of statistical information (*e.g., comments written by a user; rejections vs. accepts per user; . . .*) to the provision of context information or simple static analysis (*e.g., comment length, . . .*) [33]. Another line of thought that has been brought forth recently is the notion of community management as a collaborative effort that requires the provision of tooling to support the corresponding workflows (*e.g., assigning problematic comments to other moderators; reviewing prior decisions; . . .*) [40]. However, to date, most of this is conceptual work enhanced only by mockups and wireframes [7,33], with only a few prototypical systems being under development (e.g., [47]).

Therefore, little research exists about the acceptance of such technologies by moderators or community managers. Articles by Brunk et al. [6] and Bunde [7] analyze trust and transparency using a mocked CMSS, with limited capabilities. Nevertheless, trust and technology acceptance are core concerns regarding the adoption of such information systems in practice [36], with trust in, e.g., the system provider [55] needed to overcome the perceived risk by its user [12,36].

Empirical quantitative research often refers to the technology acceptance model (TAM) [13] and the unified theory of acceptance and use of technology (UTAUT) [59] to measure the acceptance of a given technology, with some approaches including the users' trust in the technology as an essential factor for a users' acceptance of given technology [20]. To gain some deeper insights into the critical aspect of the acceptance of CMSS by our expert interview partners, we are also addressing their thought processes and attitudes towards CMSS within this study as well.

3   Research Approach

Building upon this background, we conducted semi-structured expert interviews to generate insights for our research questions. These allowed us to find in-depth answers from practitioners in the field about their opinions, work behavior, and attitudes to the discussed developments and systems. For these reasons, and the limited number of experts available, semi-structured interviews seem to be the most suitable method for data collection [5,49]. Also, it allows us to have the interviewee test a working prototype of a CMSS designed to address the issues and requirements brought up in Sect. 2. This approach further allows us to ask follow-up questions when needed [5,49]. Since transparency in the research process is essential for qualitative research [1,8], we will go deeper into the structure of the interview guideline, the sampling process for the study in progress, and our interview setting:

In search of relevant questions for the interviews, we followed the suggestions by Rowley [49]. We generated potential questions inductively based on our theoretical background, reworked them to fit the practice case, and reduced them to the most fitting ones for the interview guideline. We structured the interview guideline according to the following three main question sets, which we derived from the existing theoretical background described in Sect. 2. After a short self-introduction of the interviewer and interviewee, the first question set covers general information about the current moderation process and used system. In addition, the fundamental attitudes toward objectivity and transparency in the moderation process and the interviewee's attitudes towards ML-based automation are covered. After the first set of questions, a functioning prototype of an ML-supported CMSS[1] is introduced, which the interviewee is asked to use to moderate a predefined set of comments. Based on this experience, the requirements for such systems [39] are discussed in the second set of questions, covering the five different aspects of team moderation, interpretability and transparency, control and correction of ML-based decisions, decision support beyond ML, and the openness of the system. The third set then includes questions regarding the acceptance of such systems, such as the potential intention to use such a system, its trustworthiness, the risks of using such a system, as well as the potential influence of system use on the organization. Finally, the last questions following the three main question sets are designed for an open discussion about issues

---

[1] https://www.moderat.nrw.

left untouched, which are important to the interviewee, and some demographic questions for further context to the statements made during the interview. An overview of the discussed topics and an exemplary question, representative of each topic, can be found in Table 1 to give an impression of the discussed content.

To find experts in the field, we have invited 24 representatives of different German news outlets to participate in our study. We received six responses from interested experts, to which we explained the planned interview procedure. We were then able to schedule three virtual interviews. The interviewed experts all operated in the field of comment moderation and were employed by one medium-sized and two of the largest national news outlets in Germany. We asked questions from the interview guideline, gave the participants an introduction to an existing prototype with the opportunity to test it, and ended with an open discussion about topics important to the respective interviewee. Each interview took between 44 and 103 min, depending on the intensity the interviews used the open discussion elements for further in-depth statements. The interviews were conducted between September and October of 2021, resulting in 214 min of recordings. The recorded interviews were transcribed by a professional transcription service[2]. The transcripts were then fine-tuned by the researchers where necessary and analyzed afterwards. The main findings of these interviews will be reported in the next section.

4 Findings

To contextualize the findings, we want to give a brief overview of our interviewee demographics: Their age spanned from 29 to 56 years, and all worked directly related to community management in their respective news outlets. They all finished their school education (Abitur; A-level equivalent), and two of the interviewees had additional Master's degrees. All of them already have several years of work experience in the field and have stayed in their respective companies for multiple years already. Despite their elevated positions, they are all still in touch with hands-on community management; however, they also have a more managerial perspective allowing them to give strategic insights beyond the mere operative ones.

In the upcoming subsections, we present the most interesting and striking findings from these interviews along with each main question set of the interview guideline. The results of the analysis are then followed by a concluding discussion in Sect. 5.

4.1 Current Process, System, and Attitudes

We interviewed all participants regarding their current moderation process, used software systems and support tools, and their attitudes towards different aspects of the moderation process.

---

[2] https://sonix.ai.

Table 1. Structure of the used interview guideline, incl. topics and representative questions

No.	Topic	Representative question (translated from German)
1. Current process, system, and attitudes		
I.	Information about the current moderation process and system setup	"Which systems do you currently use to manage your content and especially your comments?"
II.	Community management	"Which type of moderation to you currently use, pre-, post-, or mixed-moderation?"
III.	Objectivity and transparency in moderation	"Do you provide feedback about the reason for blocking a comment to the affected commentator?"
IV.	Attitude towards ML-based automation	"Would you be willing to include ML in the moderation process in general?"
—Introduction to the prototype, incl. user test—		
2. Requirements of comment moderation support systems		
V.a	Team moderation	"To which degree does the presented system cover your needs in terms of team support?"
V.b	Interpretability and transparency	"Do you miss some information you would need to understand the ML-based decision?"
V.c	Control and correction of ML-based decisions	"Can you imagine to use the decisions of the presented system alone (maybe without the ability to correct the decision)?"
V.d	Decision support beyond ML	"How useful is the presented additional commenter's information?"
V.e	Openness of the system	"Did you encounter any issues with the adaptability of the content moderation systems you have used so far in your career?"
3. Acceptance of ML-based comment moderation		
VI.a	Acceptance and intention to use	"Can you imagine that your organization would adopt such a system into its regular operations?"
VI.b	Trustworthiness of the system	"Do you consider the moderation of comments with such a system to be trustworthy?"
VI.c	Perceived risk of system Use	"Do you see risks for your work as a community manager through the use of such a system?"
VI.d	Influence on organization	"Do you see risks for your organization through the use of such a system?"
4. Closing remarks		
VII.	Open issues & discussion	"Would you like to discuss additional points with us, which have not yet been properly covered?"
VIII.	Demographics	"What is your highest level or education or academic degree?"

Noticeably, all three newspapers utilized shift operation to ensure the largest amount of moderation-coverage possible. Another common characteristic across the three outlets is the use of pre-moderation (No. II from Table 1). While one newspaper previously utilized post-moderation, they recognized a significant increase in critical comments and, thus, chose to switch their content moderation to pre-moderation. Handling rejected comments and informing commentators differed between organizations. In one case, the commentator does not receive any information, in the other cases, the commentator receives some basic information via mail (III). Additionally, while the largest newspaper was able to keep its comment section open during the night, the other two newspapers are either closing their respective comment sections during these hours or are not publishing comments until the morning, as they are not able to muster the necessary workforce to moderate comments during nighttime.

In terms of IT systems, every newspaper utilized a different system (I). While the largest newspaper has a custom solution, the other two use various applications, e.g., content management systems (CMS), with varying functions for different channels. These systems were not integrated, i.e. workers had to switch between different systems.

All newspapers agreed that user comments are critical to their online presence. Firstly, to increase customer loyalty and secondly, to increase the generated traffic (which again impacts the outlets' visibility on search engines). Basically, every interviewee could envision themselves utilizing ML-assisted content moderation to some extent (IV). However, the expected level of involvement and the degree of automation differed from newspaper to newspaper. While the largest newspaper could envision itself at some point utilizing fully automated content moderation, all newspapers agreed that the human should be kept in the loop (at least in the beginning).

4.2   Requirements of Comment Moderation Support Systems

The findings regarding the requirements' fulfillment (respectively their adequacy) for CMSS come with the limitation of the prototypical nature of the system used for demonstration and experimentation in the interviews. This entails that certain elements are not yet implemented in a way that satisfies commercial requirements for UI/UX. Nevertheless, the interviews revealed several interesting findings: First, they indicate that none of the newspapers aims for full-fledged automation at the current point in time (V.c). All seek automated support to reduce workloads but only see any potential for automation after a more extended evaluation and experimentation period. Even though not much was discussed in the literature, the interviews confirmed the importance of collaborative features in a CMSS, with ML support present (V.a). Feedback ranged from the positive acknowledgment of useful features such as assigning comments for decision and review to other community managers to requests for additional functionality (e.g., real-time exchange of moderation decisions between software clients). Furthermore, all interviewees agreed upon the necessity and helpfulness of explanations for machine decisions (V.b). While highlighting individual words with colors is uniformly considered appropriate, opportunities for further research appear to emerge for the exact configuration. One interviewee pointed out that having problematic (or anti-problematic) passages highlighted is helpful for all cases, the other two interviewees would prefer more restricted support. However, the latter were differing in their preferences of the exact configuration (e.g., only highlighting passages in selected comments vs. reducing the quantity of highlighted words) (V.d). Lastly, interviewees pointed toward existing software solutions into which they would like to integrate a CMSS (V.e). Thus, CMSS should be designed to both be able to attach to existing moderation software and/or to be able to integrate other solutions.

While this is not a complete assessment of the requirements—or the linked systems—, the results illustrate that such systems are needed and that the extant ideas are suitable guiding principles. However, the interviews also highlight the need for additional research and evaluation with practitioners, as such systems are complex and affect a critical aspect of journalism—the thin line between the right and necessity of free speech and the need for moderation to satisfy legal requirements.

4.3   Acceptance of ML-Based Comment Moderation

Regarding their acceptance factors of such systems (VI.a), it is noteworthy that all participants were interested in using such an ML-based CMSS with one organization already using a similar system in their routines. Though for one interviewee, it remained important that the system would only work as a DSS and not as a fully automated system, further stretching the importance of the human-in-the-loop approach.

The interview section about the system's trustworthiness (VI.b) also reflected the importance of the human-in-the-loop approach since the use of such a system was considered trustworthy due to its emotionless nature but not necessarily as fair without the emotional context.

This was also considered a potential risk for the community managers' work (VI.c): Their focus on the commenter in the comments section might get lost. Another identified concern is the sensitivity of the system. As with every technical test, it might miss hateful comments leading to their display on site—a condition that is perceived less likely using tight human moderation.

Another remarkable aspect of the findings is the expected impact on the trustworthiness and risks in terms of the news outlet's perception in its community (VI.d). Here, the interviewee from the mid-sized outlet stretched the potential loss of focus on the community through less engagement with the critical material as well. For them their claim for direct interaction and discussion with their smaller community is key. Machine-based moderation could harm that claim and the perceived trustworthiness of the outlet. The other two interviewees from larger outlets saw this rather differently. They currently cannot engage with their respective communities as personally as they would like to, also due to the number of critical comments that need moderation. For them, additional automation of the comment moderation process would free time they could spend on engaging directly with the community, which could, in turn, positively affect their perception in the eyes of their community.

5 Concluding Discussion

We set forth to find out more about the current state, the requirements, and the potential acceptance for the use of CMSS. Our results show various similarities and dissimilarities between the current state of the art, requirements, and adoption criteria of different newspaper outlets. For practice, our work provides insights into the current state of CMSS and their use, such as the prevalence of pre-moderation in shifts. Furthermore, adoption criteria defined by community managers can be utilized by CMSS designers to either improve their current systems or guide the development phase from the start. It became clear that the human-in-the-loop approach is preferred for the time being and that CMSS should be developed as automated support for the human community managers, relieving them from some of the burdens of their work to concentrate on their core task: engaging with their community.

Besides these valuable contributions, the study also comes with limitations. The obvious one is the limited amount of available data since only three expert interviews have been conducted. However, we argue that these three interviewees are a good representation of the market, coming from three different newspapers, with both medium-sized and large organizations being represented. Further, the interviews are only representing the German market of news outlets and the findings should therefore be interpreted in light of this cultural and regulatory context. Future research should therefore look deeper into other contexts to see, if the same results appear internationally or if differences in culture and regulation play a larger role in the acceptance of ML-based CMSS. In addition, future quantitative research could dive further into the linkages of the involved factors for accepting and adopting these systems in the community moderator's work. On that note, further research into how the use of such CMSS is perceived by the affected commenters and how the systems need to give feedback to the commenters for a higher rate of acceptance needs to be done. Besides this practitioner group, it would also be possible to conduct interviews with other academic experts in the field of journalism and hate speech prevention as well, to get a less practice-based view of the topic. Lastly, interviewing potential commentators of the general public could be worthwhile as they are affected by decisions of these systems directly during their engagement in online discussions or indirectly by the resulting shift in online debating culture [3] and the potential distortion of their freedom of expression [52].

Acknowledgments. The research leading to these results received funding from the federal state of North Rhine-Westphalia and the European Regional Development Fund (EFRE.NRW 2014–2020), Project: M●DERAT! (No. CM-2-2-036a).

References

1. Aguinis, H., Solarino, A.M.: Transparency and replicability in qualitative research: the case of interviews with elite informants. Strateg. Manag. J. **40**(8), 1291–1315 (2019)
2. Bloch-Wehba, H.: Automation in moderation. Cornell Int. Law J. **53**(1), 41–96 (2020)
3. Boberg, S., Schatto-Eckrodt, T., Frischlich, L., Quandt, T.: The moral gatekeeper? Moderation and deletion of user-generated content in a leading news forum. Media Commun. **6**(4), 58–69 (2018)
4. Brail, S.: The price of admission: Harassment and free speech in the wild, wild west. Wired_Women: Gender and new realities in cyberspace (1996)
5. Brinkmann, S.: Qualitative Interviewing. Oxford University Press, United Kingdom (2013)
6. Brunk, J., Mattern, J., Riehle, D.M.: Effect of transparency and trust on acceptance of automatic online comment moderation systems. In: Becker, J., Novikov, D. (eds.) 21st IEEE Conference on Business Informatics, pp. 429–435. Russia, Moscow (2019)
7. Bunde, E.: AI-assisted and explainable hate speech detection for social media moderators - a design science approach. In: Proceedings of the 54th Hawaii International Conference on System Sciences, pp. 1264–1273. HICSS 2021, ScholarSpace, Kauai, HI, USA (2021)
8. Burton-Jones, A., Boh, W.F., Oborn, E., Padmanabhan, B.: Editor's comments: advancing research transparency at MIS Quarterly: a pluralistic approach. Manag. Inf. Syst. Q. **45**(2), 3–8 (2021)
9. Chen, Y., Zhou, Y., Zhu, S., Xu, H.: Detecting offensive language in social media to protect adolescent online safety. In: Proceedings of the 2012 ASE/IEEE International Conference on Social Computing and 2012 ASE/IEEE International Conference on Privacy, Security, Risk and Trust, pp. 71–80. SOCIALCOM-PASSAT 2012, IEEE, Amsterdam, Netherlands (2012)
10. Cheng, J.: Report: 80 percent of blogs contain "offensive" content (2007). https://arstechnica.com/information-technology/2007/04/report-80-percent-of-blogs-contain-offensive-content/
11. Coral Project: Coral by Vox Media (2021). https://coralproject.net/
12. Das, T., Teng, B.S.: The risk-based view of trust: a conceptual framework. J. Bus. Psychol. **19**(1), 85–116 (2004)
13. Davis, F.: A Technology Acceptance Model for Empirically Testing New End-User Information Systems: Theory and Results. Ph.D. thesis, Massachusetts Institute of Technology, Massachusetts (1985)
14. Ellis, J.: What happened after 7 news sites got rid of reader comments (2015). https://www.niemanlab.org/2015/09/what-happened-after-7-news-sites-got-rid-of-reader-comments/
15. Engelke, K.M.: Enriching the conversation: audience perspectives on the deliberative nature and potential of user comments for news media. Digit. J. **8**(4), 447–466 (2020)
16. Etim, B.: The Most Popular Reader Comments on The Times (2015). https://www.nytimes.com/2015/11/23/insider/the-most-popular-reader-comments-on-the-times.html
17. Felzmann, H., Villaronga, E.F., Lutz, C., Tamò-Larrieux, A.: Transparency you can trust: transparency requirements for artificial intelligence between legal norms and contextual concerns. Big Data Soc. **6**(1), 1–14 (2019)

18. Fortuna, P., Nunes, S.: A survey on automatic detection of hate speech in text. ACM Comput. Surv. **51**(4), 1–30 (2018)
19. Gardiner, B., Mansfield, M., Anderson, I., Holder, J., Louter, D., Ulmanu, M.: The dark side of Guardian comments (2016). https://www.theguardian.com/technology/2016/apr/12/the-dark-side-of-guardian-comments
20. Gefen, D., Karahanna, E., Straub, D.W.: Trust and tam in online shopping: an integrated model. MIS Q. **27**(1), 51–90 (2003)
21. Gillespie, T.: Content moderation, AI, and the question of scale. Big Data Soc. **7**(2), 1–5 (2020)
22. Goodman, B., Flaxman, S.: European union regulations on algorithmic decision making and a "Right to Explanation". AI Mag. **38**(3), 50–57 (2017)
23. Gorwa, R., Binns, R., Katzenbach, C.: Algorithmic content moderation: technical and political challenges in the automation of platform governance. Big Data Soc. **7**(1), 1–15 (2020)
24. Herodotou, H., Chatzakou, D., Kourtellis, N.: Catching them red-handed: Realtime aggression detection on social media. In: 2021 IEEE 37th International Conference on Data Engineering (ICDE), pp. 2123–2128 (2021)
25. Hine, G.E., et al.: Kek, cucks, and god emperor trump: a measurement study of 4chan's politically incorrect forum and its effects on the web. In: Proceedings of the Eleventh International AAAI Conference on Web and Social Media, pp. 92–101. ICWSM-2017, Montral, Canada (2017)
26. Kim, J.: Moderating the uncontrollable. Intersect. Stanford J. Sci. Technol. Soc. **10**(3), 1–9 (2017)
27. Köffer, S., Riehle, D.M., Höhenberger, S., Becker, J.: Discussing the value of automatic hate speech detection in online debates. In: Drews, P., Funk, B., Niemeyer, P., Xie, L. (eds.) Tagungsband Multikonferenz Wirtschaftsinformatik 2018. MKWI 2018, Leuphana Universität, Lüneburg, Germany (2018)
28. Kolhatkar, V., Taboada, M.: Constructive language in news comments. In: Proceedings of the First Workshop on Abusive Language Online. pp. 11–17. ALW1, Vancouver, Canada (2017)
29. Kowalski, R.M., Giumetti, G.W., Schroeder, A.N., Lattanner, M.R.: Bullying in the digital age: a critical review and meta-analysis of cyberbullying research among youth. Psychol. Bull. **140**(4), 1073–1137 (2014)
30. Lazer, D.M.J., et al.: The science of fake news. Science **359**(6380), 1094–1096 (2018)
31. Lewis, S.C., Holton, A.E., Coddington, M.: Reciprocal journalism: a concept of mutual exchange between journalists and audiences. Journal. Pract. **8**(2), 229–241 (2014)
32. Liu, J., McLeod, D.M.: Pathways to news commenting and the removal of the comment system on news websites. Journalism **22**(4), 867–881 (2021)
33. Loosen, W., et al.: Making sense of user comments: identifying journalists' requirements for a comment analysis framework. Stud. Commun. Media **6**(4), 333–364 (2017)
34. MacAvaney, S., Yao, H.R., Yang, E., Russell, K., Goharian, N., Frieder, O.: Hate speech detection: challenges and solutions. PLoS ONE **14**(8), 1–16 (2019)
35. Mansfield, M.: How we analysed 70m comments on the Guardian website (2016). https://www.theguardian.com/technology/2016/apr/12/how-we-analysed-70m-comments-guardian-website
36. McKnight, D.H., Carter, M., Thatcher, J.B., Clay, P.F.: Trust in a specific technology: an investigation of its components and measures. ACM Trans. Manag. Inf. Syst. **2**(2), 1–25 (2011)

37. Mondal, M., Silva, L.A., Benevenuto, F.: A measurement study of hate speech in social media. In: Dolong, P., Vojtas, P. (eds.) Proceedings of the 28th ACM Conference on Hypertext and Social Media, pp. 85–94. HT 2017, ACM, Prague, Czech Republic (2017)
38. Muddiman, A., Stroud, N.J.: News values, cognitive biases, and partisan incivility in comment sections. J. Commun. **67**(4), 586–609 (2017)
39. Niemann, M.: Elicitation of requirements for an AI-enhanced comment moderation support system for non-tech media companies. In: Stephanidis, C., Antona, M., Ntoa, S. (eds.) HCII 2021. CCIS, vol. 1419, pp. 573–581. Springer, Cham (2021). https://doi.org/10.1007/978-3-030-78635-9_73
40. Niemann, M., Müller, K., Kelm, C., Assenmacher, D., Becker, J.: The German comment landscape. In: Bright, J., Giachanou, A., Spaiser, V., Spezzano, F., George, A., Pavliuc, A. (eds.) MISDOOM 2021. LNCS, vol. 12887, pp. 112–127. Springer, Cham (2021). https://doi.org/10.1007/978-3-030-87031-7_8
41. Nobata, C., Tetreault, J., Thomas, A., Mehdad, Y., Chang, Y.: Abusive language detection in online user content. In: Proceedings of the 25th International Conference on World Wide Web, pp. 145–153. WWW 2016, ACM Press, Montreal, Canada (2016)
42. Papacharissi, Z.: Democracy online: civility, politeness, and the democratic potential of online political discussion groups. New Media Soc. **6**(2), 259–283 (2004)
43. Park, D., Sachar, S., Diakopoulos, N., Elmqvist, N.: Supporting comment moderators in identifying high quality online news comments. In: Kaye, J., Druin, A., Lampe, C., Morris, D., Hourcade, J.P. (eds.) Proceedings of the 2016 CHI Conference on Human Factors in Computing Systems, pp. 1114–1125. CHI 2016, ACM, San Jose, CA, USA (2016)
44. Pöyhtäri, R.: Limits of hate speech and freedom of speech on moderated news websites in Finland, Sweden, the Netherlands and the UK. Ann. Ser. Hist. Sociol. **24**(3), 513–524 (2014)
45. Pritchard, S.: The readers' editor on... closing comments below the line (2016). https://www.theguardian.com/commentisfree/2016/mar/27/readers-editor-on-closing-comments-below-line
46. Reich, Z.: User comments: the transformation of participatory space. In: Singer, J.B., (eds.) et al. Participatory Journalism: Guarding Open Gates at Online Newspapers, chap. 6, pp. 96–117. Wiley-Blackwell, Chichester, UK, 1 edn. (2011)
47. Riehle, D.M., Niemann, M., Brunk, J., Assenmacher, D., Trautmann, H., Becker, J.: Building an integrated comment moderation system – towards a semi-automatic moderation tool. In: Proceedings of the HCI International 2020, Copenhagen, Denmark (2020)
48. Ross, B., Rist, M., Carbonell, G., Cabrera, B., Kurowsky, N., Wojatzki, M.: Measuring the reliability of hate speech annotations: the case of the European refugee crisis. In: Beißwenger, M., Wojatzki, M., Zesch, T. (eds.) Proceedings of the 3rd Workshop on Natural Language Processing for Computer-Mediated Communication, pp. 6–9. NLP4CMC III, Stefanie Dipper, Sprachwissenschaftliches Institut, Ruhr-Universität Bochum, Bochum, Germany (2016)
49. Rowley, J.: Conducting research interviews. Manag. Res. Rev. **35**(3/4), 260–271 (2012)
50. Rudin, C.: Stop explaining black box machine learning models for high stakes decisions and use interpretable models instead. Nat. Mach. Intell. **1**(5), 206–215 (2019)

51. Sadiq, S., Mehmood, A., Ullah, S., Ahmad, M., Choi, G.S., On, B.W.: Aggression detection through deep neural model on twitter. Futur. Gener. Comput. Syst. **114**, 120–129 (2021)
52. Sander, B.: Freedom of expression in the age of online platforms: the promise and pitfalls of a human rights-based approach to content moderation. Fordham Int'l LJ **43**, 939 (2019)
53. Schmidt, A., Wiegand, M.: A survey on hate speech detection using natural language processing. In: Ku, L.W., Li, C.T. (eds.) Proceedings of the Fifth International Workshop on Natural Language Processing for Social Media, pp. 1–10. SocialNLP 2017, Association for Computational Linguistics, Valencia, Spain (2017)
54. Siegert, S.: Nahezu jede zweite Zeitungsredaktion schränkt Online/Kommentare ein (2016). http://www.journalist.de/aktuelles/meldungen/journalist-umfrage-nahezu-jede-2-zeitungsredaktion-schraenkt-onlinekommentare-ein.html
55. Söllner, M., Hoffmann, A., Leimeister, J.M.: Why different trust relationships matter for information systems users. Eur. J. Inf. Syst. **25**(3), 274–287 (2016)
56. The Coral Project Community: Shutting down onsite comments: a comprehensive list of all news organisations (2016). https://community.coralproject.net/t/shutting-down-onsite-comments-a-comprehensive-list-of-all-news-organisations/347
57. The European Parliament: The Council of the European Union: Regulation (EU) 2016/679 of the European Parliament and of the Council of 27 April 2016 on the protection of natural persons with regard to the processing of personal data and on the free movement of such data, and repealing Directive 95/46/EC (General Data Protection Regulation). Off. J. Eur. Union **119**, 1–88 (2016)
58. Ullmann, S., Tomalin, M.: Quarantining online hate speech: technical and ethical perspectives. Ethics Inf. Technol. **22**(1), 69–80 (2019). https://doi.org/10.1007/s10676-019-09516-z
59. Venkatesh, V., Morris, M.G., Davis, G.B., Davis, F.D.: User acceptance of information technology: toward a unified view. MIS Q. **27**(3), 425–478 (2003)
60. Vosoughi, S., Roy, D., Aral, S.: The spread of true and false news online. Science **359**(6380), 1146–1151 (2018)
61. Whittaker, E., Kowalski, R.M.: Cyberbullying via social media. J. Sch. Violence **14**(1), 11–29 (2015)
62. Yin, D., Xue, Z., Hong, L., Davison, B.D., Kontostathis, A., Edwards, L.: Detection of harassment on web 2.0. In: Proceedings of the Content Analysis in the WEB, pp. 1–7. CAW2.0, Madrid, Spain (2009)
63. Yin, W., Zubiaga, A.: Towards generalisable hate speech detection: a review on obstacles and solutions. Peer J. Comput. Sci. **7**, 1–38 (2021)

Advancing the Use of Information Compression Distances in Authorship Attribution

Santiago Palmero Muñoz[1], Christian Oliva[2(✉)] (iD), Luis F. Lago-Fernández[2](iD),
and David Arroyo[1](iD)

[1] Institute for Physical and Information Technologies "Leonardo Torres Quevedo"
(ITEFI), Consejo Superior de Investigaciones Científicas (CSIC), Madrid, Spain
david.arroyo@csic.es
[2] Universidad Autónoma de Madrid, 28049 Madrid, Spain
{christian.oliva,luis.lago}@uam.es

Abstract. Detecting unreliable information in social media is an open
challenge, in part as a result of the difficulty to associate a piece of
information to known and trustworthy actors. The identification of the
origin of sources can help society deal with unverified, incomplete, or
even false information. In this work we tackle the problem of associ-
ating a piece of information to a certain politician. The use of inaccurate information is of great relevance in the case of politicians, since
it affects social perception and voting behavior. Moreover, misquota-
tion can be weaponized to hinder adversary reputation. We consider the
task of applying a compression-based metric to conduct authorship attribution in social media, namely in Twitter. In specific, we leverage the
Normalized Compression Distance (NCD) to compare an author's text
with other authors' texts. We show that this methodology performs well,
obtaining 80.3% accuracy in a scenario with 6 different politicians.

Keywords: Authorship recognition · Cyber-attribution · Normalised
compression distance

1 Introduction

Communication through social media has become an essential part of people's
lives. However, widespread misinformation and disinformation have become serious risks. Detecting unreliable information is a crucial challenge, especially when
the actors behind information sources are unknown [29]. Inaccurate and fabricated content in social media comes from a variety of sources, usually as user-
generated content or information scraped from the Internet and manually mod-
ified [17]. Attributing authorship for this type of information can help track the
related sources and find their origin.

The proliferation of non-credible information is conspicuously hazardous in
the case of politics. In the past decades, there is a significant number of examples

F. Spezzano et al. (Eds.): MISDOOM 2022, LNCS 13545, pp. 114–122, 2022.
https://doi.org/10.1007/978-3-031-18253-2_8

in which some politicians make use of ungenuine news and information to gain political advantage [13]. The capability of tracking information sources can be partially constructed by means of authorship attribution [16]. Our work will contribute to such a goal by tackling authorship attribution in Twitter for a given dataset which contains tweets from six US (United States) politicians. We propose a method to extract features from texts by comparing tweets using the Normalized Compression Distance (NCD) [8]. A K-dimensional space is constructed by selecting representatives or generators of each writing style, so that each new text is represented in this space by considering its NCD with respect to each generator. According to this representation, it is possible to train a classifier to conclude about the authorship of a text. In this work we consider the following Machine Learning (ML) models: Support Vector Machines (SVMs) and Multilayer Perceptrons (MLPs).

The remaining of the article is organized as follows. First, in Sect. 2 we discuss the state of the art about the application of NCD to Authorship Attribution in social media. In Sect. 3, we introduce the dataset used to validate our method. Then, in Sect. 4, we detail the NCD-based features construction. In Sect. 5, we briefly explain the ML used in our experiments. The results are discussed in Sect. 6, and the derived conclusions and highlights for future work are provided in Sect. 7.

2   Related Works

Research in authorship attribution has increased in recent years [2, 16, 24]. Some of the works propose the use of multivariate analysis in stylometry. Algorithms generate some vectors of frequencies which are then classified by clustering models [4–6, 15]. Others authors introduce some labeled data to improve the obtained results with different ML algorithms: from traditional models, such as K-Nearest Neighbors [14, 19, 27], or Support Vector Machines [10, 24], to Deep Learning algorithms for Natural Language Processing, such as LSTMs [21, 28] or Convolutional Neural Networks [3, 30].

Concerning Authorship Attribution in short texts from social media, the complexity of classifying the texts increases significantly. Some models like LSTMs have their performance heavily affected when dealing with this specific task [28], leaving the door open to the SVMs and CNNs. Regarding datasets, Twitter serves as a great benchmark as it allows to obtain a large pool of users and tweets from similar or different domains. Hence, most research focuses on this social media [1, 3, 11, 20, 24, 30].

Within the techniques involving Authorship Attribution, compression distances have been used with remarkable results. There are many distance-based metrics, such as the Conditional Complexity of Compression (CCC) [22], the Normalized Compression Distance (NCD) [8], or the Compression Dissimilarity Measure (CDM) [33], and also a large variety of compressors, such as PPMd, Gzip, BZip2, Zip, or LZW [12]. The most remarkable compression methods are profile-based, i.e., those that concatenate all available text from a known author and then compare an unseen text with this [33]. Other works use instance-based methods, i.e., they estimate the distance to all the available text and then group these distances using clustering methods.

3   Politicians Dataset

In this work, we use a dataset containing tweets from different politicians. We base our preprocessing on [24]. We remove those tweets marked as retweet by the metadata and tweets following the old retweet convention, which included the characters RT. We also remove non-English tweets and those with less than four tokens. Finally, tweet tags, which include usernames and hashtags, urls, numbers, dates and timestamps are replaced with the tokens REF, TAG, URL, NUM, DAT, TIM, respectively [24,26]. These replacements, especially tweet tags, are needed to avoid creating models unsuitable for authorship attribution [20].

The dataset contains approximately 1.25×10^6 tweets from 545 US politicians[1]. From the original dataset, we choose the six users who have the highest number of tweets. To break ties in the top six, we use alphabetical order. After preprocessing, the final dataset has a total of 16000 instances. For the evaluation, we generate five partitions by splitting the dataset in 80% training - 20% test. This dataset is publicly available, which facilitates reproducibility for further works and its users have not been selected by Twitter search heuristics.

4   Feature Construction: NCD Attribute Vectors

The Normalized Compression Distance (NCD) [8] is a compresion-based metric that calculates the similarity between two texts by means of a distance. Thus, two texts are similar when the distance between them is small, and they are different when their distance is large. We describe the process of generating attributes using this metric.

From text strings T, we create a set of K attribute generators $G = \{g_1, g_2, ..., g_K\}$. Each generator g_i is the concatenation of some strings from T, which are not used in the rest of the generators in G. These generators are not balanced regarding size and the number of strings in each of them can vary. However, G contains an even number of generators of each class that equals $K/6$. The procedure used in our experiments transforms text strings from T into numerical attributes by using a variant of the NCD. This variant, called the normalized conditional compressed information distance [32], is defined as:

$$D(g_j, t_i) = \frac{C(g_j :: t_i) - C(g_j)}{C(t_i)}, \tag{1}$$

where g_j is a generator and t_i is a single text string from T. $C(x)$ is the *gzip* compressed size of x, and the operator :: is the concatenation of strings. Then,

---

[1] The original dataset can be downloaded from https://www.reddit.com/r/datasets/comments/6fniik/over_one_million_tweets_collected_from_us/.

text strings from T have its distance computed to each of the generators in G forming a new set of data I. Each instance in I is an attribute vector with dimension K where each element is $i_{ij} = D(g_j, t_i)$. Finally, I is used to train a ML model. Generators G can be created not only from text strings within the original dataset T, but also using other strings from external sources. The rest of this section explains the previous [31,32] and novel procedures we have conducted to generate subsets G and I under a multi-class authorship scenario.

4.1 Disjoint Subsets

Initial set T is divided into T_{tr} and T_{test}. Then, T_{tr} is divided again into T_G and T_I. Subset G is created from T_G, and I_{tr} and I_{test} are created following the functions $D(G, T_I)$ and $D(G, T_{test})$, respectively. This way, strings that are used to create the generators G do not appear in I. Thus, G and I are disjoint subsets. For all the experiments done with this procedure we used 80% of the instances from T_{tr} to create T_G.

4.2 All Data for Training

Following the idea in [32], the Disjoint approach might leave a small subset of data for training, which could be a handicap. In this procedure, the initial set T is only divided into T_{tr} and T_{test}. Subset G is created from T_{tr}. I_{tr} and I_{test} are created following the functions $D(G, T_{tr})$ and $D(G, T_{test})$, respectively. Note that this time G and I_{tr} share T_{tr}. Every string from T_{tr} contributes to the creation of one generator. Consequently, each instance of I_{tr} has an attribute which is close to 0, because of the distance to this generator, adding some bias.

5 ML Models and Evaluation

In this section, we describe the Machine Learning (ML) models used in this work: Support Vector Machines (SVM) [9], which are one of the most robust prediction models, and Multilayer Perceptrons (MLP) [25], the most common feedforward neural network. The NCD attribute vectors will be the input to these models. We use the standard Scikit-Learn [23] implementation for SVM, and the Keras [7] implementation for MLP. A description of the evaluation is included.

5.1 Machine Learning Models

Support Vector Machine. This ML approach bases its classification on finding a hyperplane (a decision boundary) that separates the classes with maximum margin [9]. It uses kernel functions to map a non-linearly separable N-dimensional dataset onto a new high dimensional space in which linear separability is more plausible. In this work, we use linear and radial basis function (RBF) kernels.

Multilayer Perceptron. This model is the most common kind of artificial neural network, where neurons are hierarchically organized in layers, with feed-forward connections between adjacent layers. Hidden layers (neither input nor output) provide the computational processing to determine the most probable class. In this work, we use a Rectifier neural network with a single hidden layer, which is an MLP with Rectifier Linear Unit (ReLU) activation function.

5.2   Evaluation

The models' evaluation consists of a cross-validation with the five partitions described in Sect. 3. We consider the differences between the attribute vectors generation procedures described in Sect. 4. For tuning the optimal hyperparameters, we follow the grid search detailed in Table 1. We train both SVMs (linear and RBF kernels) until convergence, and the MLP for 500 epochs. To minimize the cross-entropy loss we use the Adam optimizer [18], applying checkpointing to get the best validation loss. We also add dropout and L2 regularization to every layer.

Table 1. Grid search tuning for training linear SVMs, RBF SVMs, and MLPs

Model	Hyperparam	Values
Linear SVM	C	$range[10^{-4}-10^4]$
RBF SVM	C	$range[10^{-4}-10^4]$
	γ	$range[10^{-4}-10^4]$
MLP	Units	$[100, 200]$
	Learning rate	$range[10^{-4}-10^{-1}]$
	L2 regularization	$[0, 10^{-5}, 10^{-4}, 10^{-3}, 10^{-2}]$
	Dropout	$[0, 0.1, 0.2, 0.3]$
	Epochs	500

6   Results

In this section, we show our results after following the procedures described in Sect. 4 with the models and evaluation criteria detailed in Sect. 5. In all our analyses, we use accuracy (ACC) and balanced accuracy (BAC) to compare the performance of our proposals. We train SVM with Linear and RBF kernels and MLP, applying the grid search detailed in Table 1. The three methods have been tested with the K values 18, 36, 72, and 144. We show in Fig. 1 the test accuracy for each model with the best hyperparameter settings and K value, and in Tables 2 and 3, we show more detailed results for both procedures.

There are some ideas to extract from these results. First, there is a slight increase in the performance of the MLP model against the SVM in the two approaches. In addition, regarding the procedure of the features generation, the

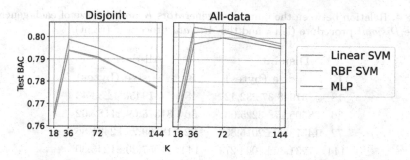

Fig. 1. Test Balanced Accuracy (BAC) versus K value for procedures *Disjoint* and *All-data* with the three models.

Table 2. Best results obtained with the *Disjoint* approach for all the models

K	Model	Hyperparams	AccTest	BACTest
36	Linear SVM	$C = 1$	0.798 ± 0.005	0.794 ± 0.006
36	RBF SVM	$C = 10$	0.798 ± 0.005	0.794 ± 0.004
		$\gamma = 0.1$		
36	MLP	$LR = 0.001$	$\mathbf{0.803 \pm 0.004}$	$\mathbf{0.799 \pm 0.003}$
		$L2 = 0$		
		$Dropout = 0.1$		

Table 3. Best results obtained with the *All-data* approach for all the models

K	Model	Hyperparams	AccTest	BACTest
72	Linear SVM	$C = 1$	0.804 ± 0.007	0.800 ± 0.008
72	RBF SVM	$C = 1$	0.806 ± 0.007	0.803 ± 0.006
		$\gamma = 10$		
36	MLP	$LR = 0.001$	$\mathbf{0.809 \pm 0.007}$	$\mathbf{0.805 \pm 0.006}$
		$L2 = 0.001$		
		$Dropout = 0.1$		

best option is All-data. However, it is worth to mention that SVMs require a much lower computational cost for training than the neural network. The MLP's need for the hyperparameters search described in Table 1 makes the SVM choice more suitable.

Concerning the K values, both $K = 36$ and $K = 72$ show the best performance. The value of K is directly related to the size of the generators, so it should not make their size larger than 32 KB [22,31]. The reason for this is that the sliding window of the *LZ77* algorithm, used in *gzip*, can only reference the last 32 KB[2]. Therefore, the point is to adjust the K value to be as higher as

---

[2] For more information visit https://datatracker.ietf.org/doc/html/rfc1951.

Table 4. Relation between the number of generators K and the size of each generator for the *Disjoint* procedure (left), and the *All-data* procedure (right).

Disjoint		All-data	
K	size (bytes)	K	size (bytes)
18	31948.37±32.42	18	31945.34±33.43
36	28505.17±3225.63	36	31378.09±1182.62
72	14513.80±2015.85	72	18169.24±2491.86
144	7231.36±1004.27	144	9057.20±1245.30

possible while making generators of size as close as possible to 32 KB. We show in Table 4 the relation between the number of generators K and the size of each generator for both the *Disjoint* (left) and *All-data* (right) procedures.

Looking at the tables, considering the size of the generators, the best values of K are 18 and 36. However, with $K = 18$ the models do not have enough information to perform well, and this is observed in the accuracy (see Fig. 1). Finally, increasing the number of generators beyond 36 reduces their size, and this also affects the models' accuracy.

7   Conclusions and Future Work

In this paper we have proposed a method to conduct authorship attribution by combining compression metrics and ML. The method has been tested on a dataset with tweets from six US politicians. We have analyzed the possibility of concluding about the politician behind a certain tweet just by measuring the NCD of this tweet with respect to a set of K writing style representatives. Such a comparison enables the classification of the tweet on the ground of ML models properly trained using a K-dimensional space of representation. This space is constructed upon K representatives or generators extracted from the original dataset. As ML models, we have used SVMs and MLPs. In our experiments we have evaluated the selection of adequate values of K, and the possibility of using as much data as possible to train and validate our models. Indeed, we distinguish two scenarios with regard to data preparation. First, we consider that none of the text samples included in the generators set are included in the text samples used to train and validate our model. Second, we consider the use of samples from the generators set as samples in the training and validation sets. In other words, we enable data reutilization. We reach the conclusion that the best option for our NCD-based authorship attribution is to use MLP, consider a $K = 36$ dimensional representation space and to re-use generators data for training and validation.

For future work, we have to bear in mind the explainability shortcomings of MLP, along with its computational burden. Our next steps in NCD-based authorship attribution will target at improving the construction of the training dataset and study the possibility of replacing MLP by SVM. Moreover, we have to take into account that in this paper we have used an implementation of the NCD using *gzip*. Additional work is required to consider alternatives to this compressor, which eventually could lead to overcome the limitations associated to the sliding window of the *LZ77* algorithm (e.g., ppmz or bzip2).

Acknowledgements. This project has received funding from the European Union's Horizon 2020 Research and Innovation Programme under grant agreement No. 872855 (TRESCA project), from Grant PLEC2021-007681 (project XAI-DisInfodemics) funded by MCIN/AEI/ 10.13039/501100011033 and by European Union NextGeneration EU/PRTR, from Comunidad de Madrid (Spain) under the project CYNAMON (no. P2018/TCS-4566), cofunded with FSE and FEDER EU funds, and from Spanish projects MINECO/FEDER TIN2017-84452-R and PID2020-114867RB-I00 (http://www.mineco.gob.es/).

References

1. Alonso-Fernandez, F., Belvisi, N.M.S., Hernandez-Diaz, K., Muhammad, N., Bigun, J.: Writer identification using microblogging texts for social media forensics. IEEE Trans. Biomet. Behav. Identity Sci. **3**(3), 405–426 (2021)
2. Aykent, S., Dozier, G.: AARef: exploiting authorship identifiers of micro-messages with refinement blocks. In: 2020 19th IEEE International Conference on Machine Learning and Applications (ICMLA), pp. 1044–1050. IEEE (2020)
3. Aykent, S., Dozier, G.: Author identification of micro-messages via multi-channel convolutional neural networks. In: 2020 IEEE International Conference on Systems, Man, and Cybernetics (SMC), pp. 675–681. IEEE (2020)
4. Baayen, H., Halteren, H., Neijt, A., Tweedie, F.: An experiment in authorship attribution, January 2002
5. Binongo, J.N.G.: Who wrote the 15th book of OZ? An application of multivariate analysis to authorship attribution. Chance **16**(2), 9–17 (2003)
6. Burrows, J.F.: Word-patterns and story-shapes: the statistical analysis of narrative style. Liter. Linguist. Comput. **2**(2), 61–70 (1987)
7. Chollet, F., et al.: Keras. http://keras.io (2015)
8. Cilibrasi, R., Vitanyi, P.: Clustering by compression. IEEE Trans. Inf. Theory **51**(4), 1523–1545 (2005)
9. Cortes, C., Vapnik, V.: Support vector networks. Mach. Learn. **20**, 273–297 (1995)
10. Diederich, J., Kindermann, J., Leopold, E., Paass, G.: Authorship attribution with support vector machines. Appl. Intell. **19**, 109–123 (2003). https://doi.org/10.1023/A:1023824908771
11. Fourkioti, O., Symeonidis, S., Arampatzis, A.: Language models and fusion for authorship attribution. Inf. Process. Manag. **56**(6), 102061 (2019)
12. Halvani, O., Winter, C., Graner, L.: On the usefulness of compression models for authorship verification. In: Proceedings of the 12th International Conference on Availability, Reliability and Security, pp. 1–10 (2017)
13. Hameleers, M., Minihold, S.: Constructing discourses on (un)truthfulness: attributions of reality, misinformation, and disinformation by politicians in a comparative social media setting. Commun. Res. (2020)
14. Hastie, T., Tibshirani, R., Friedman, J.: The Elements of Statistical Learning: Data Mining, 2nd edn. Inference and Prediction. Springer, New York (2009). https://doi.org/10.1007/978-0-387-21606-5

15. Holmes, D., Robertson, M., Paez, R.: Stephen crane and the New York tribune: a case study in traditional and non-traditional authorship attribution. Comput. Human. **35**, 315–331 (2001)
16. IARPA: Human Interpretable Attribution of Text using Underlying Structure (HIATUS) Program (2022)
17. Jursenas, A., Karlauskas, K., Ledinauskas, E., Maskeliunas, G., Rondomanskas, D., Ruseckas, J.: The Role of AI in the Battle Against Disinformation (2022)
18. Kingma, D.P., Ba, J.: Adam: a method for stochastic optimization. In: Bengio, Y., LeCun, Y. (eds.) 3rd International Conference on Learning Representations, ICLR 2015, San Diego, CA, USA, May 7–9, 2015, Conference Track Proceedings (2015)
19. Kjell, B., Addison Woods, W., Frieder, O.: Information retrieval using letter tuples with neural network and nearest neighbor classifiers. In: 1995 IEEE International Conference on Systems, Man and Cybernetics. Intelligent Systems for the 21st Century. vol. 2, pp. 1222–1226 (1995)
20. Layton, R., Watters, P., Dazeley, R.: Authorship attribution for twitter in 140 characters or less. In: 2010 Second Cybercrime and Trustworthy Computing Workshop, pp. 1–8. IEEE (2010)
21. Oliva, C., Palmero-Muñoz, S., Lago-Fernández, L.F., Arroyo, D.: Improving LSTMs' under-performance in authorship attribution for short texts. In: Proceedings of the European Interdisciplinary Cybersecurity Conference (EICC) (2022)
22. Oliveira, W., Jr., Justino, E., Oliveira, L.S.: Comparing compression models for authorship attribution. Forensic Sci. Int. **228**(1–3), 100–104 (2013)
23. Pedregosa, F., et al.: Scikit-learn: Machine learning in Python. J. Mach. Learn. Res. **12**, 2825–2830 (2011)
24. Rocha, A., et al.: Authorship attribution for social media forensics. IEEE Trans. Inf. Forensics Secur. **12**(1), 5–33 (2017)
25. Rumelhart, D.E., Hinton, G.E., Williams, R.J.: Learning Internal Representations by Error Propagation, pp. 318–362. MIT Press, Cambridge, MA, USA (1986)
26. Schwartz, R., Tsur, O., Rappoport, A., Koppel, M.: Authorship attribution of micro-messages. In: Proceedings of the 2013 Conference on Empirical Methods in Natural Language Processing, pp. 1880–1891 (2013)
27. Selj, V., Peng, F., Cercone, N., Thomas, C.: N-gram-based author profiles for authorship attribution. In: Proceedings of the Conference Pacific Association for Computational Linguistics PACLING 2003, September 2003
28. Shrestha, P., Sierra, S., González, F.A., Montes, M., Rosso, P., Solorio, T.: Convolutional neural networks for authorship attribution of short texts. In: Proceedings of the 15th Conference of the European Chapter of the Association for Computational Linguistics, vol. 2, Short Papers, pp. 669–674 (2017)
29. Theophilo, A., Giot, R., Rocha, A.: Authorship attribution of social media messages. IEEE Trans. Comput. Soc. Syst. 1–14 (2021)
30. Theóphilo, A., Pereira, L.A., Rocha, A.: A needle in a haystack? Harnessing onomatopoeia and user-specific stylometrics for authorship attribution of micro-messages. In: ICASSP 2019–2019 IEEE International Conference on Acoustics, Speech and Signal Processing (ICASSP), pp. 2692–2696. IEEE (2019)
31. de la Torre-Abaitua, G., Lago-Fernández, L.F., Arroyo, D.: A compression-based method for detecting anomalies in textual data. Entropy **23**(5), 618 (2021)
32. de la Torre-Abaitua, G., Lago-Fernández, L.F., Arroyo, D.: On the application of compression-based metrics to identifying anomalous behaviour in web traffic. Log. J. IGPL **28**(4), 546–557 (2020)
33. Veenman, C.J., Li, Z.: Authorship verification with compression features. In: CLEF (Working Notes) (2013)

Discourses of Climate Delay in American Reddit Discussions

Aline Sylla[1], Felix Glawe[1], Dirk Braun[1], Mihail Padev[1], Sina Schäfer[1], Albina Ahmetaj[1], Lilian Kojan[2,3], and André Calero Valdez[3(✉)]

[1] RWTH Aachen University, Aachen, Germany
{Aline.Sylla,Felix.Glawe,Dirk.Joachim.Braun,Mihail.Padev,Sina.Schaefer,
Albina.Ahmetaj}@rwth-aachen.de
[2] Human-Computer Interaction Center, RWTH Aachen University, Aachen, Germany
[3] Institute for Multimedia and Interactive Systems, University of Lübeck,
Lübeck, Germany
{kojan,calerovaldez}@imis.uni-luebeck.de

Abstract. Arguments that seek to justify the lack of measures to combat anthropogenic climate change have been identified in public discourse and characterized into four distinct Discourses of Climate Delay. Reddit provides a useful source of data for discourse research. While discourse on other social media platforms is prone to polarization due to echo-chamber effects, the prevalence of these effects on Reddit is disputed. We used the Reddit and pushshift APIs to acquire data from posts on the popular political communities r/democrats and r/Republican. We then used intercoder-validated deductive qualitative content analysis based on the defined Discourses of Climate Delay to identify if Reddit users employ different Discourses of Climate Delay based on their political group affiliation. We find that members of r/Republican tend to employ arguments based on preventing change, while those in r/democrats preferentially use arguments that emphasize the complexity necessary for implementing structural changes.

Keywords: Discourses of climate delay · Reddit · Republicans · Democrats

1 Introduction

Among the many challenges facing humanity in the 21st century, and despite its increasingly evident effects, anthropogenic climate change seems to be one of the most divisive issues in contemporary public discourse. Consequentially, there has been an ever-increasing range of arguments to downplay the need for action. This debate carries over into social media, where supporters of various political camps use common platforms to share their thoughts and debate about these topics. These discussions can be classified with the so-called Discourses of Climate Delay by Lamb et al. [1], which "accept the existence of climate change, but justify inaction or inadequate efforts" [1]. Lamb et al. identified different kinds of discourses ranging from a change of topic to the use of mis- or disinformation about outcomes of climate action. Since these discourses are relatively new, there has not been a lot of research concerning specific social groups. This led us to the question if any groups favor certain discourses. Since Democrats and Republicans are the prime examples of two opposing poles in this discussion in American society, we want to explore if there are differences in the usage of this theory. For this study, we chose Reddit as a sample social media platform. We compared the Democratic forum to the Republican one regarding their tendencies to outline polar behavior regarding politics and compare their discussion behavior. We will show the contents of this study in detail.

2   Related Work

We will look at three different topics on which to base our hypotheses. First, we will elaborate on the Discourses of Climate Delay. Following that, Reddit as a platform for political discussion will be explored. Lastly, we will give a description of Democrats and Republicans in the American political landscape and their differences in perception and approaches to climate change. This chapter closes with a summary of the related work and the resulting research question and corresponding hypotheses.

2.1   Discourses of Climate Delay

Discourses of Climate Delay are strategies employed to disregard the need for action to lessen or prevent climate change [1]. The difference between these discourses and other arguments opposing climate policies is as follows: Climate denialism or climate-impact skepticism do not acknowledge the scientific consensus on climate change and the negative impact on the planet. Discourses of Climate Delay, on the other hand, do acknowledge climate change as a threat [1,2]. Nevertheless, they are communicative strategies that divert attention away from action by focusing on questions such as which action is beneficial and which is not, when a certain action should be employed, who is to cover costs, and who should be held responsible for taking action in the first place [1]. Lamb et al. emphasize that this can happen with good intentions as well as maliciously, but regardless of the intentions, it prevents or delays meaningful action.

Lamb et al. state that the discourses can be subsumed under four categories: *redirect responsibility*, *push non-transformative solutions*, *emphasize the downsides*, and *surrender*.

Redirect Responsibility. Discourses in this category revolve around answering the question "who is responsible for taking climate action?" [1]. The main focus lies in shifting responsibility to either restrict the range of solutions or push responsibility onto other actors, delaying own actions or justifying inaction. Redirect responsibility discourses include the practice of whataboutism, individualism, or using the "free rider" excuse, stating that taking action allows other actors to benefit despite their inaction [1].

Push Non-transformative Solutions. Discourses in this category focus on solutions to climate change that are not disruptive to current living standards and practices while disregarding the need for more extreme measures [1]. Common discourses can be technological optimism or fossil fuel solutionism, where the main premise is that future innovations will sufficiently address climate change. Other examples include relying on and supporting voluntary action without compulsion and talking about the need for a solution for climate change and ambitious goals without acting on them or having a concrete plan to reach them [1].

Emphasize the Downsides. Discourses in this category center around negative impacts that climate policy can or could have on people or the economy [1]. They rely on the conviction that necessary change would be too disruptive and would cost too much to be desirable, compared to the consequences of inaction. Discourses in this category include appeals to social justice or well-being, which state that policies will disproportionately affect marginalized groups and make their lives more difficult, as well as deny countries or individuals the ability to participate in a modern or desired livelihood [1]. Another option is to seek policy perfectionism, where an unrealistic standard is set for a policy to be accepted, like all parties agreeing on a policy or expecting a high impact with minimal cost.

Surrender. Discourses in this category demand a refocusing of efforts towards adapting to climate change instead of trying to mitigate it or give up efforts altogether [1]. Discussion centers around the idea that mitigating climate change is impossible because it is too late to do so, it was not meant to be, or because it cannot work with the current systems in place [1]. Lamb et al. state that discourses in this category can also be religiously motivated and include a trust in God or fate as the only feasible option to choose right now.

2.2 Reddit

A cursory examination of existing research points towards Reddit as a promising data source for analyzing political discourse for several reasons.

Reddit is characterized as a "social news aggregation, web content rating and discussion" website [3], or as a "bulletin of user-submitted text, links, photos, and videos" [4]. It is evident that social media and social news sites determine what topics become foci in the contemporary discourse and popular media narrative to an ever-increasing extent [5], with Reddit outsourcing the curation, ranking, and commentary of the current topical content to its users [5].

Reddit is a well-visited website, ranking as the 18th most visited site globally and the 6th most visited in the United States in 2019 [6]. Reddit's own published statistics claim there are more than 100,000 active communities (i.e., subreddits) as of late 2021, with a total of 366 million posts created in that year [7]. Also, "aggregate user data is publicly accessible" [5] and the data can be used to "perform longitudinal studies on the whole system, and, critically, to ensure the reproducibility of the results" [3].

Reddit can be loosely described as having an "inferred" community structure [8]. In other words, most of the activity on Reddit is not centered around expanding one's network or attaining some form of social capital but rather on the discussion and commentary of specific topics and themes as defined within the communities. Users usually subscribe to subreddits but not to other users, again focusing on content rather than building a network [3].

The structure of Reddit itself mimics the structure of individual comment threads, with the landing page providing a curated list of currently popular topics. Registered users see posts from the communities they are subscribed to, as well as some popular posts, with unregistered users being shown content based on posts' current popularity [3]. Individual posts are embedded within a respective community (i.e., a subreddit).

Reddit posts are hierarchically structured in the following way: The threads are structured as a root tree, with the original (or 'self-post') at the root of the structure, first-level comments responding to the original posts, second-level comments responding to those on the level above them, etc. Users have the option to 'upvote' or 'downvote' self-posts as well as individual comments, with highly upvoted entries receiving increased visibility.

This leads to a form of self-organization [3], where adherence to so-called "rediquette" [9] is monitored by the users themselves. Adherence to further norms is generally subreddit-dependent, with norm violation and compliance being punished or rewarded based on self-defined internal rules or guidelines of that community [8]. Certain behavior that would be frowned upon in some communities is encouraged in others, leading to diverse discussion within the different subreddits.

2.3 Democrats vs. Republicans

The supporters of the parties represented in America's two-party system—the Democrats and the Republicans—differ in many more facets than just their different political stances [10–12]. Studies continue to describe psychological and behavioral differences between party members, reaching from motivation or reasoning to speech and writing patterns [10–13].

Sheldon and Nichols compared Democrats and Republicans in regard to their value systems. They found that Republicans scored higher on extrinsic values than intrinsic values, meaning that they valued financial success, popularity, and their own image more than intimacy, helping others, and growth. Democrats, on the other hand, scored higher in intrinsic values than in extrinsic values [14]. Furthermore, Democrats more commonly inhabit a more prosocial orientation, valuing community and cooperation, while Republicans inhabit a more pro-self orientation, focusing on personal gain at the expense of others if need be [14].

When talking about Democrats and Republicans, we can derive certain assumptions about the two groups by also considering the distinction between liberal and conservative people, as a conservative mindset correlates with voting for the Republican party, whereas a liberal mindset correlates with voting for the Democratic party [15]. However, these assumptions have to be taken into account with care since there are a certain amount of conservative Democrats as well as liberal Republicans [15]. The personality dimensions from the "Big Five" model can be observed differently in liberals and conservatives [16]. Liberals score high in the "openness to new experiences" dimension, characterizing them as open-minded, creative, curious, and novelty seeking, whereas conservatives have a high score in the conscientiousness dimension, making them more likely to be orderly, conventional, and organized [16].

In relation to climate change, there are also several differences between Republicans and Democrats. Historically, the Republican party changed its view on environmental politics when regulations concerning the environment were labeled as a burden on the economy by the Reagan administration [17]. The effects of this can still be observed today. Many Republican or Republican-leaning voters prioritize economic growth over environmental protection, whereas most Democratic or Democratic-leaning voters set their priorities the other way around [18]. Democrats express the need for more climate action more strongly than Republicans do [19]. Furthermore, Democrats see developing alternative energy sources as a priority over developing fossil-fuel-driven energy generation [19]. Republicans, on the other hand, are more divided over the question of energy, especially conservative Republicans, which represent the majority of Republicans, and they prioritize fossil fuels more than Democrats do [19].

Lastly, Democrats and Republicans use different language and can be observed writing about different themes on the internet. In a study conducted by Sylwester and Purver, differences in topics and expression were found between Democrats and Republicans. On Twitter, Republicans focus on themes like national identity, in-group identity, and their opponents, while Democrats focus on entertainment and culture, while using words that are more emotionally expressive than the ones Republicans use [10]. On Reddit, users can be categorized into political factions fairly accurately by their posts in political subreddits, but subtle differences can also be observed within posts that do not revolve around politics [20].

2.4 Research Question and Hypotheses

Lamb et al. identified the Discourses of Climate Delay to provide a reference point that can be used to counter misinformation and to more easily develop information strategies to challenge these discourses. This work will use this reference point to identify if there is a difference in usage of the different Discourses of Climate Delay to extend the reference point. By understanding how different groups use different Discourses of Climate Delay, one can not only develop information strategies but begin to target a specific audience for a greater effect.

As stated above, we chose the Democratic and Republican parties as groups of interest for their tendencies to show polar behavior in regards to policy and looked at their discussion behavior on Reddit. This work wants to answer the question if there are differences in the usage of the different Discourses of Climate Delay between Democrats and Republicans in Reddit discussions. To answer the questions, the following hypotheses are proposed.

Taking into consideration the differences in personality, view on climate debate, and language between Democrats and Republicans described in the previous chapter, we hypothesize that the difference will carry over into the Reddit arguments and be reflected by a different usage of Discourses of Climate Delay. Furthermore, we hypothesize that, due to their tendency to prioritize financial gain and economic well-being, Republicans lean into the *emphasize the downsides* discourse. Emphasizing the downsides often means focusing on economic losses that some policies might trigger.

On the other hand, we predict that Democrats use the *push non-transformative solutions* discourse more than the other discourses since they are open to new experiences and generally favor climate action. This discourse includes technological optimism and, in contrast to the other discourses, the actual intention to take action. Concluding, our hypotheses are the following:

- **H1**: There is a difference in the usage of Discourses of Climate Delay between Democrats and Republicans in Reddit discussions.
- **H2**: Republicans favor the *emphasize the downsides* Discourse of Climate Delay over other discourses.
- **H3**: Democrats favor the *push non-transformative solutions* Discourse of Climate Delay over other discourses.

These will be tested on a corpus of Reddit posts and comments using deductive qualitative content analysis along with descriptive statistical analyses as described in the next chapter of this work.

3   Method

In this chapter, we present and explain the method used to answer the research question and test our hypotheses. Because, to our knowledge, there have been no studies about the differences in the use of Discourses of Climate Delay between the Republican and Democratic parties, we chose a deductive qualitative approach to explore and discuss possible differences in depth and set the foundation for future broader quantitative studies. The data was gathered by scraping two party-specific subreddits—r/democrats and r/Republican—cleaned, and then analyzed to identify the discourses within the subreddits.

3.1   Groups

Our research focuses on the two dominant political parties in the U.S. [21]. The subreddit structure and the internal guidelines of the subreddits themselves offered a good separation to examine differences between the groups. Both sub-reddits state in their description or rules that they do not want supporters of the opposite party to discuss within the subreddit and that they do not want attacks against the political orientation of the subreddit, nor do they want promotion of other political parties [22,23]. We relied on the same approach as attributed to Morales et al. [24]: assuming users' adherence to the rules within the subreddits, we used their participation within the subreddits as a proxy of political group affiliation.

3.2 Data Acquisition

To explore the discourses used within the two subreddits, we scraped both sub-reddits using Python and by utilizing the official Reddit API [25] as well as the pushshift API [26]. We focused on scraping data from 2020 to minimize the chance of changes happening to the dataset while scraping (for example, by removing or deleting a comment or post) and because we anticipated a higher discussion rate due to the running presidential election in the U.S. A data point was added to our main dataset if the post contained the keyword 'climate' or 'Climate' within the post-title, the self-text of the post, or in one of the com-ments of the post. Each data point consists of the post-id, post-title, self-text, all comments made under the posts, the URL to the posts, the sum of votes (upvotes minus downvotes) for each comment, and the assignment to the sub-reddit it was derived from. Each post was stored in two separate data files: one containing the title, the self-text, URL and the comments, and the other one containing the sum of votes for all comments.

3.3 Content Analysis

We conducted a deductive qualitative content analysis based on Mayring [27]. The intercoder agreement method as described by Campbell et al. [28] was used and therefore, the main dataset was split into three parts and distributed over six coders with pairs of two receiving the same part. Because a Reddit post is not limited in its number of comments, we used the following strategy to narrow down the parts of each post and to define the recording unit: For each data point, the post-title and self-text had to be inspected. Then the keyword 'cli-mate' was searched for in the comments. The comment containing the keyword as well as its context was inspected. Context, in this case, was loosely defined as all comments needed to understand the discussion around the comment con-taining the keyword. Therefore the recording unit consisted of the title, self-text, and the comments containing the keyword plus their context. The coding unit (which could be included in the title, self-text, or comment) was defined as a sentence and the context unit as a complete comment. The four main Discourses of Climate Delay were used as the main categories: *redirect responsibility, surren-der, push non-transformative solutions*, and *emphasize the downsides*. Because the size of a discourse is not fixed, multiple discourses could be identified in one comment or self-text. An identified and categorized discourse was saved in a new data table including the following variables: Id of the post, type of text (post-title, self-text, comment plus position in the comment tree), the text itself, the categorization of the discourse, and the sum of votes (if the text was part of a comment). After the coders had completed the analysis, the coder pairs discussed, compared, and adjusted their results where necessary. Discourse identifications or classifications that could not be agreed upon by the coder pairs were noted and discussed in a final round by all coders. The so-created three data tables of the coder pairs were merged into a final dataset. Furthermore, we calculated the frequencies and relative frequencies of discourses in the groups and created boxplot diagrams on word count and the sum of votes for the discourses in both groups. The full analysis process is depicted in Fig. 1.

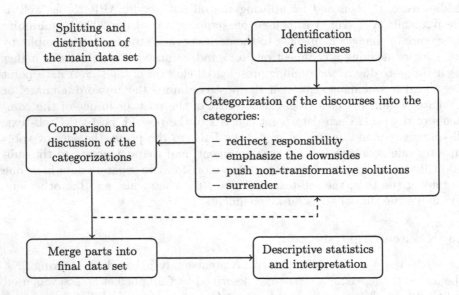

Fig. 1. Procedure of the content analysis.

4   Results

4.1   Sample Description

On the 30th June 2020 the subscription count was 123,830 for the r/Republican and 134,196 for the r/democrats subreddit. 25,287 posts were posted in 2020 within r/democrats and 27,720 within r/Republican [29]. The main data set contained 219 posts from the r/Republican subreddit and 344 posts from the r/democrats subreddit. The classification of Discourses of Climate Delay reduced the data set to 69 comments in 28 posts from r/Republican and 49 comments in 20 posts from r/democrats.

4.2   Descriptive Statistics

Reddit provides a descriptive feature through the sum of votes for each comment. Analyzing the sum of votes of comments containing a form of Discourse of Climate Delay yields a relatively uniform picture (see Fig. 2). The median of votes lies between 1 and 2—with the exception of *emphasize the downsides* in r/democrats. Since the initial vote rating is plus one (Reddit assumes that the author of a comment likes his or her own comment), this median represents a neutral activity. Either these comments did not receive many up- and downvotes or they canceled each other out. The mean of the votes is close to the median, between 0.5 and 4.8 with the exception of *redirect responsibility* in r/democrats with a mean sum of votes of 12.7. The standard deviation lies between 1.4 and 10.3 with the same exception of *redirect responsibility* in r/democrats with a standard deviation of 27.5. Those measures are close to the ones of the complete sample, which has a median of 2, a mean of 6.4 and a standard deviation of 20.

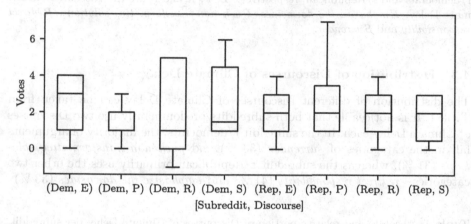

Fig. 2. Boxplots of the sums of votes per subreddit and Discourse of Climate Delay. Outliers are removed for better visibility. *Dem* and *Rep* are the subreddits r/democrats and r/Republican, respectively. *E*, *P*, *R* and *S* are the Discourses of Climate Delay: *E*mphasize the downsides, *P*ush non-transformative solutions, *R*edirect responsibility and *S*urrender.

The analysis of the word count of comments containing Discourses of Climate Delay show median word counts ranging from 50 (*surrender* in r/Republican) to 109 (*emphasize the downsides* in r/Republican) as shown in Fig. 3 with a median of 73 over all groups. The median word counts for each Discourse are higher in r/Republican than in r/democrats, except for *surrender*, where they are relatively close. The highest standard deviation (513.8) can be observed in *push non-transformative solutions* in r/Republican, while *surrender* in r/democrats has the lowest standard deviation (35.7). The standard deviation of the other discourses lies between 40.5 and 365.6.

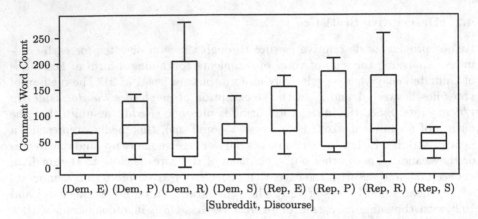

Fig. 3. Boxplot of the comment word counts in r/democrats and r/Republican for each Discourse of Climate Delay. No outliers are removed. *Dem* and *Rep* are the subreddits r/democrats and r/Republican, respectively. *E*, *P*, *R* and *S* are the Discourses of Climate Delay: *Emphasize the downsides*, *Push non-transformative solutions*, *Redirect responsibility* and *Surrender*.

4.3 Distribution of Discourses of Climate Delay

The distribution of different Discourses of Climate Delay can be taken from Table 1. It is noticeable that both subreddits predominantly use two Discourses of Climate Delay each. In the subreddit r/democrats, the majority of arguments fall in the categories of *surrender* (33 %) and *push non-transformative solutions* (31 %), whereas the subreddit r/Republican primarily uses the other two categories—*redirect responsibility* (41 %) and *emphasize the downsides* (33 %).

Table 1. Absolute and relative portion of Discourses of Climate Delay per subreddit.

Discourse of Climate Delay	r/democrats	r/Republican
Redirect responsibility	11 (22%)	28 (41%)
Emphasize the downsides	7 (14%)	23 (33%)
Push non-transformative solutions	15 (31%)	11 (16%)
Surrender	16 (33%)	7 (10%)

5   Discussion

In this chapter we will discuss the results from the previous chapter, draw connections to previous related work, identify the limitations of our approach, and consider improvements for further research.

5.1   Hypotheses

Interpreting the results we can see a duality between two groups of discourses used by Republicans and Democrats. Republicans mainly use *redirect responsibility* and *emphasize the downsides*, while the other two discourses fall behind, the next one in line being only used about half as much as *emphasize the downsides*. Meanwhile, Democrats seem to favor the two discourses that Republicans use less. The *surrender* and *push non-transformative solutions* discourses together make up almost two thirds of the occurrences of discourses in r/democrats. The divide between Democrats and Republicans in their values, their motivation, their stance on climate policy and even their Twitter behavior continues in the usage of Discourses of Climate Delay on Reddit. Therefore, H1 can be accepted: "There is a difference in the usage of Discourses of Climate Delay between Democrats and Republicans in Reddit discussions". H2 stated that "Republicans favor the *emphasize the downsides* Discourse of Climate Delay over other discourses" while H3 is "Democrats favor the *push non-transformative solutions* Discourse of Climate Delay over other discourses". Both hypotheses could not be directly confirmed, since both groups favored another Discourse of Climate Delay over the other discourses, while both our hypothesized discourses were second after that (compare Table 1). Since both hypothesized discourses still are in the favored pair of discourses of the corresponding group, we want to take a closer look at the discovered pairs.

Republicans. Based on recent work we hypothesized that Republicans favor the *emphasize the downsides* discourse over other discourses. While this is not wholly the case, the discourse is part of the pair of discourses this group mostly uses in Reddit arguments. The reasoning behind this is most likely the same as related work suggests: Republicans favor economic growth over environmental protection and their pro-self orientation leads them to argue for personal gain at the cost of others if need be [14]. Climate policy may very likely affect the economy in some way, for example non environmentally-friendly production or fossil fuels might not be financially supported by the government anymore and may by extension affect the job market. The threat of financial loss threatens Republicans in their pro-self orientation, and might lead them to arguing against that change to prevent personal losses. "*The green new deal he supports would cost 90 TRILLION dollars for 10 years. It would destroy the entire economy much worse than any climate change could ever wish of doing.*"[1]

The discourse that is used mostly by Republicans on Reddit is the *redirect responsibility* discourse. This falls in line with the discovered tendency of Republicans to try to avoid change or at least push it back by demanding that others change first. Another explanation could be derived from the time of the investigation. We examined Reddit discussion at the end of the 4-year

---

[1] https://www.reddit.com/r/Republican/comments/j6hkev/workingclass_americans_in_all_states_support/.

period of Donald Trump as president and leader of the Republican party. Donald Trump was very well known for shifting responsibility onto others, using a technique called whataboutism, which is subsumed in the *redirect responsibility* discourse [30], e.g., *"My problem with this is that in the treaty, it doesn't include China and India...THE TWO BIGGEST CONTRIBUTORS TO CLIMATE CHANGE."*[2]. Republicans may have adopted this rhetoric—particularly shifting blame towards China—from their political leader, Donald Trump, who painted China as one of America's greatest rivals, particularly in an economic sense [31].

Democrats. Recent work shows that Democrats are more open to change and inhabit a prosocial orientation [14]. They do not primarily favor the *push non-transformative solutions* discourse over all other Discourses of Climate Delay, but it is still the second most commonly used by Democrats on Reddit, which is supported by findings from recent work. Their push for change and climate action may be well-intentioned but as Lamb et al. discuss, can still result in action-delaying behavior like trusting in future technology to solve climate problems and expecting non-disruptive change to be sufficient [1]. *"Making diesel fuel from atmospheric CO2 might be the only way to go there."*[3]

Democrats, however, use the *surrender* discourse the most. One reason could be, again, the timeframe of our analysis at the end of a Republican-led presidency, which was especially disruptive regarding climate policy, e.g., in its leaving the Paris Climate Agreement [32]. Seeing policies being revoked and past action nullified might have instilled a sense of hopelessness or doom in Democrats. Another reason can be deduced from an analysis by Napier et al., who examined happiness between Democrats and Republicans and found Democrats to be less happy than their Republican counterparts [33]. Hibbing et al. suggest that while conservatives avoid negative experiences, liberals are more likely to actively search for confrontation leading to this kind of negativity bias [34]. This might lead to the conclusion that change is impossible and therefore promote the *surrender* discourse. Nevertheless, openness and push for change still plays a very prominent role in Democrat *surrender* discourse. The thought that any action might now be too late anyway leads to a shift to adaption to climate change instead of prevention. *"Come to terms with it, we're just going to have to move some coastal cities. The climate crisis is unstoppable."*[4]

To conclude this discussion, we can observe this duality between the two favored discourses of each party in regard to change. At their core *emphasize the downsides* and *redirect responsibility* are discourses that delay climate action by trying to prevent change. Meanwhile *push non-transformative solutions* and

---

[2] https://www.reddit.com/r/Republican/comments/k3njr4/paris_climate_treaty_puts_america_last/.

[3] https://www.reddit.com/r/democrats/comments/fdm1t2/whats_the_appeal_of_joe_biden/.

[4] https://www.reddit.com/r/democrats/comments/iaopl2/opinion_trump_vilifies_mask_wearing_to_get_people/.

surrender are discourses that delay climate action by (mis)guiding the wish for change in a different direction, while still allowing for a direct push for action. Therefore Republicans favor the first pair of discourses, for they are generally more skeptical of change, while Democrats, who are generally more open to change, favor the second pair.

5.2 Limitations

Several limitations to the results of this work should be considered. First of all, we cannot guarantee the completeness of the dataset, as some comments in the posts had been deleted or removed, or were otherwise not accessible, allowing for the possibility that potentially relevant information was missing. Secondly, by choosing the year 2020 as the timeframe for our research, we limited the scope of our results, even if the communities we examined have existed for much longer and are still active today. Furthermore, we had to rely on the users of the subreddits to conform to the rules of their respective communities stating that people who affiliate with another party should not post or comment in the subreddit. Finally, we only focused on the keyword 'climate', which on one hand resulted in 'false positive' posts, which discussed e.g., political climate, and on the other hand may have left out posts and comments which included Discourses of Climate Delay, but did not include the specific word 'climate'.

5.3 Further Research

To build on this work, there are some aspects to consider for future research. Firstly, one could adjust or expand the timeframe to direct or expand the scope of the analysis. Since we only analyzed Reddit discussions from the year 2020, it could be interesting to compare the results to another year that is further in the past, e.g., the year 2016 or 2012, during which presidential elections in the US were also held. Another possibility would be to compare a year of the presidential elections to a year where there was no such election, or to observe the change between 2020 and the present. Secondly, it could be interesting to analyze posts from politicians in the same way, and examine similarities and differences between the discussion behavior of private citizens and that of the policymakers that represent them. Moreover, for further research, it could be useful to expand the key words beyond 'climate', by looking at related topics like the 'Green New Deal' or 'renewable energy'. Relating to this, finding new keywords can be partially automated by utilizing text mining. Lastly, this work demonstrates the possibilities for further in-depth analysis of the apparent duality between the categories of Discourses of Climate Delay used by Republicans and Democrats, which could expand this approach and apply it to other social or ideological groups.

6 Conclusion

This work utilized a deductive qualitative content analysis to find out if Democrats and Republicans show a different usage of Discourses of Climate

Delay in online discussions on Reddit. The results of our study show that there is a difference between Democrats and Republicans in their use of Discourses of Climate Delay on Reddit. While Democrats favor *surrender* and *push non-transformative solutions* in an effort to address the need for change, Republicans do the opposite—they use *emphasize the downsides* as well as *redirect responsibility* to prevent change from happening. With that in mind, future campaigns and efforts to counter these Discourses of Climate Delay can better focus their efforts on addressing the respective target groups.

References

1. Lamb, W.F., et al.: Discourses of climate delay. Glob. Sustain. **3** (2020)
2. Dunlap, R.E., McCright, A.M., et al.: Organized climate change denial. In: The Oxford Handbook of Climate Change and Society, vol. 1, pp. 144–160 (2011)
3. Medvedev, A.N., Lambiotte, R., Delvenne, J.-C.: The anatomy of Reddit: an overview of academic research. In: Ghanbarnejad, F., Saha Roy, R., Karimi, F., Delvenne, J.-C., Mitra, B. (eds.) DOOCN 2017. SPC, pp. 183–204. Springer, Cham (2019). https://doi.org/10.1007/978-3-030-14683-2_9
4. Duggan, M., Smith, A.: 6% of online adults are reddit users. Pew Internet & American Life Project **3** (2013)
5. Weninger, T., Zhu, X.A., Han, J.: An exploration of discussion threads in social news sites: a case study of the reddit community. In: IEEE/ACM International Conference on Advances in Social Networks Analysis and Mining (ASONAM 2013), pp. 579–583. IEEE (2013)
6. Del Valle, M.E., Gruzd, A., Kumar, P., Gilbert, S.: Learning in the wild: understanding networked ties in Reddit. In: Dohn, N.B., Jandrić, P., Ryberg, T., de Laat, M. (eds.) Mobility, Data and Learner Agency in Networked Learning. RNL, pp. 51–68. Springer, Cham (2020). https://doi.org/10.1007/978-3-030-36911-8_4
7. redditinc.com: Reddit recap 2021. https://www.redditinc.com/blog/reddit-recap-2021 Accessed 08 Mar 2022
8. Datta, S., Adar, E.: Extracting inter-community conflicts in reddit. In: Proceedings of the International AAAI Conference on Web and Social Media, vol. 13, no. 01, pp. 146–157 (2019)
9. Anderson, K.E.: Ask me anything: what is reddit? Libr. Hi Tech News **32**(5), 8–11 (2015)
10. Sylwester, K., Purver, M.: Twitter language use reflects psychological differences between Democrats and Republicans. PLoS ONE **10**(9), 1–18 (2015)
11. Schreiber, D., et al.: Red brain, blue brain: evaluative processes differ in Democrats and Republicans. PLoS ONE **8**(2), 9–14 (2013)
12. Sweetser, K.D.: Partisan personality: the psychological differences between Democrats and Republicans, and independents somewhere in between. Am. Behav. Sci. **58**(9), 1183–1194 (2014)
13. Gustafson, A., et al.: Republicans and Democrats differ in why they support renewable energy. Energy Policy **141**, 111448 (2020)
14. Sheldon, K.M., Nichols, C.P.: Comparing democrats and republicans on intrinsic and extrinsic values. J. Appl. Soc. Psychol. **39**(3), 589–623 (2009)
15. Linn, E.L.: The influence of liberalism and conservatism on voting behavior. Public Opin. Q. **13**(2), 299–309 (1949)

16. Carney, D.R., Jost, J.T., Gosling, S.D., Potter, J.: The secret lives of liberals and conservatives: personality profiles, interaction styles, and the things they leave behind. Polit. Psychol. **29**(6), 807–840 (2008)

17. Dunlap, R.E., McCright, A.M.: A widening gap: Republican and Democratic views on climate change. Environment **50**(5), 26–35 (2008)

18. Smeltz, D., Sullivan, E., Wolff, C.: Republicans and democrats in different worlds on climate change. The Chicago Council on Global Affairs, October 2021

19. Funk, C., Hefferon, M.: U.S. public views on climate and energy, pp. 1–36. Pew Research Center (2019)

20. Acosta, A., Ciurea-Ilcus, S., Wegrzynski, M.: Predicting users' political support from their reddit comment history. Science **1612**(349), 310 (2016)

21. Jones, J.M.: U.S. political party preferences shifted greatly during 2021. https://news.gallup.com/poll/388781/political-party-preferences-shifted-greatly-during-2021.aspx. Accessed 17 Feb 2022

22. reddit.com: Republican. https://www.reddit.com/r/Republican/. Accessed 17 Feb 2022

23. reddit.com: Democrats: Building a better future. https://www.reddit.com/r/democrats/. Accessed 17 Feb 2022

24. de Francisci Morales, G., Monti, C., Starnini, M.: No echo in the chambers of political interactions on reddit. Sci. Rep. **11**(1), 2818 (2021)

25. reddit: reddit API documentation. https://www.reddit.com/dev/api/. Accessed 17 Feb 2022

26. pushshift.io: pushshift.io API documentation. https://pushshift.io/api-parameters/. Accessed 17 Feb 2022

27. Mayring, P.: Qualitative Inhaltsanalyse [Qualitative Content Analysis], 12 edn. Beltz Verlagsgruppe (2015)

28. Campbell, J.L., Quincy, C., Osserman, J., Pedersen, O.K.: Coding in-depth semistructured interviews: problems of unitization and intercoder reliability and agreement. Sociol. Methods Res. **42**(3), 294–320 (2013)

29. frontpagemetrics.com: Metrics for reddit. https://frontpagemetrics.com/. Accessed 17 Feb 2022

30. Pearcy, M.: "It's not accidental at all"-media literacy, "Whataboutism," and Occam's Razor. Res. Issues Contemp. Educ. **6**(2), 10–35 (2021)

31. Elms, D., Sriganesh, B.: Trump's trade policy: discerning between rhetoric and reality. Asian J. WTO Int'l Health L Pol'y **12**, 247 (2017)

32. Jotzo, F., Depledge, J., Winkler, H.: US and international climate policy under president Trump (2018)

33. Napier, J.L., Jost, J.T.: Why are conservatives happier than liberals? Psychol. Sci. **19**(6), 565–572 (2008)

34. Hibbing, J.R., Smith, K.B., Alford, J.R.: Differences in negativity bias underlie variations in political ideology. Behav. Brain Sci. **37**, 297–307 (2014)

Incremental Machine Learning for Text Classification in Comment Moderation Systems

Anna Wolters[1]([✉])[ID], Kilian Müller[2][ID], and Dennis M. Riehle[1][ID]

[1] University of Koblenz-Landau, Koblenz, Germany
{awolters,riehle}@uni-koblenz.de
[2] University of Münster - ERCIS, Münster, Germany
kilian.mueller@ercis.uni-muenster.de

Abstract. Over the last decade, researchers presented (semi-)automated comment moderation systems (CMS) based on machine learning (ML) and natural language processing (NLP) techniques to support the identification of hateful and offensive comments in online discussion forums. A common challenge in providing and operating comment moderation systems is the dynamic nature of language. As language evolves over time, continuous performance evaluations and resource-inefficient model retraining are applied to ensure high-quality identification of hate speech in the long-term use of comment moderation systems. To study the potentials of adaptable machine learning models embedded in comment moderation systems, we present an incremental machine learning approach for semi-automated comment moderation systems. This study shows a comparison of incrementally-trained ML models and batch-trained ML models used in comment moderation systems.

Keywords: Incremental learning · Text classification · Comment moderation systems

1 Introduction

Increasing online communication confronts journalists in media and news corporations with a task that is "not historically part of a journalist's daily routines" [15, p. 1022]: comment moderation. Journalists feel responsible for eliminating hate speech and other forms of abusive language in order to prevent discussions from deviating or escalating, as well as to fulfill legal obligations [5,28]. Manual comment moderation, however, becomes a time-consuming task, as journalists are usually facing large amounts of comment data [5]. For this reason, some organizations take the measure of completely banning comment sections from their websites or outsource the moderation activities to overcome the issues of comment moderation [15]. In addition to the unmanageable number of comments, comment moderation is a challenging task in itself, since journalists are

F. Spezzano et al. (Eds.): MISDOOM 2022, LNCS 13545, pp. 138–153, 2022.
https://doi.org/10.1007/978-3-031-18253-2_10

in the dilemma of eliminating hateful comments, while guaranteeing freedom of speech [28]. To find a viable solution that appropriately addresses the challenges of comment moderation, researchers and platform operators are investigating automated classification mechanisms that use ML and NLP methods to identify abusive comments [16,29,39]. These automated methods offer the possibility to keep discussion forums running, while classifying and removing hateful comments automatically [38].

Providing and operating (semi-)automated comment moderation system include resource-intensive tasks ranging from data acquisition and labeling to constant maintenance and evaluation of the system. For the system development, labeled datasets are required as one of the key resources for training machine learning models. Initial data acquisition and labeling, however, are costly and time-inefficient tasks [36]. In addition to that, there is a need for repeated evaluation of the models' performances, since language evolves continuously [17]. As a consequence, we identify the need for action to study resource-efficient and more dynamic techniques that adequately address the presented obstacles for the operation of comment moderation systems. Additionally, we expect a comment moderation system to be able to adjust to changes in the data pattern, as any real-world application must be capable of doing [4]. A concept that supports the continuous adjustment of machine learning models is *incremental learning*. In the given research, we study how incrementally-trained ML models perform in comparison to batch-trained models in the context of semi-automated comment moderation. We present a learning strategy that aligns with human-in-the-loop ML techniques, as our solution continuously integrates domain knowledge provided by moderators [43].

This paper is structured as follows. In Sect. 2, we provide background information on comment moderation systems, as well as fundamental definitions of batch learning and incremental learning. Additionally, we present the results of a structured literature search on incremental learning techniques used in text classification tasks. The applied research method is presented in Sect. 3. Next, we describe the objectives for our development process and explain the performed development steps in more detail in Sect. 4. Section 5 covers the demonstration of our learning strategy and presents the results of our iterative evaluation. Our paper closes with a concluding discussion of the research findings and limitations in Sect. 6.

2 Theoretical Background

2.1 Comment Moderation and Comment Moderation Systems

Comment moderation and, in particular, automated comment moderation with the help of information technology finds increasing interest in news outlets, online communities, and academia [16,38]. Journalists perform comment moderation in order to eliminate *hate speech* or *abusive language* from their organization's website [5]. However, definitions of terminology, such as abusive language, hate speech, or harassment, are not clearly established in academia [7]. Removing comments from the comment thread can potentially be compared to censorship [5], leaving journalists in the dilemma of removing uncivil and hateful comments, while ensuring freedom of speech [28]. Comment moderation is usually performed as pre- or post-moderation and is regulated by laws, ethics, and further guidelines [28].

Supporting technology in the form of comment moderation systems help journalists and community managers to better cope with the large amount of data and frees the journalists from their additional work as comment moderators. [39], for instance, present a data mining approach to automatically identify hateful or offensive comments. They combine textual data patterns to elements derived from the social network the comments were posted in, such as the interaction of users. [16] discuss the role of automated comment moderation on the social platform *Reddit* and demonstrate the effect of comment moderation in an online community. [5] investigate a simplified approach to automate comment moderation, in which they used a pre-defined list of swear words to identify comments of abusive language. However, contrary to their initial assumption, this approach did not present itself as a useful mechanism. Thus, more advanced techniques are necessary to support the automation of comment moderation.

2.2   Batch Learning vs. Incremental Learning

Machine learning is usually performed using *batch learning*, which is also referred to as *offline learning* [4], *single-task learning* [44], or *isolated learning* [11]. Batch learning works under the assumption that the data distribution of training and test data is static and given in the training phase of the model creation [22]. After executing the training phase and deploying the machine learning instance to production, the model is applied to classify or cluster incoming data, i.e., there is a clear distinction between the training and testing phase. In a dynamic environment, however, where the entire data distribution is not given in the training phase, machine learning instances must be able to learn continuously in order to adjust to their environment [4]. To reflect the dynamic environment in the learning instance, an incremental learning technique can be applied.

Incremental learning techniques aim at creating machine learning instances that adapt to their environments while retaining previously learned knowledge [30]. Further, incremental learning approaches are characterized by their ability to learn new classes as well as their independence from previously learned data [27]. Naturally, incremental learning is also better suited to address dynamic learning problems, in which loading large datasets into memory is not feasible [4]. *Online learning* [20], *lifelong learning* [27], *evolutionary learning* [20], or *continual learning* [23] can be used as synonyms for incremental machine learning. Frequently, however, these terms are also distinguished from one another. A learning strategy is described as *online learning* to stress that it is able to process one instance at a time, thus may be applied to data streams [1]. The term *lifelong learning*, however, is used to emphasize the idea to replicate human learning [11]. *Evolutionary learning* can be understood as a synonym to lifelong learning [20]. Incremental learning techniques can be further distinguished between batch incremental learning and single-instance learning, describing the portion of data that is processed at a time [22].

Besides their ability to work in dynamic environments, incremental learning techniques have further advantages over batch learning approaches. Incremental learning methods offer computational benefits and lead to a reduced demand in storage capacity, since a large dataset does not have to be stored in memory throughout the entire training process [30]. The key challenge in incremental learning, however, is finding the right balance between learning new knowledge and retaining previously learned information, which is known as the *stability-plasticity dilemma* [8]. In the stability-plasticity dilemma, the balance of learning and retaining knowledge is described as a design question for learning systems [8]. If a system is designed to tend to forget previously learned knowledge, it is prone to *catastrophic forgetting* [23,33].

2.3   Incremental Learning in Text Classification

Among several use cases, incremental machine learning techniques also find application in text classification (TC) tasks. In a structured literature search based on the methodology proposed by [40], the literature databases *Scopus* and *Web of Science* were searched for research that cover the usage of incremental learning techniques in text classification tasks. The search string was set to a combination of the terms *incremental learning* and *text classification*. We did not make any further restrictions in order to obtain a broader range of results. After excluding duplicate literature, a total of 19 papers were identified, which were published between 2004 and 2020. Within the identified set of literature, we recognize a shared understanding of the benefits of incremental machine learning in a variety of domains as well as a wide range of tasks. Additionally, similar observations with regard to the challenges of incremental learning are given. Examples of domains covered are the identification of spam in e-mails [37], or the detection of evidence of breast cancer in medical reports [9].

A wide range of approaches to implement incremental learning strategies for TC tasks was identified in the literature search. While the majority of the literature covers supervised machine learning, unsupervised and semi-supervised learning techniques are also included. Within the literature on supervised incremental machine learning for text classification, well-known baseline algorithms for text classification such as Naïve Bayes (NB) [18] or Support Vector Machines (SVM) [46] are studied. A multi-class approach was presented in [4], which is based on the work by [32]. In [31], a non-probabilistic approach based on the *Winnow* algorithm is investigated. Further, deep learning techniques such as neural networks, particularly Recurrent Neural Networks (RNN) and Convolutional Neural Networks (CNN), are also applied to implement an incremental learning strategy for TC tasks [9,12,30]. Within the set of literature focusing on unsupervised techniques, different clustering strategies are presented [14,21,37]. Additionally, ensemble learning is covered, which yields the advantage to better balance learning new information and forgetting formerly learned knowledge by continuously evaluating and exchanging classifiers within the ensemble [35].

Lastly, semi-supervised methods are also presented, which additionally offer the resource-efficient advantage to include labeled as well as unlabeled data for a TC task using incremental learning [19,36,41]. Further, in [3], a bibliometric survey on incremental learning in text classification is presented.

Despite the differences in the usage of incremental learning in text classification, similar motivational factors and a shared understanding of the benefits were identified. Incremental learning is used to address high memory utilization, which is a common concern in batch learning [4,30,46]. Further, the lack of adaptability of batch learning techniques motivates the use of incremental learning techniques as well as its inefficiency, particularly with regard to maintenance tasks such as completely retraining machine learning models [4,34]. Incremental learning is used to prevent performance degradation of machine learning models used in production, i.e., to guarantee high classification performance over time [34,46]. Similarly, a set of common concerns was identified. As textual data is usually linked to a high dimensionality of the feature space, the constant increase of the feature space due to continuous learning of new knowledge is a common concern [10,18]. In the set of literature examined in our literature search, catastrophic forgetting is also considered as a potential issue for incremental learning in text classification [30].

3   Research Approach

Our research connects incremental learning in text classification tasks with comment moderation systems. This paper is based on the architecture and moderation process of a research project presented by [29]. In this research, we aim at developing dynamic machine learning models for semi-automated comment moderation systems using incremental machine learning. Our research follows a design science approach based on the Design Science Research Methodology (DSRM) proposed by [26], using a problem-centered approach. The artifacts of our research are machine learning models that are able to learn incrementally when embedded in a semi-automated comment moderation system. Additionally, we present a testing environment to support the comparison of incrementally-trained and batch-trained ML models in the context of comment moderation systems.

First, according to [26], researchers are demanded to identify the research problem in order to capture the complexity of the problem. In line with that, our research is firstly motivated and introduced: semi-automated text classification approaches used in comment moderation systems are affected by the dynamic nature of language. We study a flexible learning technique that continuously adjusts to the environment and contrast it to traditional batch learning (Sects. 1 and 2). Second, objectives for the research outlet must be defined. Third, the artifact's design is planned, and the actual development is performed. We define requirements for a dynamic learning approach embedded in comment moderation systems and apply the requirements to the artifact development (Sect. 4). Next, the developed artifacts are demonstrated and evaluated with regard to their ability to continuously learn new knowledge and in comparison to techniques based on batch learning (Sect. 5). We perform an iterative performance evaluation based on common performance metrics to compare both learning techniques. Thus, this section also covers the evaluation phase according to the methodology by [26]. Last, the paper closes with a discussion of the research findings and an outlook on future research (Sect. 6).

4 Incremental ML in Comment Moderation Systems

4.1 Design Objectives

For our research, we consider a semi-automated comment moderation system where the extent of incoming comments that are automatically moderated is controlled by the level of certainty of the machine learning instance as measured by the prediction probability. Manual moderation is only performed if the machine learning instance is not able to assign the comment a label with a probability above a pre-defined threshold. Thus, a certain amount of moderation must still be performed manually, which will be used as the foundation for incrementally updating the machine learning instance. During the operation of a CMS, each manual moderation activity generates a labeled data instance as a by-product. Our goal is to incorporate a single-instance incremental learning technique, in which the machine learning model is updated after processing manual moderation decisions performed by a user. In this way, a resource-efficient and continuous learning strategy is created, and human knowledge provided in the form of the labeled comment is continuously integrated.

   As a testing environment, we create a simplified comment moderation system. We simulate a steady data flow and manual moderation activities with the help of a labeled dataset. A manual moderation decision is simulated by deriving the true label of a data instance from the labeled dataset. Given that, the application does not rely on user input, but makes use of the knowledge provided in the labeled dataset. A continuous arrival of new data is replicated by processing one data instance at a time, chronologically ordered based on the creation timestamp of the data instances. Further, we aim at contrasting an incremental learning technique with batch learning. To do so, we additionally create batch-trained classifiers and use them as a reference for the subsequent evaluation and incremental training procedure. In order to better observe the adaptation of the models and the effect of incremental learning, time-intensive training of the models in advance is deliberately avoided, while we perform proper batch learning on the benchmark models. For the ML models that will subsequently be trained incrementally, we train the models in advance to guarantee that their initial performance is at least better than random guessing (i.e., validation accuracy: 50%).

4.2 Development

We study incremental learning approaches based on three different algorithms: Naïve Bayes (NB), Adaptive Boosting (AdaBoost), and Logistic Regression

144   A. Wolters et al.

(LR). The algorithms were selected because of their simplicity and suitability for incremental learning [21,24,45]. NB is a prominent algorithm for incremental text classification tasks, as its simplicity allows for a straightforward update of the classifier [21]. An incremental learning variant of a NB classifier updates its prior probability by turning the posterior probability to the new prior probability [21]. While in regular adaptive boosting, the weight of an observation is changed based on the entire training set, incremental AdaBoost uses sampling with replacement based on a Poisson distribution [24]. As a base estimator, we use simple tree-based classifiers. For incremental LR, the incremental adjustment is performed by updating the logistic regression parameters using stochastic gradient descent [45]. For each algorithm, we develop a batch-trained and incrementally-trained ML model. We implemented the algorithms that will be trained incrementally using the Python library *river* and thereby fulfill the goal to create ML models based on single-instance incremental learning [22].

For the model training, we additionally use the Python packages *scikit-learn* [25] and *scikit-optimize*[1] as well as *spacy*[2] and *NLTK*[3] for preprocessing the textual data. The model training is based on a labeled dataset, some of which is publicly available [2]. The dataset contains around 430,000 German comments and covers the period from November 2018 to July 2021. A binary labeling was used to differentiate the comment data between *rejected (positive)*, i.e. hateful or offensive comments, and *accepted (negative)* instances [2]. With the help of community managers from a German newspaper as well as crowd workers the dataset was labeled. Only around 25,000 data instances, roughly 6% of the entire dataset, are labeled as positive, thus making the dataset highly imbalanced.

Prior to applying ML algorithms on the data, the dataset is preprocessed using common NLP techniques. We apply stop word removal, lemmatization, lowercase conversion and remove special and single characters. Further, we use the *term frequency-inverse document frequency* (TF-IDF) weighting scheme to vectorize the textual data due to its simplicity and suitability for incremental learning. The implementation of the vectorization for the incrementally-trained models supports a continuous extension of the feature space when new tokens appear in the comment data, which appropriately reflects a continuous learning behavior [6]. Next, hyperparameter tuning is performed using *GridSearch* and *Bayesian Optimization* using *scikit-learn* and *scikit-optimize*. We apply well-established and commonly used techniques and additionally align the data preparation steps with the suggestions by [2] in order to simplify the learning process and focus on the comparison of the learning techniques.

Based on the preprocessed data and optimal hyperparameter settings, we perform the (initial) training of the classifiers. For the batch-trained models, we created a balanced subset of the entire dataset (∼34,000 instances). For a reduced initial performance, only a subset of the newly created balanced dataset is used to initially train the models that will perform incremental learning in the

---

[1] https://scikit-optimize.github.io/.
[2] https://spacy.io/.
[3] https://www.nltk.org/.

subsequent step ($\sim$4,000 instances). The data samples in the subset were randomly sampled. It is important to note that we utilized the oldest data available in the dataset for the (initial) training and newer data for the performance evaluation in order to correctly represent the time dimension, as we aim at understanding how the performance of ML models changes while language evolves over time. Further, there is no overlap between data used for the training and evaluation, and the dataset for the evaluation immediately follows the training dataset in time.

The final part of the development step covers the testing environment used for incrementally updating the classifiers, as well as to evaluate their performance. For the development, we used the Python library *streamlit*[4] that supports the creation of web applications for data science tasks. We use the application to simulate the constant data flow and moderation activities, as well as to trigger the incremental model updates. In the given case, the data flow is paused until a comment is processed and, if necessary, an update iteration of the machine learning model is performed. As specified above, the update of a model is triggered when the certainty of the ML instance for classifying an incoming comment based on the prediction probability falls below a pre-defined threshold. A false classification does not initiate an update.

5   Demonstration and Evaluation

For the performance evaluation, we apply *prequential evaluation*, or *test-then-train* evaluation, which is a well-known technique to evaluate the performance of data streams [1,4,13]. The term *prequential* is the short form for *predictive sequential* [1]. The first step in the prequential evaluation is computing the predictions for each incoming data instance. In a second step, every single instance is used to update the classifier [13]. We use a modification of the prequential evaluation since we restrict the update of the classifiers to the manual moderation decision, whereas we evaluate the performance by updating the performance metrics for each incoming instance. Further, we apply immediate feedback, i.e., whenever a manual moderation activity is simulated, the data flow is paused [4,37]. This ensures that we keep the chronological order of the comments based on their creation timestamp. We evaluate the performance outcome of the incremental model with regard to varying values for the threshold for the prediction probability as well as the observation period.

The performance evaluation is based on the metrics accuracy, the area under the receiver operating curve (ROCAUC), precision, and recall. In combination, these performance metrics allow for a comprehensive and appropriate evaluation of the classifiers' performances, when evaluated on imbalanced datasets. Based on simple cross-validation, we determine the starting performance of each classifier based on a validation set. As we study a single-instance incremental learning approach, we apply the API for metrics provided by the Python package *river*. The metrics are updated based on the true label and the predicted

---

[4] https://streamlit.io/.

Table 1. Initial performance per classifier

Classifier	Initial performance metrics			
	Accuracy	ROCAUC	Precision	Recall
NB (BL/IL)	0.70/0.63	0.77/0.71	0.74/0.62	0.61/0.67
AB (BL/IL)	0.66/0.53	0.72/0.52	0.66/0.51	0.66/0.55
LR (BL/IL)	0.70/0.60	0.76/0.64	0.74/0.60	0.61/0.54

label or the prediction probability. In Table 1, the initial performance values, i.e., the starting point for the subsequent evaluation, for the batch-trained models (BL) and models that will be incrementally-trained (IL) are depicted. In the subsequent performance evaluation, the metrics of both types of classifiers will be updated after processing a single instance. The results in Table 1 indicate a decent performance for each batch-trained classifier. These results justify the use of the models as performance benchmarks in the given research. Each classifier that will be incrementally trained in the subsequent step, shows a reduced initial performance as desired. Each of the weak classifiers performs better than random guessing, i.e., the previously defined design objective is fulfilled. In addition to the performance metrics, we also record the number of misclassifications performed by each model in the subsequent performance evaluation. Further, we additionally save the label of each instance that was used to perform an incremental update in order to get more insight into the training dataset.

We executed the performance evaluation in an iterative manner to study the effect of different parameter settings on the classifiers' performances. First, we focused on the effect of varying threshold values for the prediction probability, i.e., we regulated the amount of manual comment moderation in our system. Naturally, a higher prediction probability creates a larger number of comments that must be manually moderated in the semi-automated setting. A larger amount of manual moderation, however, also implies more frequent updates of the incrementally-trained models. We noticed, that a higher frequency of incremental updates of the model leads to fewer misclassifications performed by the incrementally-learned classifier. Additionally, a high increase in the accuracy as well as the ROCAUC score of the incremental models was recorded. However, in the given context, a high accuracy might give a misleading impression of the true performance, since the dataset is imbalanced. For the incrementally-trained models, we observe a strong decline in the recall and/or precision of the classifiers. As compared to the incrementally-trained models, the batch-trained models, however, rather show slight performance degradation with regard to the development of the classifiers' accuracy and ROCAUC score. However, they also demonstrate a constant value for their recall scores. Based on these initial observations, we came to the interim conclusion that the batch-trained classifiers outperform the incrementally-trained models with regard to their ability to properly identify the minority class. We attribute this observation to the differences in the distribution of the training data. While we used a balanced dataset for the batch training, which is a common practice to allow for proper distinction between classes, the incrementally-trained models work on an imbalanced dataset. Thus, we continued our evaluation by incorporating sampling strategies to the incremental learning process.

First, we incorporated random undersampling of the majority class to the incremental learning process. The sampling strategy extends our set of parameters by the desired class ratio for the data sampling. We executed different performance evaluations using varying parameter settings for the desired class ratio, as well as the threshold for the prediction probability and the observation horizon. The results, however, indicated that undersampling the majority class does not improve the incremental learning process. Rather, undersampling showed a worse performance than in previous iterations of our evaluation. In particular, we noticed a strong increase in the number of misclassifications performed by the incrementally-trained models.

Second, we therefore applied random oversampling of the minority class instead of undersampling the majority class. We were able to see minor performance improvements as compared to previous iterations where no sampling strategy was used. Therefore, we continued applying oversampling to the incremental learning approach and observed that an equal ratio between both classes creates the best results. Most likely, oversampling outperforms undersampling in the given context, as undersampling reduces the training dataset for the incremental model updates [42]. Still, the loss in the classifiers' precision and recall value remain. In several cases, however, the significance of the loss is reduced when oversampling with an equal ratio between the classes was applied. Still, an indication of a potential competitiveness of incremental learning techniques with batch-trained models is the lower number of misclassifications performed by an incrementally-trained ML model. For the comparison between incremental learning and batch learning, we additionally observed that the incrementally-trained models are able to outperform their batch-trained counterpart with regard to the accuracy. However, the batch classifiers showed more stable results, particularly concerning the recall and precision value.

In Fig. 1, exemplary results of our research are presented. The figure shows the performance development of each incrementally-trained classifier based on the selected performance metrics. In the legend of the performance plot, the starting value for each metric of each classifier is given. The results for the AdaBoost, Naïve Bayes, and Logistic Regression classifier are depicted as dashed, dotted, and solid lines, respectively. For each incrementally-trained classifier, oversampling with an equal ration between both classes was applied. Additionally, the threshold for the prediction probability was set to 80% and the performance development was observed over the course of three months with equals an amount of roughly 36,500 comments. Figure 1 shows the performance development of the classifiers after processing each of the comments in the evaluation dataset. Interestingly, the development of the accuracy, ROCAUC, and recall score of each incrementally-trained classifier show a similar pattern. For the accuracy of each classifier, a rather strong increase can be observed at the

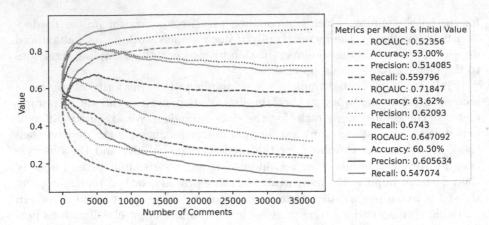

Fig. 1. Performance development of incrementally-trained models (--- AdaBoost, ······ Naïve Bayes, —— Logistic Regression)

beginning of the observation period, while the slope of the increase is reduced after around one third of the observation horizon. Similarly, each model shows an increase in its ROCAUC score at the beginning of the observation period and a slight decrease of the score after processing around 8,000 comments. In roughly the last third of the observation period, the values for the ROCAUC scores appear to be rather stagnant. Additionally, the final ROCAUC scores are very close to the initial performance scores. While we observe a constant decline of the classifiers' recall values, the development of the precision score differs. Here, the logistic regression model demonstrates a slight decrease at the beginning of the observation period, but shows a rather constant value after processing around 5,000 comments. Both remaining models, however, show a very strong decline in their precision at the beginning of the observation and a reduced but still constant decrease towards the end of the observation period. Still, neither the recall nor the precision value of any incrementally-trained classifier demonstrates an improvement during the observation.

In addition, we observed differences in the training datasets for the incremental learning for each classifier. These differences concern the size of the datasets as well as the given distribution between the classes, indicating different levels of confidence between the classifiers and among the classes. The Logistic Regression classifier appears to have a rather high level of confidence in its predictions, since the training dataset for incrementally updating the classifier was rather small. Additionally, data instances from the minority class are slightly less underrepresented, accounting for about 14% of the training data set. For the NB and AdaBoost classifier, however, the training dataset always roughly reflects the overall distribution of the classes. The training set for the incremental Naïve Bayes classifier contains around a third of the evaluation dataset, while more than half of the dataset was used for updating the incrementally-trained AdaBoost classifier.

We come to the conclusion that the batch-trained classifiers outperform incrementally-trained models with regard to the proper identification of hate speech, i.e., correctly classifying the positive class. These inclusive results indicate that more in-depth research on the reasons for the demonstrated developments is necessary. We conclude that the incrementally-trained models are not able to properly distinguish between classes and thus fail to properly identify hate speech in comment data. The monitoring of the development of the performance metrics over the course of time shows that the incrementally-trained classifier are not fully able to compete with batch-trained ML models.

6   Concluding Discussion and Future Work

In our research, we investigated how incrementally-trained ML models perform in comparison to batch-trained ML models in the context of semi-automated comment moderation systems. In a testing environment, we simulated a continuous data flow as well as manual moderation decisions, which we used to incrementally train the underlying machine learning model. In several performance evaluations, we compared incrementally-trained ML models to batch-trained models when embedded in a comment moderation system.

In each evaluation iteration, it became evident that the ability of a machine learning model which is continuously learned on incoming comments to compete against batch learning is limited. In several cases, we observed fewer misclassifications performed by the incrementally-trained classifiers than the batch-trained models. Still, the performance development of the incrementally-trained models showed insufficient improvements, since the incremental training of the classifier does not improve the precision and recall score of the model. Possibly, the lack of improvement is attributed to the underlying data the incremental training was performed on. Although we incorporated sampling strategies, we regard the imbalance in the dataset as a potential cause for the insufficient improvement. Additionally, the high dimensionality of the feature space and its constant increase might be a possible reasoning for the classifier's difficulties to properly distinguish and learn both classes. More advanced sampling strategies and feature selection techniques might be appropriate to improve the data and thus the incremental learning [18]. Further, our research is limited with regard to the evaluation metrics used. Nevertheless, it became evident that oversampling the minority class when updating the classifier incrementally improves the performance of the classifier with regard to properly identify abusive language. Contrary to that, undersampling caused weaker performances of the incremental classifiers due to the reduction in the training dataset. Given the current limitations of our research, we regard a combination of traditional batch learning and incremental updates of the classifier as an appropriate technique. It would ensure a constant level of classification quality in the long-term use of the semi-automated comment moderation system, as well as circumvent complete retraining steps of the classifier in the future.

Besides the limitations regarding the results of the incremental training, our study is also limited with regard to the simulation of semi-automated comment moderation. We assumed that manual moderation decisions are strictly made in the chronological order and without any delay. Still, our research opens up the debate on incremental machine learning techniques for comment moderation systems and introduces the use of more dynamic learning strategies in semi-automated comment moderation systems. Future work should aim at understanding the observed behavior in more detail, and finding solutions to improve the outcome of an incremental learning technique embedded in semi-automated comment moderation systems.

References

1. Ashfahani, A.: Autonomous deep learning: incremental learning of deep neural networks for evolving data streams. In: IEEE International Conference on Data Mining Workshops, ICDMW 2019, Beijing, China, pp. 83–90 (2019)
2. Assenmacher, D., Niemann, M., Müller, K., Seiler, M., Riehle, D.M., Trautmann, H.: RP-Mod & RP-Crowd: moderator- and crowd-annotated German news comment datasets. In: Proceedings of the NeurIPS Datasets and Benchmarks 2021, Virtual, pp. 1–14 (2021)
3. Barve, Y., Mulay, P.: Bibliometric survey on incremental learning in text classification algorithms for false information detection. Libr. Philos. Pract. **2020**, 2388–2392 (2020)
4. Bittencourt, M.M., Silva, R.M., Almeida, T.A.: ML-MDLText: an efficient and lightweight multilabel text classifier with incremental learning. Appl. Soft Comput. **96**, 1–15 (2020)
5. Boberg, S., Schatto-Eckrodt, T., Frischlich, L., Quandt, T.: The moral gatekeeper? Moderation and deletion of user-generated content in a leading news forum. Media Commun. **6**, 58–69 (2018)
6. Brants, T., Chen, F., Farahat, A.: A system for new event detection. In: Proceedings of the 26th International ACM SIGIR Conference on Research and Development in Information Retrieval, Toronto, Canada, pp. 330–337 (2003)
7. Brunk, J., Niemann, M., Riehle, D.M.: Can analytics as a service save the online discussion culture? - The case of comment moderation in the media industry. In: Proceedings - 21st IEEE Conference on Business Informatics, CBI 2019, Moscow, Russia, pp. 472–481 (2019)
8. Carpenter, G.A., Grossberg, S.: The art of adaptive pattern recognition by a self-organizing neural network. Computer **21**, 77–88 (1988)
9. Chen, D., Qian, G., Shi, C., Pan, Q.: Breast cancer malignancy prediction using incremental combination of multiple recurrent neural networks. In: Liu, D., Xie, S., Li, Y., Zhao, D., El-Alfy, E.S. (eds.) ICONIP 2017. LNCS, vol. 10635, pp. 43–52. Springer, Cham (2017). https://doi.org/10.1007/978-3-319-70096-0_5
10. Chen, Z., Huang, L., Murphey, Y.L.: Incremental learning for text document classification. In: Proceedings 2007 International Joint Conference on Neural Networks, Orlando, USA, pp. 2592–2597 (2007)
11. Chen, Z., Liu, B.: Lifelong machine learning. In: Synthesis Lectures on Artificial Intelligence and Machine Learning, vol. 10, pp. 1–145 (2016)

12. D'Andecy, V., Joseph, A., Cuenca, J., Ogier, J.M.: Discourse descriptor for document incremental classification comparison with deep learning. In: Proceedings of the International Conference on Document Analysis and Recognition, ICDAR, Sydney, Australia, pp. 467–472 (2019)
13. Dawid, A.P.: Present position and potential developments: some personal views: statistical theory: the prequential approach. J. Roy. Stat. Soc. Ser. A (General) **147**, 278–292 (1984)
14. Doan, T., Kalita, J.: Overcoming the challenge for text classification in the open world. In: 2017 IEEE 7th Annual Computing and Communication Workshop and Conference, CCWC 2017, Las Vegas, USA, pp. 1–7 (2017)
15. Ferrucci, P., Wolfgang, J.D.: Inside or out? Perceptions of how differing types of comment moderation impact practice. Journal. Stud. **22**, 1010–1027 (2021)
16. Jhaver, S., Birman, I., Gilbert, E., Bruckman, A.: Human-machine collaboration for content regulation. ACM Trans. Comput. Hum. Interact. **26**(5), 1–35 (2019)
17. Karjus, A., Blythe, R., Kirby, S., Smith, K.: Quantifying the dynamics of topical fluctuations in language. Lang. Dyn. Change **10**, 86–125 (2020)
18. Katakis, I., Tsoumakas, G., Vlahavas, I.: On the utility of incremental feature selection for the classification of textual data streams. In: Bozanis, P., Houstis, E.N. (eds.) PCI 2005. LNCS, vol. 3746, pp. 338–348. Springer, Heidelberg (2005). https://doi.org/10.1007/11573036_32
19. Liu, L., Liang, Q.: A high-performing comprehensive learning algorithm for text classification without pre-labeled training set. Knowl. Inf. Syst. **29**, 727–738 (2011). https://doi.org/10.1007/s10115-011-0387-3
20. Losing, V., Hammer, B., Wersing, H.: Incremental on-line learning: a review and comparison of state of the art algorithms. Neurocomputing **275**, 1261–1274 (2018)
21. Ma, H., Fan, X., Chen, J.: An incremental Chinese text classification algorithm based on quick clustering. In: Proceedings 2008 International Symposiums on Information Processing (ISIP), Moscow, Russia, pp. 308–312 (2008)
22. Montiel, J., et al.: River: machine learning for streaming data in Python. J. Mach. Learn. Res. **22**, 1–8 (2020)
23. Moons, E., Moens, M.F.: Clinical report classification: continually learning from user feedback. In: Proceedings of the IEEE 34th Symposium on Computer-Based Medical Systems, CBMS, Virtual, pp. 455–460 (2021)
24. Oza, N.: Online bagging and boosting. In: Conference Proceedings - IEEE International Conference on Systems, Man, and Cybernetics, Waikoloa, USA, vol. 3, pp. 2340–2345 (2005)
25. Pedregosa, F., et al.: Scikit-learn: machine learning in Python. J. Mach. Learn. Res. **12**, 2825–2830 (2011)
26. Peffers, K., Tuunanen, T., Rothenberger, M.A., Chatterjee, S.: A design science research methodology for information systems research. J. Manag. Inf. Syst. **24**, 45–77 (2007)
27. Polikar, R., Upda, L., Upda, S.S., Honavar, V.: Learn++: an incremental learning algorithm for supervised neural networks. IEEE Trans. Syst. Man Cybern. Part C (Appl. Rev.) **31**, 497–508 (2001)
28. Pöyhtäri, R.: Limits of hate speech and freedom of speech on moderated news websites in Finland, Sweden, The Netherlands and the UK. Ann. Ser. Hist. Sociol. **24**, 513–524 (2014)
29. Riehle, D.M., Niemann, M., Brunk, J., Assenmacher, D., Trautmann, H., Becker, J.: Building an integrated comment moderation system – towards a semi-automatic moderation tool. In: Meiselwitz, G. (ed.) HCII 2020. LNCS, vol. 12195, pp. 71–86. Springer, Cham (2020). https://doi.org/10.1007/978-3-030-49576-3_6

30. Shan, G., Xu, S., Yang, L., Jia, S., Xiang, Y.: Learn#: a novel incremental learning method for text classification. Expert Syst. Appl. **147**, 1–11 (2020)

31. Siefkes, C., Assis, F., Chhabra, S., Yerazunis, W.S.: Combining winnow and orthogonal sparse bigrams for incremental spam filtering. In: Boulicaut, J.-F., Esposito, F., Giannotti, F., Pedreschi, D. (eds.) PKDD 2004. LNCS (LNAI), vol. 3202, pp. 410–421. Springer, Heidelberg (2004). https://doi.org/10.1007/978-3-540-30116-5_38

32. Silva, R., Almeida, T., Yamakami, A.: MDLText: an efficient and lightweight text classifier. Knowl. Based Syst. **118**, 152–164 (2017)

33. Singh, B., Sun, Q., Koh, Y.S., Lee, J., Zhang, E.: Detecting protected health information with an incremental learning ensemble: a case study on New Zealand clinical text. In: Proceedings - 2020 IEEE International Conference on Data Science and Advanced Analytics, DSAA 2020, Virtual, pp. 719–728 (2020)

34. Song, S., Qiao, X., Chen, P.: Hierarchical text classification incremental learning. In: Leung, C.S., Lee, M., Chan, J.H. (eds.) ICONIP 2009. LNCS, vol. 5863, pp. 247–258. Springer, Heidelberg (2009). https://doi.org/10.1007/978-3-642-10677-4_28

35. Srilakshmi, V., Anuradha, K., Bindu, C.S.: Optimized deep belief network and entropy-based hybrid bounding model for incremental text categorization. Int. J. Web Inf. Syst. **16**, 347–368 (2020)

36. Tang, X.L., Han, M.: Ternary reversible extreme learning machines: the incremental tri-training method for semi-supervised classification. Knowl. Inf. Syst. **23**, 345–372 (2010). https://doi.org/10.1007/s10115-009-0220-4

37. Taninpong, P., Ngamsuriyaroj, S.: Tree-based text stream clustering with application to spam mail classification. Int. J. Data Min. Model. Manag. **10**, 353–370 (2018)

38. van Aken, B., Risch, J., Krestel, R., Löser, A.: Challenges for toxic comment classification: an in-depth error analysis. In: Proceedings of the Second Workshop on Abusive Language Online, ALW2, Brussels, Belgium, pp. 33–42 (2018)

39. Veloso, A., Meira Jr, W., Macambira, T., Guedes, D., Almeida, H.: Automatic moderation of comments in a large online journalistic environment. In: International AAAI Conference on Web and Social Media, ICWSM 2007, Boulder, USA, pp. 1–8 (2007)

40. vom Brocke, J., Simons, A., Niehaves, B., Riemer, K., Plattfaut, R., Cleven, A.: Reconstructing the giant: on the importance of rigour in documenting the literature search process. In: Proceedings of the 17th European Conference on Information Systems, ECIS 2009, Verona, Italy, pp. 1–12 (2009)

41. Wang, D., Al-Rubaie, A.: Incremental learning with partial-supervision based on hierarchical Dirichlet process and the application for document classification. Appl. Soft Comput. **33**, 250–262 (2015)

42. Wegier, W., Ksieniewicz, P.: Application of imbalanced data classification quality metrics as weighting methods of the ensemble data stream classification algorithms. Entropy **22**, 1–17 (2020)

43. Wu, X., Xiao, L., Sun, Y., Zhang, J., Ma, T., He, L.: A survey of human-in-the-loop for machine learning. Future Gener. Comput. Syst. **135**, 364–381 (2022)

44. Xia, R., Jiang, J., He, H.: Distantly supervised lifelong learning for large-scale social media sentiment analysis. IEEE Trans. Affect. Comput. **8**, 480–491 (2017)

45. Xie, Y., Willett, R.: Online logistic regression on manifolds. In: Proceedings - ICASSP IEEE International Conference on Acoustics, Speech and Signal Processing, Vancouver, Canada, pp. 3367–3371 (2013)
46. Zhang, B., Su, J., Xu, X.: A class-incremental learning method for multi-class support vector machines in text classification. In: Proceedings - International Conference on Machine Learning and Cybernetics 2006, Dalian, China, pp. 2581–2585 (2006)

Author Index

Printed in the United States
by Baker & Taylor Publisher Services

Printed in the United States
by Baker & Taylor Publisher Services